汉英对照湖湘经典丛书
HUNAN CULTURAL CLASSICS(Chinese-English)

郑燕虹　蒋洪新　尹飞舟　主编
Edited by Zheng Yanhong, Jiang Hongxin and Yin Feizhou

曾国藩诗文选

Selected Poetry and Prose of Zeng Guofan

尹飞舟、乐国斌　译
Translated by Yin Feizhou and Le Guobin
唐浩明　编
Edited by Tang Haoming

岳麓書社·长沙
Changsha: Yuelu Publishing House

◆◆◆

本书系湖南省“十四五”时期社科重大学术和文化研究专项
“湖湘经典英译与传播研究”（编号：21ZDAZ21）阶段性成果

总序

习近平总书记指出："中华优秀传统文化是中华民族的文化根脉，其蕴含的思想观念、人文精神、道德规范，不仅是我们中国人思想和精神的内核，对解决人类问题也有重要价值。要把优秀传统文化的精神标识提炼出来、展示出来，把优秀传统文化中具有当代价值、世界意义的文化精髓提炼出来、展示出来。"[1]

湖湘文化作为中华优秀传统文化的重要组成部分，自然也应当"提炼出来、展示出来"。国学大师钱基博（1887—1957）先生在《近百年湖南学风》中说道："湖南之为省，北阻大江，南薄五岭，西接黔蜀，群苗所萃，盖四塞之国。其地水少而山多，重山叠岭，滩河峻激，而舟车不易为交通。顽石赭土，地质刚坚，而民性多流于倔强，以故风气锢塞，常不为中原人文所沾被。抑亦风气自创，能别于中原人物以独立。人杰地灵，大儒迭起，前不见古人，后不见来者，宏识孤怀，涵今茹古，罔不有独

1《习近平谈治国理政》第三卷，第 314 页。外文出版社 2020 年 6 月第 1 版。

立自由之思想，有坚强不磨之志节。湛深古学而能自辟蹊径，不为古学所囿。义以淑群，行必厉己，以开一代之风气，盖地理使之然也。”[1]湖南虽居“四塞之地”，然湘人却始终葆有“胸怀天下”的气度与理想。经上古本土文化、中原文化、楚文化的多元文化影响，湖湘大地先后出现了屈原（约前 340—约前 278）、贾谊（前 200—前 168）、周敦颐（1017—1073）、王夫之（1619—1692）、陶澍（1779—1839）、魏源（1794—1857）、胡林翼（1812—1861）、曾国藩（1811—1872）、左宗棠（1812—1885）、谭嗣同（1865—1898）、黄兴（1874—1916）、蔡锷（1882—1916）、毛泽东（1893—1976）、蔡和森（1895—1931）、刘少奇（1898—1969）等一大批杰出人才。他们建功立业，写下了大量的经典著作。这些著作蕴含着忧国忧民的爱国精神、学以致用的经世精神、敢为人先的创新精神、以天下为己任的担当精神、“先天下之忧而忧，后天下之乐而乐”的奉献精神。这些精神，在中华民族文化发展史上具有极其重要的地位。

推动湖湘文化走出去，既是弘扬民族精神、发展中华文化、为世界文化增添光彩的需要，也是向世界展示湖南形象、促进文明交流互鉴的需要，是我们义不容辞的责任与使命。而揆诸现实，对湖湘文化经典的翻译与出版传播却不尽如人意。纵观近年来国家高级别对外翻译出版工程的实施情况，鲜有全译本、丛书译本的湖湘经典译著入选。即便有经典著作入选，多以湖湘古典文学作品为主，兼有近代湖湘名人的传记和诗文，选题的广度和

1 钱基博《近百年湖南学风》，第 1 页。岳麓书社 2010 年 1 月第 1 版。

深度均有待拓展。这些翻译和研究的成果相对零散，系统性不强。基于上述缘由，由国务院学位委员会学科评议组成员、湖南师范大学郑燕虹教授领衔的课题组提出，要结合现代国际社会和文化复兴的需求，翻译打造一批真正代表湖湘精神的文化精品走向世界，从而更好地展现中华文化的博大精深、有容乃大、异彩纷呈。

正是怀持这份对湖湘文化的敬重和传承弘扬湖湘文化的使命担当，课题组召集了包括欧洲科学院院士张隆溪教授、欧洲科学院院士蒋洪新教授、美国新泽西海洋学院杨孝明教授、教育部新世纪优秀人才支持计划入选者曾艳钰教授、“芙蓉学者”余承法教授、“潇湘学者”尹飞舟教授、蒋莉华教授等在内的10余位知名专家，以及何正兵、邓天文、彭天笑、侯奇焜、梁斌、刘云雁、谢敏敏、乐国斌、郭萍等一批青年学者，组成了一支实力强、结构优、潜力大的湖湘文化翻译与传播研究团队，并以“湖湘经典英译与传播研究”为题成功申报了湖南省“十四五”时期社科重大学术和文化研究专项项目。课题成员着眼湖湘文化的源流历程，从中选取最具有代表性人物的经典作品，将其译成英文，竭力为外国读者呈现高水准的湖湘文化系列丛书。

这套“汉英对照湖湘经典丛书”的编选构想主要有两个方面：一是以人物为线索，选编湖湘文化代表性人物的经典作品，以期借助历史人物的影响力产生最佳传播效果；二是以作品为线索，选编上述人物作品之外、最能体现湖湘文化精神、影响深远的湖湘经典诗文，向世界推介更多具有湖湘特色、体现中国精神、蕴藏中华美学精神的优秀文化。丛书有以下三个鲜明特点：

一是宏阔的学术视野。协同推进湖湘经典的英译与传播研究，是一种全新的尝试。它不囿于研究某个作品、某个个人、某个时期、某一思想，而是对整个湖湘经典的整体、系统的英译和传播进行综合研究，显示出宏阔的学术研究视野。

二是鲜明的跨学科意味。丛书既注重语言、文学、文化及翻译的本体研究，又综合运用历史学、哲学、传播学等多学科交叉的研究方法，尤其注重吸收中英对比、中外文化交流方面的成果，更加丰富立体地呈现湖湘经典的文化魅力。

三是强烈的创新意识。丛书选择具有普遍性、代表性和湖湘特色的经典进行英译，具有鲜明的独特性、地域性和多元性，与当前我国构建中国特色哲学社会科学体系深度契合。

“千红万紫安排著，只待新雷第一声。”湖湘文化蕴含着经世致用、爱国奉献、敢为人先等精神特质，深入开展湖湘经典英译与传播工作，对于推动中华文化更好走向世界将产生积极深远的影响。我们相信，在湖湘文化“走出去”过程中，只要坚持将文化经典摆在首位，把湖湘特色和世界潮流结合起来，把继承传统与关注当下结合起来，湖湘文化在世界文化百花园中一定会展现出独特的魅力，大放光彩。

黄友义

中国翻译协会常务副会长

Preface to the *Hunan Cultural Classics*

"China's finest traditional culture is the cultural lifeline of the Chinese nation," said Xi Jinping, General Secretary of the CPC Central Committee. He went on to say, "Its visions, concepts, values and moral norms are the core of Chinese thinking, and they also hold invaluable references to resolving problems of humanity. We should extract the cream of traditional Chinese culture, and display those elements that are still relevant in the world today."[1]

The culture of Hunan Province, as an indispensable part of traditional Chinese culture, should also be "extracted and displayed." Mr. Qian Jibo(1887—1957), a master of traditional Chinese learning, said in *The Style of Scholarship in Hunan in the Past Hundred Years*: "Hunan borders on the Yangtze River in the north, embraces the Five Mountain Ridges in the south, and adjoins Guizhou and Sichuan in the west. Virtually enclosed by mountains and waters, Hunan has been inhabited by different ethnic groups. Its rugged mountains and treacherous rivers make transportation difficult either by land or by water. The land of Hunan is rocky and hard; the local people are tough and strong-willed by nature.

1 Xi Jinping: *The Governance of China (III)*, page 367. Foreign Languages Press, June, 2020.

It has its own unique culture and ethos almost free from the influence of the Central Plains. As a fair place which produces outstanding people, Hunan has many remarkable scholars, unparalleled in history or even in the future. All of them have harbored an unwavering commitment to independence and freedom, visionary insights, and wisdom drawn from both ancient and contemporary times. Deeply rooted in classical learning, they have blazed new trails without being encumbered by tradition. Upholding righteousness for collective interests, they have conducted themselves with high standards to herald this distinctive spirit of their era, behind all of which is Hunan's geographical context." Even though residing in such a rather confined region, people in Hunan have always embraced the vision and magnanimity of "caring for all under heaven." Thanks to the multicultural influences of ancient native culture, the Central Plains culture and the Chu culture, Hunan has cultivated and produced a large number of outstanding talents, such as Qu Yuan(340BC—278BC), Jia Yi(200BC—168BC), Zhou Dunyi(1017—1073), Wang Fuzhi(1619—1692), Tao Shu(1779—1839), Wei Yuan(1794—1857), Hu Linyi(1812—1861), Zeng Guofan(1811—1872), Zuo Zongtang(1812—1885), Tan Sitong(1865—1898), Huang Xing(1874—1916), Cai E(1882—1916), Mao Zedong(1893—1976), Cai Hesen(1895—1931), and Liu Shaoqi(1898—1969). They achieved a great deal in the causes they fought for and left us with a large number of classic works, which are imbued with the patriotic spirit of caring for the country and the people, the application of learning to praxis, the daring innovation of things new and unattempted, the ambition of taking on responsibilities for all the world as one's own, and the noble self-sacrifice "to feel the anxiety before all others feel it under heaven, and feel the joy after all others feel it in the world." These are qualities that have contributed significantly to the development of Chinese culture.

To promote Hunan culture beyond its borders is not only answering the need of propagating the national ethos, developing Chinese culture, and adding splendor to world culture, but is also answering the need to display Hunan in the best light and help the mutual exchange and understanding of different cultures; it is our unshakable obligation and mission.

However, the current situation of the translation and publication of Hunan cultural classics are far from satisfactory. Few fully translated Hunan classics series have been included in national translation and publication projects. What has been shortlisted were some classic literary works, along with some biographies and poems written by Hunan celebrities in the early 20th century, resulting in a selection limited both in breadth and depth. The translation of Hunan cultural classics has been done in a piecemeal and unsystematic manner. Therefore, a team of scholars headed by Professor Zheng Yanhong of Hunan Normal University, who is also a member of the Discipline Review Group of the Academic Degrees Committee of the State Council of China, has proposed to translate and publish a series of representative Hunan classics, in response to contemporary international interests and China's pursuit of cultural rejuvenation, so as to exhibit the profundity, inclusiveness, and diversity of Chinese culture.

It is with this deep respect for the representatives of Hunan culture and the sense of mission that many scholars are working on this publication project. Apart from Professor Zheng Yanhong, the team is made up of more than 10 renowned experts, including Professor Zhang Longxi and Professor Jiang Hongxin, both foreign members of Academia Europaea, Professor Yang Xiaoming of the New Jersey Maritime Institute, Professor Zeng Yanyu, an inductee of the New Century Excellent Talent Support Program of the Ministry of Education, Professor Yu Chengfa, a Furong Scholar, Professor Yin Feizhou, a Xiaoxiang Scholar, and Professor Jiang Lihua, as well as a group of young scholars such as Dr. He Zhengbing, Dr. Deng Tianwen, Dr. Peng Tianxiao, Dr. Hou Qikun, Dr. Liang Bin, Dr. Liu Yunyan, Dr. Xie Minmin, Dr. Le Guobin, and Dr. Guo Ping. With the title *Study of the English Translation and Dissemination of Hunan Classics*, the project has been designated as a key project of the 14th Five-Year Plan of Hunan Province in Philosophy and Social Science Research. The project team members focus on the history of Hunan culture, select the most representative classic works, translate them into English, and try to present a high-quality Hunan cultural series to the readers outside of China.

Structurally, the Chinese-English Edition of Hunan Classics follows two threads. The first puts emphasis on authors. Classic works by representative figures of Hunan culture are to be presented to leverage their influence to attract readers. The second focuses on works. In addition to the works of the above-mentioned famous figures, more works, both prose and poetry, are also included in the collection for their manifestation of specific Hunan cultural features and their profound influence so that they can best display the Hunan local characteristics as well as the spirit of Chinese culture and aesthetics.

The series has three distinctive features as follows:

First, it presents a broad scholarly vision. It is a completely new effort to coordinate translation and communication studies of Hunan classics. This series demonstrates a broad academic vision in a comprehensive study of Hunan classics as a whole with systematic research on its translation and communication rather than focusing on an individual work or writer, or a certain period of time, or a particular trend of thought in isolation.

Second, it is distinctively interdisciplinary. The series is not just an ontological study in linguistics, literature, culture, and translation, but also a multi-dimensional representation of Hunan classics approached from multiple disciplines including history, philosophy, and communication, with special attention to absorbing the achievements in cultural exchange between China and foreign countries.

Third, it is driven by a strong sense of innovation. The series selects renowned and representative Hunan classics for English translation with a stress on the work's uniqueness, regional features, and diversity. It deeply aligns with the current trend of construction of a philosophy and social science system with Chinese characteristics in China.

As depicted in the poem by Zhang Weiping in the Qing Dynasty, "A thousand buds, red or purple, are ready for the first thunder of spring."With the spiritual qualities of patriotic dedication, practical application, and innovative boldness, the classics of Hunan culture are likewise ready for their journey abroad. The translation and dissemination of Hunan classics will have a positive impact on promoting Chinese culture to the world. During this process, it is imperative to combine local traits with global trends and to associate traditional thinking with current concerns. We believe that Hunan culture with its unique charm and flavor will be appreciated by people from different countries.

Huang Youyi
Executive Vice President
Translators Association of China

前　言

（一）

清嘉庆十六年（1811），曾国藩出生在湖南湘乡县一个普通的耕读之家。身为私塾教师的父亲麟书给他取名为子城，字伯涵。当时他的曾祖父还健在，祖父正当中年，经营着田产，是家中的当家人。五岁时，他的曾祖父去世。在以后漫长的岁月里，这个家一直是三代同堂。他上有大两岁的姐姐，后来父母又给他生了四个弟弟、三个妹妹。这是一个人口众多的大家庭。祖父能干，父亲勤勉，虽人口众多，但日子还过得下去，家中的五个男孩都可以读书，只不过功名科举，对这个家庭来说是艰难的。

他的父亲在经过十七次考试后，才在四十三岁那年考取秀才，一生功名止于此。他本人从十四岁参加考试，每次都以落榜结束，直到道光十三年（1833），他开始时来运转。第七次考试时他考取秀才，这年他二十三岁。随后，他进入当时湖南省的最高学府岳麓书院深造。第二年他考中举人。接下来，经过两次失败后，在他二十八岁时，也就是道光十八年（1838），他高中进士，并顺利通过朝考，入翰林院为庶吉士，登上科举考试的顶峰。在千军万马过独木桥的科考时代，农家子弟的他是极为罕见的幸运儿。就在这时，他自己将名字改为国藩，号涤生。他以雄心勃勃的姿态，迎接前程似锦的未来。

两年后，曾国藩通过翰林院的散馆考试，留在翰苑做一个从七品衔的翰林院检讨。从那时起，直到四十二岁离开北京，他做了十二年的太平京官。他把这段时期的京官做得花团锦簇，风光无限。十二年京官生涯带给他最大的好处是，他通过自觉刻苦的修身自律，完成了自我人格的升华。

曾国藩进京的第二年，便跟着唐鉴，与倭仁、吴廷栋等一班志同道合的朋友一道，从格物致知、正心诚意的修身做起，储备日后治国平天下的大能量。他研习立诚、主敬、静心、谨言、有恒五门功课，且躬身力行，以每天写日记的方式，以慎独的高度，严格地苛求自己，逐渐去掉身上的许多毛病，为后来的艰难大事业奠定了坚实的人格基础。

京官生涯带给他另外的好处是，锻炼了他的才干，为他提供了足够的位望。

曾国藩官运的亨通为常人所不及。史载他十年七迁，而且遍兼五部。所谓十年七迁，指他在二十八岁到三十七岁之间的十个年头里，获得了七次升迁。三十七岁那年，他一次性地连升四级，由从四品衔的中级官员，一下子跃进到从二品衔的朝廷大员序列。这样的机遇，在官场中非常罕见。所谓遍兼五部，指他在道光二十九年（1849），至咸丰二年（1852）这几年里，朝廷六部，除户部外，他以礼部侍郎的身份相继兼任过兵部、工部、刑部、吏部侍郎。这种经历，让他的才干得到全方位的历练，又广结人脉。命运给了他常人少有的青睐。

朝野都看到，一颗新星正在京师冉冉升起，不用多久，此人必将入阁拜相，走进最高的权力圈。然而，命运便就在这时，为他做了另外一番安排。

（二）

咸丰二年六月，他又得到一个好差事，那就是主考江西乡试。这趟差使，除了给他通常的许多好处外，还有一个特别的好处，那就是他可以在乡试完毕回家探亲。他离家整整十二年了。十二年间，他的祖母祖父相继去世，他的父母也逐年变老。这段时期，父亲与几个弟弟跟他在京师还见过面，唯独没有再见过面的母亲，成了他心中最大的牵挂。他太想见母亲了！而这次，他有机会如愿以偿。他向皇上请准两月的探亲假，怀着巨大的憧憬，离京踏上江西乡试主考之路。

岂料，上天给了他最大的惩罚。半途之中，他接到母亲去世的讣告。他只得辞职，立即改道还乡，为母亲办理丧事。

几乎就在同时，一年多前在广西起义的太平军，杀出广西进入湖南，一路攻城略地，势如破竹。在围攻湖南省城长沙八十多天后，转而北上，轻易地拿下湖北重镇汉阳。消息传到北京，朝廷一片惊惶。咸丰帝火速任命曾国藩为湖南团练大臣，帮助地方政府维持社会治安，打击乘乱而起的动乱势力。

经过几番思考与犹豫后，曾国藩领下这道圣旨。咸丰二年十二月，他赶赴长沙，做起团练大臣来。团练大臣也需要自己的武装力量。在请示朝廷同意后，他在长沙建起一个民团。民团有一千余人，这一千余人全部来自他的家乡湘乡县。他按照明朝名将戚继光建戚家军的办法，将一千余人编成三个营，严格训练，期望他们能在战争中发挥大作用。

他的这些做法，令湖南省政府部门不能理解。因训练事，他又与驻扎在长沙的军方产生磨擦。在一场内斗之后，曾国藩决定离开长沙。他的这支千人大团，被带到湖南的南部重镇衡州府。在那里，他遇到了天赐良机。

他的好朋友湖南新宁人江忠源，因带领勇丁成功阻击太平军的功劳，而受到朝廷的信任。他请求曾国藩在湖南募勇训练，作为他的兵源的补充。此事得到了朝廷的同意。曾国藩借此在衡州招募万人，组建水师与陆军两支人马，各五千人十个营，加上八千随军长伕，号称两万。这支队伍建成不久，江忠源战死于安徽。于是，曾国藩自然而然地成了这支人马的统帅。咸丰四年（1854）正月，曾国藩带着这支人马在衡州府誓师出征。这支人马，便是日后声名赫赫的湘军。

湘军在经过几次败仗后，咸丰四年八月二十七日，攻破武昌、汉阳，一时声誉鹊起。朝廷对曾国藩及其湘军寄予极大希望。但湘军一进入江西，便身陷困境。接下来两年多里，仗打得多不顺利：败仗多，胜仗少；被动多，主动少；士气低迷多，军心昂扬少。总之，一句话：逆境多，顺境少。咸丰七年（1857）二月，曾国藩的父亲去世。借此机会，他离开战场回家休养。

在为父亲守丧的一年多时间里，曾国藩对出山五年的岁月，作了深刻的反思。在痛苦的思索中，他更多地是检讨自己的不足。通过这一番的反思与检讨，他的心志更加坚定，而行事方式也更加成熟与圆融了。

咸丰八年（1858）六月，曾国藩奉旨重返战场。他挺过三河之役的惨败，迎来时局剧变所带给他的转机。咸丰十年（1860）春，太平军一举踏平江南大营，席卷整个苏南，军锋凌厉，锐不可当。朝廷在四顾无人的危急中，不得不重用曾国藩及其湘军：任命曾国藩为两江总督。在熬过九个年头的客寄虚悬的尴尬局面后，曾国藩终于有了地方实权。有了这个实权，他在人事与粮饷两个方面，开始走出困境，步入坦途。不久，咸丰帝去世，慈禧掌权。慈禧调整过去咸丰帝对曾氏又用又疑的政策，令曾国藩统辖江苏、安徽、江西及浙江四省，所有四省的文武官员一律由曾国藩节制。这就意味着把整个东南战场交给曾国藩一人。随之，又晋升他为协办大学士，再次向天下表明朝廷对他的信任。

同治三年（1864）六月十六日，湘军中的劲旅吉字营，在曾氏胞弟曾国荃的率领下，攻破太平天国的都城天京。此一事实，宣告经过十余年的艰苦激战，湘军取得了最终胜利。朝廷封曾国藩为一等侯，他的弟弟曾国荃封一等伯。非皇亲国戚而兄弟同日并封侯伯，古往今来，没有先例。

诚如古人所说，日中则昃、月盈则亏，接下来的日子，曾国藩过得并不舒畅。捻战的不顺，令他抑郁。天津教案的处置，更让他身负骂名。他身心交瘁，彻底垮了下来。同治十一年（1872）二月初四日，曾国藩因脑中风，而突然病逝于两江总督任上，虚岁六十二岁。朝廷为之辍朝三日，谥为文正。

（三）

中国的先贤认为一个人应当在三个领域里努力，并有所建树。

这三个领域分别为：道德、事功、著述。这就是所谓的“三立”，即立德、立功、立言。曾国藩从年轻时代起，就信奉这个理念。他努力向圣贤看齐，千辛万苦地把平定天下的事业做成功。同时，他一生手不释卷，对各门学问都有很大的兴趣，尤其对诗与古文所下的功夫最多。他所编辑的两部诗文集《经史百家杂钞》与《十八家诗钞》，是晚清以来读书人案头上必备的书籍。他勤于创作，尽管军政公务繁忙，仍然为后世留下不少诗文。现存的《曾国藩全集》诗文卷中收有他的诗作三百三十多首，词作八首，古文一百六十多篇。

他的诗文，在近代中国文学史上有很大的影响与很高的地位。

为文上，他看重扬雄、韩愈的文风，在刚柔相济的审美观中，更偏向阳刚之美，讲究气势宏大、声调铿锵，正如钱基博所说：“湘乡曾国藩以雄直之气，宏通之识，发为文章”，“异军突起而自为一派，可名为湘乡派。一时流风所被，桐城而后，罕有抗颜行者”。

对于诗，他更偏重杜甫的沉郁忧思。后人认为，他是晚清同光体的开创者。

特别值得指出的是，作为封建末世乱局中的砥柱，他的奏折有“晚清第一奏折”之称。他的不少奏折在其生前便已传诵海内，被疆吏们视为奏章范本。

作为闻名遐迩的曾氏家族的家长，他身后流传甚广的曾文正公家书，其知名度与影响面，甚至远过于他精心创作的诗词与古文。要全面了解曾国藩，不能不读一读他写给子弟们的家书；况且，他的那些布局谨严、字句讲究的家书，也是他的文章中的一部分。

所以，这本诗文集，在精选他的诗词古文的同时，也选录了若干篇他的奏折、家书代表作，以便让我们更好认识这位被誉为“最后一个集中国传统文化大成”的曾文正公。

目前尚未发现曾国藩的作品被译成外文出版。由于曾国藩是中国近代史上极有影响的人物，国外学术界对曾氏的研究成果还是不少的。美国的一些中国学研究大家在其著作中都对曾氏有过论述，如马士的《中华帝国对外关系史》、黑尔的《曾国藩与太平天国》、芮玛丽的《同治中兴：中国保守主义的最后抵抗（1862—1874）》、孔飞力的《中华帝国晚期的叛乱及其敌人：1796—1864年的军事化与社会结构》、费正清与刘广京的《剑桥中国晚清史》、柯文的《在中国发现历史：中国中心观在美国的兴起》等。其中黑尔对曾国藩的研究尤其令人瞩目。他的《曾国藩与太平天国》是美国学术界第一本对曾国藩进行全面研究的著作，对其生平思想、治军、筹办洋务以及文学成就等都有论述。

关于这本选集，需要说明的有两点：第一，所选的诗文，均出自岳麓书社2011年《曾国藩全集》（修订版）。第二，诗文之排列，以时间先后为序。

唐浩明

Introduction

I

In 1811 [1], during the reign of the Qing Emperor Jiaqing, Zeng Guofan was born into a family of farmers and educators in Xiangxiang County, Hunan Province. His father, Zeng Linshu, who was a private school teacher, named him "Zicheng" and gave him the courtesy name "Bohan."[2]

His grandfather managed the family's land, and after his great grandfather's death when Zeng Guofan was five years old, three generations of the family lived under the same roof. Zeng Guofan was the second eldest of a large family, with four sisters and four younger brothers. Led by a capable grandfather and a hard-working father, the family managed to get by despite its size. All five boys had access to schooling, however, only Zeng Guofan achieved success through imperial examinations.[3]

It was only after sitting for the county-level imperial exam for the 17th time that Zeng Guofan's father finally passed to become a *xiucai* [4]at the age of 43.

Zeng Guofan sat for his first county-level imperial exam at the age of 14 but failed to pass it until his seventh attempt at the age of 23. Soon after, he attended the highest seat of learning in Hunan, Yuelu Academy, and passed the provincial imperial exam the following year to become a *juren*. [5] At the age of 28, he passed the national imperial exam on his third attempt and

1 All dates throughout this book are presented according to the Chinese lunar calendar.

2 A courtesy name is given upon adulthood.

3 Imperial examinations at the county-level were held annually; examinations at the provincial and the national level were usually held triennially.

4 *Xiucai* is the title for a scholar who has passed the county-level imperial exam.

5 *Juren* is the title for a scholar who has passed the provincial exam.

became a *jinshi*. [1] After passing the palace examination presided by the emperor, he reached the pinnacle of the imperial exam system when he was appointed to Hanlin Academy as an official *shujishi*. [2] His successful navigation of this system was all the more extraordinary given his farming background and the highly competitive nature of the exams. Subsequently, he changed his name from "Zicheng" to "Guofan" and assumed the pen name "Disheng," eagerly embracing a promising future with a heart full of ambition.

Two years later, Zeng Guofan passed the exam at Hanlin Academy and stayed on as an imperial historiographer at the associate seventh rank. He spent 12 years serving as an imperial official in Beijing, leaving the capital at the age of 42 with an illustrious career. This period was underscored by a determination to strengthen his integrity through self-cultivation and strict self-discipline.

During his second year in Beijing, Zeng Guofan learned from Tang Jian. [3] Together with like-minded friends, such as Wuqigeli Woren [4] and Wu Tingdong, [5] Zeng Guofan broadened his knowledge base and refined his character to better equip himself to govern the country and promote world peace in the future. He focused on five areas that he incorporated into his daily life: sincerity, respect, meditation, circumspection, and perseverance. He held himself to a high standard by keeping a diary and exercising caution in his

1 *Jinshi* is the title for a scholar who has passed the national exam.

2 *Shujishi* is a temporary post for new-comers in Hanlin Academy during their internship.

3 Tang Jian (1778-1861) was a famous neo-Confucianist in the late Qing Dynasty. He was appointed as chamberlain of ceremonials during the reign of Emperor Daoguang.

4 Woren (1804-1871), or Wesin in Manchu pronunciation, was a famous neo-Confucianist in the late Qing Dynasty. He was appointed as grand secretary of the imperial cabinet during the reign of Emperor Tongzhi.

5 Wu Tingdong (1793-1873) was a famous neo-Confucianist in the late Qing Dynasty. He was appointed as Vice Minister of Punishment during the reign of Emperor Tongzhi.

private life, whittling away at his faults to morally prepare himself for what the future held for him.

Life as an official in Beijing also afforded him opportunities to demonstrate his competence, thereby earning sufficient respect from his peers.

Zeng Guofan had an extraordinary career. He was promoted seven times across five government ministries over ten years beginning when he was 28. At the age of 37, he was promoted a remarkable four times within one year, from a fourth-rank midlevel official to a second-rank senior official. Moreover, during a period of just three years, Zeng served Emperors Daoguang and Xianfeng as the vice minister of four ministries successively: war, works, punishments, and personnel. He did this while also holding down his post as Vice Minister of Rites, thereby leaving the Ministry of Revenue as the only one of the six ministries he did not lead. Being tested in this way made him more well rounded with his personal network expanded. There was no doubt that fate was on his side.

The government and the public recognized that a new political star was rising in the capital. His path toward leadership and the highest government circle appeared unstoppable. Fate, however, had different plans.

II

In the sixth month of the second year of Emperor Xianfeng's reign (1852), Zeng Guofan received a plum commission. He was appointed chief examiner of the provincial imperial exam in Jiangxi Province. In addition to the usual benefits, this commission would allow him to return home to visit family after the provincial imperial exam. During the 12 years he had been away, his paternal grandparents had died, and his parents had grown frail. Although his father and younger brothers had visited him in the capital, Zeng Guofan worried about his mother, whom he had not seen since leaving home. Seizing his chance, he pleaded with the emperor for 20 days' leave to visit family and then departed Beijing for his new commission in Jiangxi.

However, the greatest misfortune befell him: he was notified of his mother's death on his journey to Jiangxi. He resigned his commission and returned home to mourn his mother.

Around the same time, the Taiping rebels, who had fought in Guangxi more than a year earlier, coalesced into an unstoppable force that shifted its focus from Guangxi to Hunan, steamrolling through cities and plundering along the way. After more than 80 days besieging Changsha, the capital of Hunan, the Taiping rebels turned north and seized the strategic town of Hanyang in Hubei Province. News of the rebels' victories sparked a panic in the imperial government. Emperor Xianfeng quickly appointed Zeng Guofan to head a civil defense corps in Hunan to help the local government maintain order and fight against the ensuing riotous forces.

After much consideration, Zeng Guofan accepted the post and headed to Changsha in the 12th month of the second year of Emperor Xianfeng's reign (1852). As the head of the civil defense corps, he needed to establish a force of his own. With the imperial government's permission, he raised a one-thousand-strong corps filled solely with people from his hometown, Xiangxiang County. In a nod to the famed Ming Dynasty general Qi Jiguang, Zeng Guofan raised a fighting force based on family ties and then divided them into three battalions. He drilled them relentlessly in preparation for the decisive role that they would play against the Taiping rebels.

Zeng Guofan's methods perplexed the Hunan provincial

government and caused friction with the military stationed in Changsha. Infighting prompted him to leave Changsha and shift his one thousand troops to Hengzhou Prefecture, a strategic stronghold in southern Hunan. There, a divine opportunity presented itself.

Jiang Zhongyuan was a native of Xinning in Hunan and a good friend of Zeng Guofan. He had won the trust of the imperial government in return for leading a local militia to thwart the Taiping rebels. He urged Zeng Guofan to recruit troops in Hunan to supplement his army. Zeng Guofan enlisted ten thousand troops in Hengzhou and established a navy and an army, each with 10 battalions totaling five thousand troops. The addition of eight thousand conscripted laborers brought the total number of troops to approximately twenty thousand. Soon after these armed forces were established, Jiang Zhongyuan was killed fighting in Anhui Province, thus making Zeng Guofan their new commander-in-chief. In January of the fourth year of Emperor Xianfeng's reign (1854), Zeng Guofan rallied the armed forces in Hengzhou, marking the beginning of the renowned Xiang Army (Hunan Army).

On the 27th day of the eighth month in the fourth year of Emperor Xianfeng's reign (1854), the Xiang Army overcame previous defeats to recapture Wuchang and Hanyang from the Taiping rebels, quickly establishing the army's reputation. The imperial government had high hopes for Zeng Guofan, but his army would soon become bogged down in Jiangxi. Over the next two years, victories often proved elusive and the army expressed little initiative, leading to low morale among the troops. In short, adversity outweighed any advantages. The passing of his father in the second month of 1857 afforded Zeng Guofan the opportunity to lick his wounds, and he left the battlefield for home.

For more than a year, Zeng Guofan mourned his father and

contemplated the five years he led the army, painfully examining his faults. This reflection and self-criticism fortified his resolve and cultivated a maturity and sense of ease that he previously did not have.

In the sixth month of the eighth year of Emperor Xianfeng's reign (1858), Zeng Guofan was ordered to return to the battlefield. After a disastrous defeat at the battle of Sanhe Town in Anhui, a change in the political climate turned things around. In the spring of 1860, the Taiping rebels captured the Jiangnan military base (one of the two military bases established by the imperial government to fight the Taiping rebels) and steamrolled through southern Jiangsu province. Desperate to find anyone trustworthy, the imperial government was forced to turn again to Zeng Guofan and his Xiang Army to suppress the Taiping rebels, appointing Zeng Guofan the Viceroy of Liangjiang (present-day Jiangsu, Anhui, and Jiangxi provinces). After nine humbling years, Zeng Guofan finally had real local power that allowed him to address issues of personnel and provisions that had plagued his Xiang Army. Soon after, Emperor Xianfeng died, Emperor Tongzhi succeeded to the throne, but it was Empress Dowager Cixi who came to power. Whereas Emperor Xianfeng had used Zeng Guofan despite harboring misgivings about him, Empress Dowager Cixi gave him free rein over Jiangsu, Anhui, Jiangxi, and Zhejiang provinces, putting all civil and military officials in those areas under his command. This meant that the entire southeast battlefield was entrusted solely to him. He was soon promoted to Deputy Grand Secretary (Vice Prime Minister), further demonstrating the imperial government's confidence in him.

On the 16th day of the sixth month in the third year of Emperor Tongzhi's reign (1864), under the leadership of Zeng Guofan's younger brother, Zeng Guoquan, an elite squad in the Xiang Army called the Jizi Battalion defeated the Taiping rebels and captured Tianjing (present-day Nanjing), the capital of the Taiping Heavenly Kingdom. This victory came at the cost of more than ten years of arduous and intense fighting by the Xiang Army. Out of respect, the imperial government awarded Zeng Guofan and Zeng Guoquan, the titles of first-class marquis and first-class count, respectively, which was an unprecedented honor for officials from non-imperial families.

As the ancients used to say, the sun travels westward after midday, and the moon wanes after turning full. In the years that followed, contentment and joy eluded Zeng Guofan. His unsuccessful fight against the peasant-led Nian Army in northern China and the handling of the Tianjin Massacre [1] caused depression and blackened his reputation. Mental and physical exhaustion followed, and on the fourth day of the second month in the 11th year of Emperor Tongzhi's reign (1872), Zeng Guofan died of a stroke at the age of 62. Out of respect, the imperial government suspended official activities for three days and granted him the posthumous title "Wenzheng."[2]

III

The ancient sages believed that one should strive to make contributions in three areas: virtue, meritorious service, and writing. This concept, also known as the three achievements (*sanli*), is what Zeng Guofan had championed since his youth. He strove to emulate the sages and underwent innumerable hardships to bring peace and stability to the country. At the same time, he was a studious man who devoted his life to all manner of learning, and to poetry and classical Chinese prose in particular. He compiled two collections of poetry and prose, namely, *A Collection of*

1 The Tianjin Massacre occurred in 1870 when Tianjin civilians attacked Catholic churches in protest against forceful evangelization.

2 The literal meaning of "Wenzheng" is "literary and righteous."

One Hundred Classics and Historical Writings and *A Collection of Poems by Eighteen Poets*, which have been indispensable to scholars since the late Qing Dynasty. Despite being steeped in military and political affairs, Zeng Guofan was also a diligent writer who left behind many poems for later generations. *The Complete Works of Zeng Guofan*, which is in print, contains more than 330 poems, eight *ci*-poems, [1] and more than 160 works of classical Chinese prose.

His literary works have had a strong influence on the history of modern Chinese literature and are highly regarded.

As for classical Chinese prose, his writing style follows that of literary figures such as Yang Xiong [2] and Han Yu, [3] and his aesthetic sense integrates power and grace with a strong masculine presence and a grand sonorous tone. According to Qian Jibo, [4] "Zeng Guofan's writing style flows from a place of masculinity, morality, and extensive knowledge." Qian continued, "He emerged as the representative of a new school of literature called the Xiangxiang school. For a time, his style was so popular it was almost unrivaled after the decline of the Tongcheng school."[5]

In terms of poetry, Zeng Guofan favored the melancholy of the Tang Dynasty poet Du Fu. Later generations considered him to be the founder of the Tong-Guang [6] style of the late Qing Dynasty.

In particular, he remained a stalwart during the chaotic

1 *Ci* is a type of lyric poetry that uses various poetic meters derived from a base set of fixed pattern forms. The rhythmic and tonal pattern of *ci*-poems are based upon certain, definitive musical song tunes (*cipai*).

2 Yang Xiong (53 BC-AD 18) was a Chinese philosopher, poet, and politician of the Western Han Dynasty known for his philosophical writings and *fu*-poetry compositions.

3 Han Yu (768-824), courtesy name Tuizhi (Chinese: 退之), was a Chinese historian, poet, philosopher, and politician during the Tang Dynasty who significantly influenced the development of Neo-Confucianism.

4 Qian Jibo (1887-1957) was a conservative Confucian scholar, landed gentry, and Chinese language professor at Tsinghua University, St. John's University, Hunan Normal University, and National Central University (Nanking).

5 The Tongcheng school originated in Tongcheng County, Anhui Province. It was the most influential school of the Qing Dynasty.

6 An abbreviation of Emperor Tongzhi and Emperor Guangxu.

final throes of feudalism, and his memorials to the throne are considered the best of the late Qing Dynasty. During his lifetime, many were extensively read throughout China and were regarded as templates by frontier officials.

As the head of the renowned Zeng family, Zeng Guofan's family letters were widely available after his death, and they remain far more influential than his poems and classical Chinese prose. A full understanding of Zeng Guofan would be incomplete without reading his family letters, which are meticulously composed and should be considered part of his classical Chinese prose.

As such, this collection includes selected memorials to the throne and family letters to be considered alongside Zeng Guofan's poetry and prose, thus painting a fuller picture of "the last embodiment of traditional Chinese culture."

Zeng Guofan's works have not been found translated into foreign languages for publication. With Zeng Guofan being a highly influential figure in modern Chinese history, there have been research achievements on him in the academic circles abroad. Some Chinese studies experts in the United States have discussed the Zeng Guofan in their works, such as H. B. Morse's *The International Relations of the Chinese Empire*, W. J. Hail's *Tseng Kuo-fan and the Taiping Rebellion*, M. C. Wright's *The Last Stand of Chinese Conservation: The Tungchih Restoration*, 1862—1874, P. A. Kuhn's *A Rebellion and It Enemies in Late Imperial China: Militarization and Social Structure*, 1796—1864, J. K. Fairbank and Kwang-Ching Liu's *Cambridge History of China in the Late Qing Dynasty*, and P. A. Cohen's *Discovering History in China*. Among them, Hail's *Tseng Kuo-fan and the Taiping Rebellion* is particularly noteworthy. Being the first comprehensive study of Zeng Guofan in the American academic community, Hail's monograph discusses Zeng's life philosophy, military governance, preparations for the

Westernization Movement, and literary achievements.

There are two points to note about this collection.First, the selections are taken from the revised edition of *The Complete Works of Zeng Guofan*, published by Yuelu Publishing House in 2011.Second, the selected writings are arranged in chronological order.

Tang Haoming

目 录

Contents

目　录

诗

02　岁暮杂感十首（选二）
06　寄郭筠仙浙江四首
10　忆弟二首
14　温甫读书城南寄示二首
18　送妹夫王五归五首
24　酬九弟（选一）
28　小池
30　题《箸筤谷图》
34　次韵何廉昉太守感怀述事十六首（选一）
36　沅甫弟四十一初度
44　忮求诗二首

词

56　贺新郎——题钱楞仙同年《玉堂归娶图》二首

文

62　烹阿封即墨论
68　送郭筠仙南归序
74　求阙斋记
80　送唐先生南归序
88　原才
94　君子慎独论
98　欧阳生文集序
108　圣哲画像记
130　英雄诫子弟

Contents

Poems

Ten Poems on Random Year-end Thoughts (Two Selections) 03
Four Poems to Guo Yunxian in Zhejiang Province 07
Two Poems to My Brothers 11
Two Poems to My Brother Guohua at Chengnan Academy 15
Five Poems to My Homebound Brother-in-Law Wang Daipin 19
To My Brother Guoquan (One Selection) 25
The Little Pond 29
On "The Green Bamboo Valley" 31
A Response to He Lianfang's 16 Nostalgic Poems (One Selection) 35
In Celebration of My Brother Guoquan's 41st Birthday 37
Two Poems on Envy and Greed 45

Ci-poems

To the Tune of *Hexinlang* Two *Ci*-poems on the Painting"Going Home to Marry in Jade Hall" 57

Prose

On Boiling Echeng Officials and Rewarding Jimo Officials 63
Foreword to *Bidding Goodbye to Guo Yunxian on His Southward Journey Back Home* 69
Records from the Imperfection-seeking Chamber 75
Foreword to *Bidding Goodbye to Master Tang on His Southward Journey Back Home* 81
On Discovering Talented People 89
On Exercising Caution in Solitude 95
Foreword to the *Collected Works of Ouyang Sheng* 99
Portraits of Sages 109
Outstanding Figures on Educating Their Children 131

140 箴言书院记
148 《王船山遗书》序
158 书赠仲弟六则
168 劝学篇示直隶士子
180 湘乡昭忠祠记
190 罗忠节公神道碑铭
206 大界墓表
216 《湖南文征》序

奏折

226 应诏陈言疏
246 备陈民间疾苦疏
264 遵旨复奏借俄兵助剿发逆并代运南漕折
278 参翁同书片
286 拟选聪颖子弟赴泰西各国肄业折

家书

300 致诸弟 (1842)
316 谕纪鸿 (1856)
320 谕纪泽 (1858)
328 致澄弟 (1860)
332 致澄弟 (1861)
338 谕纪泽、纪鸿 (1862)
342 致沅弟 (1863)
348 致沅弟 (1864)
352 致澄弟 (1864)
356 谕纪泽、纪鸿 (1871)

A Note to Zhenyan Academy 141
An Introduction to *Posthumous Works of Wang chuanshan* 149
Six Notes to My Brother Guohuang 159
A Note to Encourage Learning Among Hebei Scholars 169
A Note on Zhaozhong Ancestral Temple in Xiangxiang County 181
Inscription on Luo Zenan's Tombstone 191
Inscription on the Dajie Gravestone 207
Foreword to *Hunan Anthology* 217

Memorials to the Throne

Memorial in Response to an Imperial Edict 227
Memorial on the People's Hardships 247
Memorial on Russia's Offer to Suppress the Taiping Rebel Army and Transport Northbound Grain in Response to an Imperial Edict 265
Memorial Attachment to Impeach Weng Tongshu 279
Memorial on the Selection of Bright Young Scholars to Study in the West 287

Family Letters

To My Brothers(1842) 301
To Jihong(1856) 317
To Jize(1858) 321
To My Brother Guohuang(1860) 329
To My Brother Guohuang(1861) 333
To Jize and Jihong(1862) 339
To My Brother Guoquan(1863) 343
To My Brother Guoquan(1864) 349
To My Brother Guohuang(1864) 353
To Jize and Jihong(1871) 357

诗

Poems

岁暮杂感十首（选二）

道光十四年(1854),二十四岁的曾国藩考中举人。这年年底,他来到北京,参加明年春天的礼部会试。遗憾的是，他未考中。因道光十六年有恩科会试，这是一个好机会，于是曾国藩没有回湖南老家，而是留在北京，寓居长郡会馆，刻苦攻读四书五经，以待恩科再试。道光十五年十二月，在寒冷而寂寞的北京古城,他写下十首七律,题为《岁暮杂感十首》。这里选取其中的第一、二两首。

第一首写的是独在异乡为异客的作者的思念家乡之情，他想象着北归的大雁会为他带来故乡的消息。第二首具体地写他对家乡高嵋山的怀念。

芒鞋镇日踏春还，
残腊将更却等闲。
三百六旬同逝水，
四千余里说家山。
缁尘已自沾京雒，
羌笛何须怨玉关。
为报南来新雁到，
故乡消息在云间。

Ten Poems on Random Year-end Thoughts (Two Selections)

In the 14th year of Emperor Daoguang's reign (1834), Zeng Guofan passed the provincial imperial exam to become a *juren* at the age of 24. In autumn that same year, he traveled to Beijing for a national imperial exam that would be held by the Ministry of Rites the following spring. Unfortunately, he did not pass. He remained in Beijing to take a special imperial exam that would be held in 1836. While boarding at Changjun Guild Hall, he dedicated himself to studying the Four Books and Five Classics of Confucianism. Then, in the cold and lonely Beijing in the twelfth month of 1835, he composed ten *qilü*-poems [1] titled "Ten Poems on Random Year-end Thoughts." The first two poems are presented below.

In the first poem, the poet recounts the homesickness that he feels as a lonely stranger in a far-off land. He imagines that swan geese returning from the south will bring him news from home. In the second poem, the poet reminisces about Mount Gaomei, which is located in his hometown.

After a spring outing in straw sandals,
I remain at ease even as the year turns.
One year's time flows by like a river,
As I reminisce about my home thousands of miles away.
My black horse stains with dust from travel to the capital,
Qiang flute is heard without reproaching Yumen Pass.
Swan geese [2] fly north from the south,
Delivering news from home over the clouds.

1 *Qilü* is a type of eight-line poem that has seven characters per line and follows strict prosodic rules.

2 Swan geese are often considered messengers in traditional Chinese literature.

高嵋山下是侬家，
岁岁年年斗物华。
老柏有情还忆我，
夭桃无语自开花。
几回南国思红豆，
曾记西风浣碧纱。
最是故园难忘处，
待莺亭畔路三叉。

My home sits at the foot of Mount Gaomei;
Nature presents a beautiful spectacle every year.
The old cypress trees still remember me;
The fine peach trees blossom at will.
I often recall the red beans in the south,
And the west wind gently passing through the screen door.
The most memorable place back home,
Remains the Oriole Pavilion by the forked road.

寄郭筠仙浙江四首

道光二十年(1840)九月,会试落第的郭嵩焘离京投浙江学政罗文俊之幕。这年十一月,新任翰林院检讨之职的曾氏,写了四首七律寄给郭嵩焘。

郭嵩焘字筠仙,湖南湘阴人,是曾氏的终生挚友、儿女亲家。郭氏于道光二十七年中进士,入翰林院,历官苏松粮道、两淮盐运使、署理广东巡抚,晚年出任驻英、法公使。

这四首诗抒发了诗人对友谊的珍惜,对孤寂中的朋友的安慰,以及初入官场的自我感叹。

一病多劳勤护惜,
嗟君此别太匆匆。
二三知己天涯隔,
强半光阴道路中。
兔走会须营窟穴,
鸿飞原不计西东。
读书识字知何益?
赢得行踪似转蓬。

碣石逶迤起阵云,
楼船羽檄日纷纷。

Four Poems to Guo Yunxian in Zhejiang Province

After failing the imperial exams, Guo Songtao left Beijing in the ninth month of the 20th year of Emperor Daoguang's reign (1840) to join Luo Wenjun, the educational commissioner of Zhejiang. In the 11th month that same year, Zeng Guofan took time from his new appointment as a historiographer at Hanlin Academy to write four *qilü-* poems, which he sent to Guo Songtao.

Guo Songtao, courtesy name Yunxian, was a native of Xiangyin County, Hunan Province. He was a lifelong friend to Zeng Guofan and the father-in-law to one of his daughters. Guo Songtao entered Hanlin Academy after passing the national imperial exam in 1847. He served as the grain commissioner of the Su-Song region (Suzhou and Songjiang), the salt commissioner of the Lianghuai region (areas north and south of the Huai River), and the acting governor of Guangdong Province. In later years, he served as an envoy to Great Britain and France.

In the following poems, the poet expresses the value he places on friendship, comforts lonely friends, and reflects on life as an official.

Take care as you are busy and ailing;
Alas, you left in such haste.
A handful of confidants scatter to the winds;
Journeys occupy much of our time.
Rabbits learn to tend burrows;
Flying swan geese heed direction.
What good is reading books?
Only to wander in life like floating grass seeds.

Dense clouds loom over meandering Mount Jieshi,
Warships and maneuvers intensify by the day.

螳螂竟欲当车辙，
髋髀安能抗斧斤？
但解终童陈策略，
已闻王歙立功勋。
如今旅梦应安稳，
早绝天骄荡海氛。

无穷志愿付因循，
弹指人间三十春。
一局楸枰虞变幻，
百围梁栋借轮囷。
苍茫独立时怀古，
艰苦新尝识保身。
自愧太仓縻好爵，
故交数辈尚清贫。

向晚严霜破屋寒，
娟娟纤月倚檐端。
自翻行箧殷勤觅，
苦索家书展转看。
宦海情怀蝉翼薄，
离人心绪茧丝团。
更怜吴会飘零客，
纸帐孤灯坐夜阑。

However, like a mantis hoping to block a war wagon,
How could a hip or a thigh contend with an ax?
As soon as Zhong Jun [1] emerges with a brilliant strategy,
Reports arrive of young Wang Xi's [2] exploits.
Let the traveler sleep free of homesickness today,
For young warriors cleared the borders of foes.

Ambition makes way for routine;
Thirty years passes in an instant.
The chessboard foretells change;
Trees grow thick with a hundred rings.
Boundless solitude encourages nostalgia;
A taste of distress may keep one safe.
My good fortune in the capital shames me,
For my old friend is still in need.

A heavy frost breaks through the house at dusk;
An elegant slip of a moon rests upon the eaves.
I rummage through the travel case,
Scrambling for letters from home to read anew.
The true feelings of an official are as flimsy as a cicada's wings;
The traveler's thoughts are entangled as though by caterpillar silk.
Pity the lone visitor in Wu County,
Sitting at night by a paper screen lit by a lonely lamp.

1 Zhong Jun, posthumously known as "Zhong Tong," was a famous young strategist during the reign of Emperor Wu in the Han Dynasty.

2 Wang Xi was a famous strategist during the reign of Emperor Ping in the Han Dynasty.

忆弟二首

道光二十二年（1842）十月十二、十四日两天，在对岁月飞逝的感叹声中，作者写下两首思念远在故乡的四个弟弟的七律。

曾国藩有四个弟弟，按族中排行，分别为四弟国潢、六弟国华、九弟国荃、季弟国葆。这四个弟弟在后来的战争年代中，都成了他的重要帮手。此时他们都在家乡忙着读书求学，应付科举考试。但求取功名对他们来说是一桩难事，当时他们连秀才都没有一人考中。

第一首，写的是对四个弟弟的一齐想念。在最后一句中，我们仿佛看到一个望断天涯、愁肠百结的游子正站在眼前。

第二首，是专门写给九弟的。在北京大哥家住了一年半的老九，这年七月离京回家。作者想起四年前回家途中，在襄阳渡襄水时遇到的危难，就问九弟：你这次过襄水时，情况如何？

无端绕室思茫茫，
明月当天万瓦霜。
可惜良宵空兀坐，
遥怜诸弟在何方？
纷纷书帙谁能展，
艳艳灯花有底忙。
出户独吟聊妄想，
孤云断处是家乡。

Two Poems to My Brothers

On the 12th and 14th days of the tenth month in the 22nd year of Emperor Daoguang's reign (1842), Zeng Guofan lamented the quick passing of time and composed the two *qilü*-poems below out of nostalgia for his brothers, who were still living in his hometown.

From oldest to youngest, his four younger brothers were named Guohuang, Guohua, Guoquan, and Guobao. In later years, they would become trusted wartime aides, but they were still home diligently preparing for the imperial exams when he wrote these poems. However, scholarly honors did not come as easily for his brothers, none of whom even passed the county-level imperial exam.

The first poem relates how deeply Zeng Guofan misses his brothers, with the last sentence painting a picture of a burden-weary traveler standing before us far from home.

The second poem is dedicated to his brother Guoquan, who lived with the poet in Beijing for a year and a half before returning home in the seventh month of 1842. Zeng Guofan recalled the peril he faced four years earlier while crossing the Xiang River (in Xiangyang of Hubei Province) on the way home. He asks Guoquan, how it was crossing the Xiang River this time.

Around the house I aimlessly pace;
The moon shines on the roof tiles like frost.
Alas, as I sit alone on this fine night,
I ask from afar, where are my brothers?
Who will crack open these books?
Busy are the lanterns shining so bright.
I go out to chant alone, wishing in vain,
For the lonely clouds to float to my hometown.

忽忆他时襄水上，
恶风半夜撼春雷。
舟人捩舵声同泣，
客子扶床面已灰。
仰荷皇天全薄命，
信知浮世等轻埃。
汝今归去复何似？
回首世途诚险哉。

Once while crossing the Xiang River,
An evil wind shook the night with spring thunder.
The boatman turned the rudder with a sob;
The passengers paled as they gripped their berths.
I entrusted my ill-fated life to Heaven,
Knowing I was no more than specks of dust in this world.
How was your return journey?
The world is indeed a treacherous place.

温甫读书城南寄示二首

这两首诗作于道光二十三年（1843）。此时他的六弟国华（号温甫）正在长沙城南书院读书。城南书院即湖南第一师范学院的前身。

第一首夸奖六弟眼下正是出山朝云，希望他专心攻读，以求出类拔萃；又叹息自己终日陷于事务及应酬之中，蹉跎了岁月。

第二首是诗人对长沙的美好回忆。九年前，曾氏在岳麓书院读书，对文化名城长沙记忆深刻。诗中提到的城南妙高峰、岳麓山下的爱晚亭、岳麓山上的大禹碑以及市中心古长沙国定王旧居等，都是长沙有名的风景区及远古遗存。通过对它们的想念，诗人写出了他对长沙古城以及对自己那段求学岁月的怀念。

十年长隐南山雾，
今日始为出岫云。
事业真如移马磨，
羽毛何得避鸡群。
求珠采玉从吾好，
秋菊春兰各自芬。
嗟我蹉跎无一用，
尘埃车马日纷纷。

Two Poems to My Brother Guohua at Chengnan Academy

Written in the 23rd year of Emperor Daoguang's reign (1843), the next two poems relate to the poet's brother Guohua, under the pen name Wenfu, who was studying in Changsha at Chengnan Academy.[1]

The first poem describes a future that awaits Guohua if he studies hard and makes a name for himself. The poet then laments the time that has been wasted while he is bogged down with work and social niceties.

In the second poem, the poet recalls fond memories of living and studying in Changsha, the cultural city where he attended Yuelu Academy almost a decade earlier. The poem highlights scenic and historic sites, including Miaogao Peak in the south, Autumn-Admiring Pavilion at the foot of Yuelu Mountain, the Da Yu stele at the top of Yuelu Mountain, and the royal residence of the ancient Changsha Kingdom in the city center. The poet guides the reader through these sites to express his nostalgia for the ancient city and the years he spent at school there.

Concealed for ten years in the misty southern mountains,
Now is the time to emerge from your cave.
A career is like encouraging horses to work,
The challenge is to avoid blending in with the flock.
People seek talents to their own liking;
Chrysanthemums and orchids each have their own day.
Alas, I waste time to no avail;
Riding in a carriage amid dust day to day.

1 The predecessor of "Hunan First Normal University."

岳麓东环湘水回，
长沙风物信佳哉！
妙高峰上携谁步？
爱晚亭边醉几回。
夏后功名余片石，
汉王钟鼓拨寒灰。
知君此日沉吟地，
是我当年眺览来。

The Xiang River[1] running east of Yuelu Mountain,
The scenery in Changsha is wonderful!
With whom did you walk on Miaogao Peak?
I often got tipsy by the Autumn-Admiring Pavilion.
The Xia Dynasty's glory is engraved into slab stone;
The bell and drum of the Han King have cooled down;
Where you stand muttering to yourself,
Was where I once gazed into the distance?

1 This Xiang River runs in Hunan Province.

送妹夫王五归五首

道光二十四年（1844）五月，曾氏胞妹国蕙之夫王待聘（在家族内被称之为率五）来到北京投奔内兄。王待聘希望在翰林院做官的内兄，为他在翰苑谋得一个小差事，借内兄的提携，今后做一名小官吏。

王待聘的这个自我人生规划，从根本上来说就是错误的。一则翰苑门槛极高，身无功名的他是不可能迈进去的。二则此时的曾氏只是翰林院的下层官员，并无能力在此地安插私人。留妹夫在京师住了三个月后，曾氏无可奈何地将王待聘打发回家，临分手时赠送了他这五首诗。

“牛衣岁月即羲皇”，是这五首诗的核心内容。曾氏劝告妹夫：不要羡慕官场，安居乡里，夫妻恩爱，虽清贫却无忧无虑，这就是上好岁月。

飘然弃我即山林，
野服黄冠抵万金。
滚滚污尘得少辟，
茫茫歧路一长吟。
梁鸿旅食妻孥共，
苏季贫归忧患深。
东去大江芦荻老，
皇天飒飒正秋霖。

Five Poems to My Homebound Brother-in-Law Wang Daipin

In the fifth month of the 24th year of Emperor Daoguang's reign (1844), Wang Daipin, the husband of Zeng Guofan's younger sister Guohui, joined the poet in Beijing. He had hoped that, as an official at Hanlin Academy, Zeng Guofan would use his connections to find him a job and someday guide his entry into officialdom.

Unfortunately, Wang Daipin's plan was not well thought out. First, he lacked the scholarly achievements required to enter such a lauded institution as Hanlin Academy. Second, at that time, Zeng Guofan was a low-level official with no leverage to exercise favoritism. After three months in the capital, Zeng Guofan finally sent him home with the five poems below.

The five poems are based on the line, "Even Fuxi [1] loves simple living." Zeng Guofan advises his brother-in-law not to envy the life of an official. Instead, he exhorts him to enjoy a peaceful life in the countryside with his loving wife. Nothing could be better than a poor but honest life free from worries.

Leaving me for the mountains,
Simple clothes worth some gold.
Keep the billowy dust away;
Sing a song on the lengthy forked road.
Liang Hong [2] shared humble food with his wife and children;
Su Qin [3] returned home impoverished and in misery.
East along the Yangtze reeds grow old;
Heaven whistles for the wind amidst the autumn rain.

1 Fuxi was counted as the first of the Three Sovereigns at the beginning of the Chinese dynastic period and credited along with his sister and wife Nüwa with creating humanity.

2 Liang Hong was a famous writer of the Eastern Han Dynasty. He had a respectful and loving wife.

3 Su Qin was a famous strategist of the Warring States period. He had a haughty wife.

荆楚楩楠夹道栽，
于人无忤世无猜。
岂知斤斧联翩至，
复道牛羊烂漫来！
金碧觚棱依日月，
峥嵘大栋逼风雷。
回头却羡曲辕栎，
岁岁偷闲作弃材。

高嵋山下草芊绵，
去国蹉跎今六年。
村老半闻悲薤露，
人间容易即桑田。
炎云凉雨有翻覆，
舞榭歌台况变迁。
莫讶荣枯无定态，
君今犹守旧青毡。

Phoebe and Pine trees line narrow lanes;
Men without defiance appear innocent.
Alas, axes strike in quick succession;
Cattle and sheep turn and scatter!
Colorful roof corners rise up against the heavens;
Towering trees brace against thunder and wind.
They look back with envy upon the twisted old oak,
Reveling in a long leisurely life.

Grasses grow dense down Mount Gaomei;
Six years I have been away from home.
Half of the village elders have passed on;
Change is the norm in this world.
They alternate like hot clouds and cool rains;
Change marks the dance hall and the singing stage.
Be not surprised that nothing is fixed;
You still hold fast to the old norms.

有齐季女吾弟行，
操臼君家老孟光。
曾是弋凫相劳飨，
犹闻雏凤已轩昂。
秦嘉上计心情薄，
王霸躬耕身世忘。
织屦辟纩终古事，
牛衣岁月即羲皇。

老弟三年困省门，
寒山无律可回温。
由来命分政须尔，
久信文章不足尊。
南雁乖违少书信，
西风牢落对乾坤。
因君传语告予季，
失马亡羊莫更论。

A pious young lady keeps my brother company,
Just as Meng Guang[1] managed the home.
Together you are soul mates;
The young phoenix readies for flight.
Though promoted, Qin Jia[2] bore regrets;
Wang Ba[3] chose to retire to the farm.
Shoemaking and weaving make traditions;
Even Lord Fuxi loves simple living.

Brother you are trapped in Hunan for three years;
The cold mountain warms up on a whim.
Destiny is just as fickle as this,
Years of writing are not enough for respect.
Few family letters arrive from the south;
Only the west wind offers comfort here.
Pass my words down to my brothers;
Think no more over lost horses and goats.

1 Meng Guang was the loyal wife of Liang Hong.

2 Qin Jia was a poet of the Eastern Han Dynasty. He missed his wife terribly when he was appointed to a post in Luoyang, the capital.

3 Wang Ba was a famous hermit of the Western Han Dynasty. He returned to a farming life after resigning from the imperial government.

酬九弟（选一）

这首诗写于道光二十四年（1844），是名曰《酬九弟四首》中的第四首。

之所以选取这首诗，是因为它的开头两句很有名。前面说过，曾氏有四个弟弟，除开最小的那个外，其他三个都已成年，这两句则是对这三个弟弟的评价。做大哥的评价弟弟，不足为奇；奇的是后来的情形，与这些评语一一吻合。

辰君指四弟国潢，他生在庚辰年。“平正”二字，用来评价老四。老四终生既无功名，又无战功，守在老家一辈子。平者，平凡、平庸。正者，规规矩矩，走正道。对于老四，这是最恰当的评语。午君指壬午年出生的六弟国华。老六的突出特色是特立独行，与众不同。评价最高的是老九沅甫（国荃），诗人称之为曾家的白眉。汉代有“马氏五常，白眉最良”之说，即兄弟五人中长着白眉的那个最优秀。后来的事实证明，老九的确是他四个弟弟中的最优秀者。

辰君平正午君奇，
屈指老沅真白眉。
入世巾袍各肮脏，
闭门谐谑即支离。

To My Brother Guoquan (One Selection)

Composed in the 24th year of Emperor Daoguang's reign (1844), this is the last in a series of four poems titled "To My Brother Guoquan."

This poem was selected for the first two verses, which are quite famous. As mentioned previously, Zeng Guofan had four younger brothers, three of whom had reached adulthood by this time. In the first two verses, he evaluates his adult brothers, which was not surprising for an elder brother. The surprising part was that his evaluations proved to be prophetic.

Zeng Guofan's brother Guohuang, also known as Chenjun, was born in 1820, making him the fourth child in the Zeng family. The poet evaluates him with the Chinese word "pingzheng" which literally means ordinary and upright. Guohuang neither left home nor distinguished himself with military or scholarly pursuits. He led an ordinary and principled life. Zeng Guofan's brother Guohua, also known as Wujun, was born in 1822, making him the sixth child in the Zeng family. He was distinctly independent and unconventional. Guoquan, who had the courtesy name Yuanfu, was the ninth child in the Zeng family and the brother whom the poet lauded most, even going so far as to call him the "white eyebrows" of the family. This nickname comes from a popular saying during the Han Dynasty, "Of the five Ma brothers, the one with white eyebrows was the most exceptional." [1] Indeed, Guoquan later proved to be the most exceptional of the poet's brothers.

Guohuang is upright, and Guohua unique;
Guoquan stands out as the White Eyebrows among us.
In officialdom, people get tainted;
Even banter behind closed doors may bode ill.

1 Ma Liang was a famous strategist of the Eastern Han Dynasty.

中年例有妻孥役，
识字由来教养衰。
家食等闲不经意，
如今漂泊在天涯。

In middle age, I support my wife and children;
Literacy has yet to save me from a poor education.
Homemade food has been taken for granted;
Now I drift aimlessly to the ends of the earth.

小池

这首诗作于道光二十六年（1846）。

屋后有一个干枯的小池塘，一夜大雨后池塘盛满了水。作者联想到，若此时有一条蛟龙在池塘的话，它一定可以借着满塘池水而腾飞。枯池喻平凡之地，蛟龙喻有志之人，雨水喻机遇。作者借此表达的意思是：只要胸怀大志，即便处于卑下，也可借机遇大展身手。

这首诗更像一个生于卑微之家的年轻人的励志之作，故而有人认为写于道光四年。那时曾氏还是年方十四岁的农家子弟，见屋后小池一夜涨水，有感而作。

屋后一枯池，
夜雨生波澜。
勿言一勺水，
会有蛟龙蟠。
物理无定资，
须臾变众窍。
男儿未盖棺，
进取谁能料？

The Little Pond

Zeng Guofan composed this poem in the 26th year of Emperor Daoguang's reign (1846).

It refers to a dried-up pond located behind a house. It fills up with water overnight after a heavy rain. The poet wonders if a legendary dragon capable of summoning storms and floods could be in the pond preparing to soar up, powered by the rainwater. This imagery of a simple plot of land flourishing into something extraordinary expresses how seizing opportunities enables ambitious people to display their talents no matter how humble their positions are.

This poem suggests the determination of a young man born into a humble family, leading some people to believe it was composed in 1824 when Zeng Guofan was just a 14-year-old boy from the countryside.

Behind the house lies a dried-up pond;
The night rain whips up billowing waves.
Do not scorn a spoonful of water,
For a flood dragon lives beneath the surface.
Nothing in nature is fixed;
A shape is transformed in an instant.
Until the lid is nailed onto his coffin,
Who can say he won't strive to achieve?

题《篬筤谷图》

曾氏在京日久，乡愁日深。他思念家乡，除想念住在老家的亲人外，也怀念家乡的青山绿水，怀念日出而作日落而息的纯朴简单的乡间生活。同在京城做官的湖南人孙鼎臣家里有一幅画，画的是长满青翠幼竹的幽深山谷。此画乃著名画家、钱塘人戴熙所作。曾氏非常喜欢这幅画，向孙鼎臣借回家细细观摩。道光二十六年（1846），赏画之余，曾氏写下了这首诗。

诗中写出了作者对官场生态的厌烦，对回归乡野的渴望。

我家湘上高嵋山，
茅屋修竹一万竿。
春雨晨锄斸玉版，
秋风夜馆鸣琅玕。
自来京华昵车马，
满腔俗恶不可删。
洞庭天地一大物，
一从北渡遂不还。

On "The Green Bamboo Valley"

Zeng Guofan's feeling of nostalgia deepened as his time in Beijing stretched out. He missed not only his family but also the charming natural beauty of his hometown and the simplicity and routine of rural life. A fellow official from Hunan named Sun Dingchen also lived in Beijing. His home displayed a painting of a remote verdant valley lush with green bamboo by Dai Xi, a celebrated painter from present-day Hangzhou, Zhejiang Province. Zeng Guofan was so enamored with the painting that he borrowed it from Sun Dingchen and brought it home to study it. Then, in the 26th year of Emperor Daoguang's reign (1846), he was inspired to compose the poem below.

Here, the poet expresses his weariness with officialdom and his yearning to return to nature.

My home lies at the foot of Hunan's Mount Gaomei,
A thatched cottage around which ten thousand bamboo sway.
On rainy spring mornings, I dig for jade slates,
Upon which I compose poetry on windy autumn evenings.
Vehicles bring noise from the capital;
My heart cannot wrench out the coarseness.
Dongting Lake sprawls out of sight;
I crossed it heading north and have yet to go back.

苦忆故乡好林壑，
梦想此君无由攀。
嗟君与我同里社，
误脱野服充朝班。
一别簹筤谢猿鹤，
十年台省翔鹓鸾。
鱼须文笏岂不好！
却思乡井长三叹。

钱唐画师天所纵，
手割湘云落此间。
风枝雨叶战寒碧，
明窗大几生虚澜。
簿书尘埃不称意，
得此亦足镌疏顽。
还君此画与君约，
一月更借十回看。

Sweet are the memories of the woods and ravines back home;
But one cannot roam them within a dream.
We once worshipped at the same village shrine;
Foolishly shedding ordinary clothes for official garb.
I bid farewell to the green bamboo, to the monkeys and cranes,
Ten years ago, when I left my home to become an official.
Of course, being an official has its benefits!
Yet homesickness remains with me for three deep sighs.

The painter from Qiantang was gifted by Heaven;
He scooped up Hunan clouds and painted them here.
Wind and rain battle branches and leaves against the cold;
Bright windows create the illusion of waves.
Dust-laden books appear out of place;
Yet, they reduce the feeling of rigidity.
Now I return it to you, confessing,
I will have asked to borrow it ten more times within a month.

次韵何廉昉太守感怀述事十六首（选一）

何廉昉即何栻，当时为江西省建昌府知府。他到任不久便城池失守，妻儿遇难，遭到朝廷的严厉处分。咸丰八年（1858）除夕，心事沉重的何栻一口气写了十六首七律，并寄给曾氏。

何栻的诗打动了曾氏及其身边的幕僚们，众人纷纷作诗奉和。曾氏也在咸丰九年正月，用了三天时间写下十六首奉和诗。这首诗为这组诗中的第一首。诗中气氛悲愤压抑，既是对何栻的同情，也是当时诗人自我境遇的真实写照。结尾两句传诵甚广，道出古往今来的一个普遍现象：真正的奇才异人，总是难以出人头地的。

域中哀怨广场开，
屈宋而还第二回。
幻想更无天可问，
牢愁宁有地能埋！
秦瓜钩带何人种？
社栎支离几日培？
大冶最憎金踊跃，
那容世界有奇材！

A Response to He Lianfang's 16 Nostalgic Poems (One Selection)

He Lianfang, also known as He Shi, was the prefect of Jianchang Prefecture, Jiangxi Province. Soon after his taking office, Jianchang fell into enemy hands. His wife and children died, and he was harshly disciplined by the imperial government. On New Year's Eve of the eighth year of Emperor Xianfeng's reign (1858), a heavy-hearted He Lianfang wrote sixteen *qilü*-poems, which he sent to Zeng Guofan.

Zeng Guofan and his aides were so moved by He's poems that they were inspired to write poems of their own. In the first month of 1859, Zeng Guofan responded to He Lianfang by writing 16 poems over three days. Below is the first in the series. It creates an atmosphere of stifling grief and indignation, not only sympathizing with He Lianfang but also revealing some true feelings of the poet himself. The celebrated last two verses expose a common thread between the past and the present: Extraordinary individuals rarely gain the recognition they deserve.

The public square of grievances opens,
As though reliving the banishment of Qu Yuan and Song Yu.[1]
Harboring no illusions that Heaven will answer;
It would be better to bury such grief!
The Marquis of Dongling[2] grew melons for life;
The useless oak tree lived long, safe and sound.
The great swordsmith despises the metal that flies when his hammer strikes;
Brilliant talents aren't allowed in this world!

1 Qu Yuan and Song Yu were famous poets during the Warring States period. They were both banished from the State of Chu.

2 The Marquis of Dongling lost his rank and was reduced to being a melon farmer after the fall of the Qin Dynasty.

沅甫弟四十一初度

同治三年（1864）六月十六日，湘军吉字营在曾国荃指挥下，攻进了太平天国都城天京城。这意味湘军取得决定性的胜利。这年八月二十日，是曾国荃虚岁四十一岁生日。在曾国藩看来，无论是对国家，还是对家族而言，曾老九都是大功臣。基于褒奖功臣之心，曾氏精心撰写了十三首七言绝句，作为对九弟的生日贺礼。

第一首，总体写曾老九从军七年来的艰难与功劳。第二、三、四、五、六、七、八、九首诗写老九求学、从军的经历。第十、十一、十二、十三首诗，以大哥之身份，劝九弟功成身退，以宽阔胸怀面对荣誉与诽谤。

九载艰难下百城，
漫天箕口复纵横。
今朝一酌黄花酒，
始与阿连庆更生。

陆云入洛正华年，
访道寻师志颇坚。
惭愧庭阶春意薄，
无风吹汝上青天。

In Celebration of My Brother Guoquan's 41st Birthday

On the 16th day of the sixth month in the third year of Emperor Tongzhi's reign (1864), Zeng Guoquan led the Xiang Army's Jizi Battalion to capture Tianjing, the capital of the Taiping Heavenly Kingdom, and won a decisive victory. A few months later, on the 20th day of the eighth month the same year, Zeng Guoquan celebrated his 41st birthday. Zeng Guofan considered his brother a hero to both the country and the Zeng family. To honor his extraordinary service, Zeng Guofan meticulously composed 13 *qijue*-poems [1] as a birthday gift to Zeng Guoquan.

The first poem describes the hardships and the contributions that formed his seven-year military career. Poems two through nine revolve around his experience as a scholar and a new military recruit. In poems 10 through 13, Zeng Guofan assumes the role of the elder brother and advises Zeng Guoquan to retire after his success and to keep an open mind about the good and bad he may hear about himself.

Nine challenging years to take one hundred towns;
The air is filled with widespread rumors.
Now pour a cup of chrysanthemum wine,
In celebration of my brother's birthday.

Just as Lu Yun [2] arrived in Luoyang [3] as a youth,
You were determined to seek a good mentor.
It is a shame that the doorsteps were unwelcoming;
No wind carried you skyward.

1 *Qijue* is a type of four-line poem that has seven characters per line and follows strict prosodic rules.
2 Lu Yun was a famous writer of the Western Jin Dynasty.
3 Luoyang was the capital of the Western Jin Dynasty.

几年橐笔逐辛酸，
科第尼人寸寸难。
一剑须臾龙变化，
谁能终古老泥蟠？

庐陵城下总雄师，
主将赤心万马知。
佳节中秋平剧寇，
书生初试大功时。

楚尾吴头暗战尘，
江干无土著生民。
多君龛定同安郡，
上感三光下百神。

濡须已过历阳来，
无数金汤一剪开。
提挈湖湘良子弟，
随风直薄雨花台。

邂逅三才发杀机，
王寻百万合重围。
昆阳一捷天人悦，
谁识中军血染衣！

Several years grinding away with the pen,
You failed the imperial exams again and again.
Hoisting a sword transformed you into a dragon;
Who spends his life coiled waiting in old mud?

In Luling town, the great army rallies;
The commander's loyalty known to all.
During the mid-Autumn Festival, the enemy is quelled;
The scholar's battle debut is a success.

Dark war clouds churn at the Chu-Wu border;
The battles at Luling and Anqing (riverside) are no place for the living.
You warriors who suppressed the rebels,
Feel the blessing of a hundred gods of all kinds.

The Battle of Ruxu is in the books;
You seized countless fortresses.
You nurtured Hunan's children.
You led the charge at Yuhuatai[1] like wind riders.

Three commanders fought at the Battle of Kunyang;
Wang Xun's[2] million-man army encircled rebels.
Heaven and man rejoiced at the victory;
But who saw the heroes' bloodstained clothes?

1 Yuhuatai, located in Nanjing, was once the capital of the Taiping Heavenly Kingdom.
2 Wang Xun commanded an army of one million to suppress an insurrection against the Xin Dynasty.

平吴捷奏入甘泉，
正赋周宣六月篇。
生缚名王归夜半，
秦淮月畔有非烟。

河山策命冠时髦，
鲁卫同封异数叨。
刮骨箭瘢天鉴否？
可怜叔子独贤劳。

左列钟铭右谤书，
人间随处有乘除。
低头一拜屠羊说，
万事浮云过太虚。

已寿斯民复寿身，
拂衣归钓五湖春。
丹诚磨炼堪千劫，
不借良金更铸人。

黄河余润沾三族，
白下饥民活万家。
千里亲疏齐颂祷，
使君眉寿总无涯。

I was in the middle of my dreams at night,
When news of victory came as spring water.
The rebel king was captured alive at midnight,
Beauty was seen by the moonlit Qinhuai River.

Imperial appointments come in time;
Two brothers knighted at the end of campaigns.
Does Heaven know the arrows that wounded and scarred?
Alas, little brother, you worked alone so hard for us!

Praise on the left, and slander on the right;
There are ups and downs in life.
Remember Tuyangyue,[1]
He brushed superficial matters aside like clouds.

Having reached a certain age and proven yourself as a commander,
Retire to a life of leisure.
Your devotion has passed the tough trials;
Do not lend gold to influence people.

The Yellow River enriches the Zeng family;
You've given thousands in Nanjing new life.
Relatives from near and far pray as one,
Wishing you great longevity.

1 Tuyangyue was a hermit during the Warring States period. After helping the King of Chu flee, he declined the king's offers of a reward.

童稚温温无险巇，
酒人浩浩少猜疑。
与君同讲长生诀，
且学婴儿中酒时。

Children are mild-mannered and innocent;
Drunkards are not plagued by misgivings.
As for the secret of longevity,
Take a lesson from toddlers and drunkards.

忮求诗二首

同治九年（1870）六月初四日，曾氏在赴天津处理教案前夕，给两个儿子留下一封类似遗嘱的信。信上说：我在读先贤的书籍时，发现圣贤教育别人修身的言论虽然千言万语，而其中最重要的话只有四个字：不忮不求。所谓忮，就是嫉妒；何谓求，就是贪婪。他告诫儿子，一个人若不忮不求，则心地干净，要二子在此四字上痛下功夫。

信后，曾氏抄录自己所作的不忮不求诗两首，希望儿子们时常诵读。

曾氏能作典雅工整的古体诗，同时也能作通俗易懂的浅白诗。他做湘军统帅时，就特为不识字的勇丁创作《爱民歌》《解散歌》等军歌。勇丁们一听就懂，且琅琅上口，易于记诵，故而流传甚广。这两首不忮不求诗，就属于浅白诗一类。

不忮

善莫大于恕，
德莫凶于妒。
妒者妾妇行，
琐琐奚比数。

Two Poems on Envy and Greed

On the fourth day of the sixth month in the ninth year of Emperor Tongzhi's reign (1870), Zeng Guofan wrote a letter similar to a will for his two sons. He was leaving for Tianjin to take on the case of missionaries who had been killed there. He wrote, "When I read the books of the ancient sages, I find that despite page upon page about cultivating one's moral character, their lessons could really be distilled into four words: neither envy nor greed." He taught his sons that freeing oneself of envy and greed brings peace of mind and encouraged them to apply this lesson to their own lives.

Zeng Guofan enclosed the letter with two of his own poems on "neither envy nor greed," hoping that his sons would often read them.

Zeng Guofan could compose everything from elegant, classical poems to simple, easily understood verses. While commander-in-chief of the Xiang Army, he wrote military songs, such as "Take Care of the People" and "Dismissal," for illiterate soldiers. Catchy and easily memorized, the songs were extremely popular among soldiers. The following two poems on "neither envy nor greed" fall into the category of simple poetry.

Be Not Envious

Forgiveness is the greatest virtue;
Envy is the wickedest ill.
To be envious is to be inferior,
Concerned with trivialities.

己拙忌人能，
己塞忌人遇。
己若无事功，
忌人得成务。

己若无党援，
忌人得多助。
势位苟相敌，
畏逼又相恶。

己无好闻望，
忌人文名著。
己无贤子孙，
忌人后嗣裕。

争名日夜奔，
争利东西骛。
但期一身荣，
不惜他人污。

闻灾或欣幸，
闻祸或悦豫。
问渠何以然？
不自知其故。

The clumsy envy the gifted;
The unfortunate envy the lucky.
He who achieves nothing,
Envies those who are accomplished.

He who is without support,
Envies those who have people to back them.
He turns rivals into enemies;
He views those he dislikes as a threat.

Lacking a good reputation,
He envies those who have made a good name.
Lacking worthy offspring,
He envies those with successful children.

He seeks fame day and night;
He scrambles for profits east and west.
With eyes only for his own glory,
He doesn't hesitate to smear others.

He revels in news of war;
He delights in tales of woe.
When asked, why so?
He himself does not know.

尔室神来格，
高明鬼所顾。
天道常好还，
嫉人还自误。

幽明丛诟忌，
乖气相回互。
重者灾汝躬，
轻亦减汝祚。

我今告后生：
悚然大觉悟。
终身让人道，
曾不失寸步。
终身祝人善，
曾不损尺布。
消除嫉妒心，
普天零甘露。
家家获吉祥，
我亦无恐怖。

Your home is frequented by spirits,
both good and evil.
Natural law favors generosity in return for good fortune.
Wallowing in envy is self defeating.

Envy is accompanied by evil things;
Bad luck will persist at one's side.
Serious matters wreck our health;
Petty ones sabotage our wealth.

Today, I say to the next generation:
You must awaken.
Yielding the path to others,
Has yet to slow me down.
Wishing others well,
Has yet to cost me gold.
Dispel any envy,
Then sweet dew shall fall upon the world.
Every household shall reap good fortune;
We shall have no fear.

不求

知足天地宽，
贪得宇宙隘。
岂无过人姿，
多欲为患害。

在约每思丰，
居困常求泰。
富求千乘车，
贵求万钉带。

未得求速偿，
既得求勿坏。
芬馨比椒兰，
磐固方泰岱。

求荣不知餍，
志亢神愈忲。
岁燠有时寒，
日明有时晦。

时来多善缘，
运去生灾怪。

Be Not Greedy

Contentment broadens the mind like the boundless horizon;
Greed narrows even the universe.
Those who are not gifted,
Discover that undue desire leads to misfortune.

The frugal long for abundance;
When troubled, they yearn for peace.
The affluent crave countless vehicles;
With high rank, they hunger for untold rewards.

In need, people seek quick gain;
Once obtained, they claim permanent possession.
To be as fragrant as orchids,
And as steadfast as Mount Tai.

Greed for glory is never sated;
Burning ambition stokes more want.
Warm weather may turn cold;
Celestial bodies may dim.

Fate may be kind;
Luck may give way to disaster.

诸福不可期，
百殃纷来会。

片言动招尤，
举足便有碍。
戚戚抱殷忧，
精爽日凋瘵。

矫首望八荒，
乾坤一何大！
安荣无遽欣，
患难无遽憨！

君看十人中，
八九无倚赖。
人穷多过我，
我穷犹可耐。
而况处夷途，
奚事生嗟忾？
于世少所求，
俯仰有余快。
俟命堪终古，
曾不愿乎外。

Good fortune is never certain;
Trouble may come in droves.

A few words incite blame;
One deed provokes obstructions.
If we harbor our sorrows,
Our spirits wither and wane.

Raise your head to gaze at the world;
How vast is the universe!
Do not be quick to celebrate honors;
Do not embrace rancor when meeting adversity!

Behold, nine of ten people,
Are dependent on something.
If others are poorer,
My poverty is bearable.
And if I am on a level path,
What could draw a sigh from me?
Demand less from the world,
And daily life will abound with happiness.
Leave everything to fate;
I am no exception.

词

Ci-poems

贺新郎
——题钱楞仙同年《玉堂归娶图》二首

曾氏词作很少,我们现在能看到的仅《浪淘沙》六首,以及所录的这两首《贺新郎》。

钱楞仙名振伦,浙江归安(今湖州)人,系曾氏进士同年。道光十八年(1838),钱振伦在金榜题名后,即请假回家完婚。行前请人画了一幅《玉堂归娶图》,遍请京师名流为之题诗。曾氏这两首词即作于此时。钱振伦晚年回忆此事说:曾涤生相国题《贺新郎》二阕,同时诸作俱无能出其右者。

第一首写钱振伦的金榜题名、洞房花烛轰动一时。小俩口恩爱缠绵,令世人羡慕。第二首,词人想象新婚之夜,小夫妻的亲密对话、山盟海誓,真个是神仙美眷,人间少有。

一

艳福如斯也!
记年华,同年二百,君其少者。
刚是凤池骞翥后,又结鸳鸯香社。
看此去雕鞍宝马。
袍是烂银裳是锦,算美人名士真同嫁。
好花样,互相借。

To the Tune of Hexinlang

Two *Ci*-poems on the Painting "Going Home to Marry in Jade Hall"

Zeng Guofan composed few *ci*-poems. Those that are still available include six *ci*-poems to the tune of *Langtaosha* and the two *ci*-poems below to the tune of *Hexinlang*.

Qian Zhenlun, courtesy name Lengxian, was a native of Huzhou, Zhejiang. He and Zeng passed the national imperial exam in the same year, the 18th year of Emperor Daoguang's reign (1838). Afterward, Qian asked for leave to return to his hometown to get married. Before journeying home, he asked an artist to render a painting titled "*Going Home to Marry in Jade Hall*" and invited distinguished scholars in Beijing to compose poems on the painting. The two *ci*-poems below were composed impromptu by Zeng. Recalling this event in his later years, Qian noted that these two *ci*-poems to the tune of *Hexinlang* were superior to all other improvised poems on the painting.

The first *ci*-poem describes Qian's success on the imperial exam and his upcoming wedding festivities, with the affectionate young newlyweds drawing the admiration of all. In the second *ci*-poem, Zeng imagines the intimate conversations and affectionate vows of the young couple on their wedding night and underlines the rarity of such a happy and contented couple.

1

To be so lucky in love!
In retrospect, of the successful candidates, you are the youngest.
Having passed the imperial exam, you take a beautiful bride.
Look at your decorated Ferghana horse.
A robe of silver and a dress of brocade, the beauty and the scholar are newlyweds.
The exquisite pattern is now shared.

淋漓史笔珊瑚架。
说催妆，新诗绮语，几人传写？
才子风流涂抹惯，莫把眉痕轻画。
当记取初三月夜。
欲问大罗天上事，恐小姑群婢同惊讶。
属郎语，声须下。

二

寂寞深闺里。
忆东风，泥金乍报，若何欢喜？
撤帐筵阑停烛夜，细问当时原委。
更密询烧香侍婢。
西舍东邻多士女，但骈头附耳夸双美。
不能答，笑而已。

郎君持赠无多子。
献妆台，宫衣一袭，鸾书一纸。
又剩有红绫饼餤，合卺同尝甘旨。
珍重说天恩如此。
明年携得神仙眷，料趋朝不过花砖矣。
同梦者，促君起。

The historian's pen rests upon a coral shelf.

How many bridegrooms are capable of capturing their bride's beauty and their union's sweetness in verse?

The young scholar is familiar with the brush; do not be hasty with the arch of the bride's brow.

Remember your tender moments spent under the crescent moon.

I want to ask about the wedding but fear that I might astonish the maidservants.

When speaking of the nuptials, lower your voice.

2

A lonely bedroom chamber.

In retrospect, upon receiving news of the imperial exam, could one be more joyful?

After the wedding ceremony, late at night, the candles are snuffed out,

And she enquires about the whole story.

She even asks the incense maidservant for details.

Scholars and belles in the neighborhood whisper admiringly, "What a blessed couple!"

Unable to respond, the bride just smiles.

The groom bears a few gifts: a dressing table, a palace dress, and an engagement note.

Wrapped in red silk are cakes and pies, delicacies to be enjoyed when sharing the nuptial cup.

Thanks to the emperor's kindness!

Next year, the groom will take along his bride, set to rise to a high rank.

The loving bride awakens her groom.

文

Prose

烹阿封即墨论

此文作于道光二十三年（1843），是一篇考场中的论文。这次考试的参与者为翰林院、詹事府的官员。翰詹官员每六年大考一次，考试成绩决定着他们的升迁与否。因此，朝廷与参加者都很重视。这次考试的考场设在圆明园正大光明殿，考试的内容是一赋一诗一论文，时间为一整天。

烹阿封即墨一事，见于《史记·田敬仲完世家》。大意是说，齐国管理阿城的官员不办实事，专门贿赂齐威王身边的人，为他说好话。管理即墨的官员为民办实事，但因不巴结齐威王身边的人，故而没有人为他说好话。齐威王派人下去调查，发现真相后，将阿城官员投铁锅煮死，而封赏即墨官员。

曾氏借此发表议论：贤明的领导者应该像齐威王那样重实绩，重调查，不轻信人言，奖罚分明。

曾氏这篇论文为主考官所赏识，总成绩列第六名，因此而升为从五品翰林院侍讲。

On Boiling Echeng Officials and Rewarding Jimo Officials

This essay was written in the 23rd year of Emperor Daoguang's reign (1843) as part of an examination given to officials from Hanlin Academy and Zhanshi House. [1] Officials from these institutions took this examination every six years to determine whether they would be promoted, thus making it important to the imperial court as well. This examination was held in the Palace of Heavenly Purity at Yuanmingyuan (also known as the Garden of Gardens). The day-long examination consisted of composing one *fu*, [2] one poem, and one essay.

The story of boiling the officials in Echeng and rewarding the officials in Jimo was recorded in "The Hereditary Household of Tian Jingzhong" from Records of the Grand Historian. Officials in Echeng Town in the state of Qi failed to uphold their duties, preferring instead to bribe the people around King Wei of Qi to speak well of them. Officials in Jimo Town took their posts seriously; however, nobody commended them because they refused to fawn over those surrounding the king. After sending investigators after the truth, the king ordered the officials in Echeng to be boiled in an iron wok and the officials in Jimo to be rewarded.

Zeng Guofan took advantage of the exam to introduce this concept: a wise leader should follow the example of King Wei in setting a high value on genuine achievements and the truth. He should question what others say and implement strict rules for reward and punishment.

The imperial examiner recognized the brilliance of Zeng's essay, ranking it sixth out of all the participants. Consequently, Zeng was promoted to Imperial Tutor of the associate fifth rank at Hanlin Academy.

1 Zhanshi House was an organ of the imperial government. It was established to handle the imperial family's internal affairs.

2 A type of descriptive prose interspersed with verse.

夫人君者，不能遍知天下事，则不能不委任贤大夫。大夫之贤否，又不能遍知，则不能不信诸左右。然而左右之所誉，或未必遂为荩臣；左右之所毁，或未必遂非良吏。是则耳目不可寄于人，予夺尤须操于上也。

昔者，齐威王尝因左右之言而烹阿大夫，封即墨大夫矣。其事可略而论也。自古庸臣在位，其才莅事则不足，固宠则有余。《易》讥覆𫗧，《诗》赓鹈梁，言不称也。彼既自惭素餐，而又重以贪鄙，则不得不媚事君之左右。左右亦乐其附己也，而从而誉之。誉之日久，君心亦移，而位日固，而政日非。已则自矜，人必效尤。此阿大夫之所为可烹者也。

As a king cannot be expected to be omniscient, he has to entrust worthy officials with specific tasks. As a king cannot be certain that his officials are worthy, he has to trust those around him. However, officials praised by those close to the king may not be loyal, and officials slandered by those close to the king may not be unethical. Therefore, a king cannot let others be his eyes and ears; he has to make his own decisions himself.

Long ago, King Wei of the state of Qi ordered that officials from Echeng be boiled to death while those from Jimo be rewarded as a result of what people around him said. This matter is worth consideration. Since ancient times, mediocre officials maintained their power despite their incompetence because they excelled at currying favor with the king. *The Book of Changes* and *The Book of Songs* both satirized inept officials who failed to do their jobs, yet still enjoyed all the privileges associated with them. The shame of their own inadequacies failed to override their avarice or loathsome behavior as they sought out people near the king to speak well of them. Those collaborators, in turn, were happy to benefit from the arrangement. In time, the king grew to believe the assessments of those around him. As incompetent officials became more established, the state of the country spiraled downward. And, with inflated confidence on display, others followed the bad example of these inept officials. This made officials from Echeng so deserving of their severe punishment.

若夫贤臣在职，往往有介介之节，无赫赫之名，不立异以徇物，不违道以干时。招之而不来，麾之而不去。在君侧者，虽欲极誉之而有所不得。其或不合，则不免毁之。毁之而听，甚者削黜，轻者督责，于贤臣无损也。其不听，君之明也，社稷之福也，于贤臣无益也。然而贤臣之因毁而罢者，常也。贤臣之必不阿事左右以求取容者，又常也。此即墨大夫之所为可封者也。夫惟圣人赏一人而天下劝，刑一人而天下惩，固不废左右之言，而昧兼听之聪，亦不尽信左右之言而失独照之明。夫是以刑赏悉归于忠厚，而用舍一本于公明也夫。

Virtuous officials reject favoritism and refuse to violate the natural law for the sake of the times: they value integrity and rebuff fame. They do not heed the beckoning of others. Those who praise them within earshot of the king receive nothing in return. Virtuous officials who rankle those who have the king's ear become the target of ill will. If the king accepts the slander, he may censure or even dismiss them from office; this will not harm virtuous officials. The king who rejects the baseless slander is wise; although beneficial to the country, this will not profit virtuous officials. However, virtuous officials often resign from office after being vilified. They also often refuse to ingratiate themselves with people around the king. This made officials from Jimo so deserving of their reward. A sage rewards one person to encourage the same behavior in others and punishes another to warn people against repeating the same mistake. He retains enlightenment by listening to what people around him have to say but makes sagacious decisions by not completely relying on them. Therefore, punishments and rewards should be measured based on loyalty and virtues, and promotions and demotions should be decided based on fairness and openness.

送郭筠仙南归序

道光二十五年（1845）四月，参加两届会试均告失意的郭嵩焘，离京回湖南。临别时，曾氏写了这篇文章送给他。好友分别，写诗写文章赠送，是古时文人常态。

曾氏以材与器作为话题。材，指材料的本身；器，指材料制成器具后的功用。对人来说，材好比天生资质，器好比经过学习历练后所具有的办事才干。曾氏认为，人必须通过尽可能多的雕琢而成为器，否则资质再好也会为世所抛弃。曾氏借此鼓励好友，切不可因小挫而丧志，期盼他经过反复磨砺而终成大器。

凡物之骤为之而遽成焉者，其器小也；物之一览而易尽者，其中无有也。郭君筠仙与余友九年矣，即之也温，挹之常不尽。道光甲辰、乙巳两试于礼部，留京师，主于余，促膝而语者四百余日，乃得尽窥其藏。甚哉！人不易知也。将别，于是为道其深，附于回路赠言之义，而以吾之忠效焉。

Foreword to *Bidding Goodbye to Guo Yunxian on His Southward Journey Back Home*

In the fourth month of the 25th year of Emperor Daoguang's reign (1845), Guo Songtao left Beijing for Hunan Province after having sat two imperial examinations. Prior to his departure, Zeng Guofan wrote him this essay. The practice of presenting a departing friend with a poem or an essay was common among ancient scholars.

The essay discusses "material," which may be likened to innate talent, and "instruments," which may be likened to acquired competence. Zeng argues that innate talent must be honed sufficiently before developing into an instrument that can be employed in society. In this way, Zeng encourages his friend to refrain from letting minor setbacks make him lose heart and hopes that repeated honing enables him to develop into an outstanding talent.

An instrument that is quickly produced serves little purpose, and one that is obvious to the naked eye often contains nothing. Dear Yunxian, we have been friends for over nine years. We enjoy a warm friendship that has sustained us through thick and thin. In the 24th and 25th years of Emperor Daoguang's reign (1844 and 1845, respectively), you sat two imperial examinations held by the Ministry of Rites; I was in the capital and oversaw the examinations. After more than 400 days of close communication, we have taken the measure of each other as a friend. Indeed! Knowing another person is not easy. At your departure, I offer these words to explain the significance of our friendship and demonstrate my loyalty to you.

盖天生之材，或相千万，要于成器以适世用而已。材之小者，视尤小者则优矣。苟尤小者，琢之成器，而小者不利于用，则君子取其尤小者焉。材之大者，视尤大者则绌矣。苟尤大者不利于用，而大者琢之成器，则君子取其大者焉。天赋大始，人作成物。《传》曰："人不天不因，天不人不成。"不极扩充追琢之能，虽有周公之材，终弃而已矣。

余所友天下贤士，或以德称，或以艺显，类有以自成者。而若筠仙躬绝异之姿，退然深贬，语其德若无可名；学古人之文章，入焉既深，而其外犹若钮铻而不安其无所成者，与匠石斫方寸之木，斤之削之，不移瞬而成物矣。及乎裁径尺之材以为榱桷，不

Millions of people are inherently talented, but competence must be acquired before it can serve society. Those gifted with a small talent may be superior to those gifted with an even smaller one. However, if the smaller talent is honed and developed into a useful instrument, and the small talent remains uncultivated, then the superior man will choose the smaller talent. Those gifted with a great talent may be inferior to those gifted with an even greater one. However, if the greater talent remains uncultivated, and the great talent is honed and developed into a useful instrument, then the superior man will choose the great talent. Inherent talent does not materialize without human development. It has been said, "The law of Heaven will not change for the sake of man; a man cannot achieve much unless he follows the law of Heaven." Without expending the utmost effort to nurture one's talent, even one as gifted as the Duke of Zhou shall be discarded by society in the end.

I have befriended many distinguished people. Some are known for their morality, and others are known for their talents. They tend to boast about their own accomplishments. However, my friend Yunxian takes a unique stance: he is so humble and self-deprecating that his morality seems not worth mentioning. He is extremely well-versed in classical literature but appears uneasy about having achieved nothing. A craftsman's square inch of wood is easily turned into a product with some quick cutting. A log one foot

阅日而成矣。及至伐连抱之梗枏，为天子营总章太室之梁栋，经旬累月而不得成焉。其器俞大，就之俞艰。浅者欲以一概律之，难矣。且所号为贤者，谓其绝拘挛之见，旷观于广大之区，而不以尺寸绳人者也。若夫逢世之技，智足以与时物相发，力足以与机势相会，此则众人之所共睹者矣。君子则不然，赴势甚钝，取道甚迂，德不苟成，业不苟名，艰勤错迕，迟久而后进。铢而积，寸而累。既其纯熟，则圣人之徒，其力造焉而无扞格，则亦不失于令名。造之不力，歧出无范，虽有瑰质，终亦无用。

孟子曰："五谷不熟，不如荑稗。"诚哉斯言也！筠仙勖哉！去其所谓扞格者，以蕲至于纯熟，则几矣。人亦病不为耳。若夫自揣既熟，而或不达于时轨，是则非余之所敢知也。

thick emerges as a rafter after less than one day of chopping and smoothing. And a thick and straight sandalwood tree is felled and cut to be transformed into ridgepoles and beams for the imperial chambers only after many months of chopping and smoothing. The bigger the instrument, the harder it is to make. Superficial people would like to generalize the above but to little avail. Furthermore, those who are considered sages are free of tunnel vision; they take a broad view of the larger picture rather than measure people by a petty standard. If a talented person is wise enough to adapt to the times and society and powerful enough to take advantage of opportunities, then he will become known to others. The superior man, however, does not act this way. He adapts slowly and takes a circuitous path. With no desire to establish his personal or professional reputation, he remains diligent and perseveres. Little by little, he gains experience; step by step, he makes progress. Once proficient, he becomes a disciple of Confucius. His competence has developed without inconsistencies, and he also enjoys a good reputation. If he does not strive to acquire competence, he becomes confused with nothing to guide him. His talents will serve no purpose in the end.

Mencius said, "If the five grains do not ripen, they are worse than tares." It is so true of my friend Yunxian! Once that which is incompatible with proficiency is eliminated, he will be nearly there. Others are concerned about achieving nothing. A person may consider himself proficient, but he may not have kept up with the times. This is not something that I would presume to know.

求阙斋记

这篇文章写于道光二十五年（1845）。此时曾氏年三十五岁，官从四品侍讲学士，仕途可谓顺利。更令他欣慰的是，他的祖父母、父母都还健在，而且妻子儿女、兄弟姐妹一应俱全。据他自己说，这样的家庭，京师四品以上的官员中找不出第二人。

《易经》说“日中则昃，月盈则食”，曾氏相信这个理念。他认为自己的家庭如同日之将中、月之将盈，必须得保留些缺陷，“昃”与“食”的到来才会推迟。这些缺陷即阙，须体现于自身上，比如说他本人的荣耀、享受等，都宜减少而不宜追求。

出于这样的思考，他将北京寓所命名为求阙斋，并为之作记。

国藩读《易》，至《临》而喟然叹曰：刚侵而长矣。至于八月有凶，消亦不久也，可畏也哉！天地之气，阳至矣，则退而生阴；阴至矣，则进而生阳。一损一益者，自然之理也。

Records from the Imperfection-seeking Chamber

This article was written in the 25th year of Emperor Daoguang's reign (1845) when 35-year-old Zeng Guofan was basking in a successful career as an Imperial Tutor of the associate fourth rank. He, however, was even more gratified to learn that his grandparents and parents were still in good health and that his wife, children, and siblings were all well. He asserted that no official in Beijing of equal or higher rank was in as fortunate a situation.

The Book of Changes reads, "The sun travels westward after midday, and the moon wanes after turning full." Zeng embraced this philosophical idea and concluded that his family was almost at the same stage of perfection as the midday sun and the full moon. Consequently, his family needed to retain some deficiencies in order to defer its inevitable decline. He believed that these deficiencies were imperfections that had to be reflected in himself. For example, he believed that his family would benefit if he were to negate rather than pursue some of his own glory and enjoyment.

This understanding inspired him to name his residence in Beijing the Imperfection-seeking Chamber and make it the subject of a short essay.

Whenever I read the divination of the *lin* hexagram in *The Book of Changes*, I sigh, "*Yang* [1] is becoming more dominant." However, the eighth month is a season for *yang* to diminish and *yin* [2] to become dominant, so the ominous time is coming. I cannot help but be afraid! In heaven and on earth, when *yang* diminishes, it will retreat, and *yin* will become dominant; when *yin* reaches a peak, it will transform into *yang*. This is the law of nature.

1 *Yang* is the masculine, or positive, life energy in traditional Chinese medicine and philosophy.

2 *Yin* is the feminine, or negative, life-energy in traditional Chinese medicine and philosophy.

物生而有耆欲，好盈而忘阙。是故体安车驾，则金舆鏓衡不足于乘；目辨五色，则黼黻文章不足于服。由是八音繁会不足于耳，庶羞珍膳不足于味。穷巷瓮牖之夫，骤膺金紫，物以移其体，习以荡其志，向所扼捥而不得者，渐乃厌鄙而不屑御。旁观者以为固然，不足訾议。故曰："位不期骄，禄不期侈。彼为象箸，必为玉杯。"积渐之势然也。而好奇之士，巧取曲营，不逐众之所争，独汲汲于所谓名者。道不同不相为谋，或贵富以饱其欲，或声誉以厌其情，其于志盈一也。夫名者，先王所以驱一世于轨物也。中人以下，蹈道不实，于是爵禄以显驭之，名以阴驱之，使之践其迹，不必明其意。若君子人者，深知乎道德之意，方惧名之既加，则得于内者日浮，将耻之矣。而浅者哗然骛之，不亦悲乎！

People are born with interests and desires; they like abundance and overlook deficiencies. Consequently, even if one rides in an imperial carriage, one's body will not be sated; even if one wears colorful embroidered clothes, one's eyes will not be sated. Similarly, even listening to an ensemble of traditional instruments will be insufficient to sate one's ears; even tasting a feast of fine delicacies will be insufficient to sate one's tongue. Once the needy man from an impoverished area suddenly enjoys high office and privilege, luxury alters his body, extravagance shifts his thinking, and what he once clutched so tightly is gradually disdained and discarded; bystanders accept this as natural and, thus, undeserving of criticism. As the saying goes, "A high position makes one proud; a high salary makes one extravagant. One who eats with ivory chopsticks will insist on drinking from jade cups." This represents an accumulation over time. The unconventional man is ingenious and skillful by nature; he does not pursue what the crowd seeks, and he is only eager for fame. People who walk different paths cannot share the same plans. Some chase wealth to indulge material desires, while others pursue fame to satisfy spiritual desires; the aspiration for abundance is the same. Fame began as a tool the ancient sages utilized to regulate the world. A man of mediocre moral character does not tread on solid ground; he can be encouraged to walk the right path by rank, nobility, and fame, the meaning of which he does not understand. The superior man knows the true meaning of morality, so he fears that his moral cultivation, which lags far behind any fame he has gained, will cause him to feel even vainer, thus he is ashamed of his fame. However, he who has superficially cultivated his moral character still clamors to make a name for himself – is that not sad?

国藩不肖，备员东宫之末，世之所谓清秩。家承余荫，自王父母以下，并康强安顺。孟子称“父母俱存，兄弟无故”，抑又过之。《洪范》曰：“凡厥庶民，有猷有为有守，不协于极，不罹于咎，女则锡之福。”若国藩者，无为无猷，而多罹于咎，而或锡之福，所谓不称其服者欤？于是名其所居曰“求阙斋”。凡外至之荣，耳目百体之耆，皆使留其缺陷。礼主减而乐主盈。乐不可极，以礼节之，庶以制吾性焉，防吾淫焉。若夫令问广誉，尤造物所靳予者，实至而归之。所取已贪矣，况以无实者攘之乎？行非圣人而有完名者，殆不能无所矜饰于其间也。吾亦将守吾阙者焉。

Being unworthy, I am ashamed to serve at Hanlin Academy, which is known for nobility and integrity. My ancestors have enabled my family, beginning with my grandparents' generation, to be healthy and at peace. This even exceeds the description of happiness given by Mencius, "One's parents are alive, and one's siblings are safe and sound." According to the classic *"The Great Plan"*,[1] "The ordinary people who can plan and act while maintaining their integrity, who neither conform to perfection nor make big mistakes, they are entitled to good fortune." I have neither planned nor acted, and I have made big mistakes; yet, I have been endowed with good fortune – is this not inappropriate? Therefore, I named my residence "the Imperfection-seeking Chamber." All the glories from the outside world and all the desires from within oneself leave room for imperfection. Etiquette demands moderation; music demands fullness. However, music should not be extreme, and etiquette is necessary to regulate the mind and prevent indulgence. As for a good reputation, the creator of the universe does not grant it easily; achievement and virtue precede fame. The pursuit of fame is greed, to say nothing of fighting for fame when one has yet to achieve anything. The conduct of some does not conform to a sage, yet they are equally famous; it is highly unlikely that the lives of such people are not fraught with hypocrisy. I would rather cherish my imperfection as an anachronism.

1 Known as Hong Fan in Chinese pinyin, *"The Great Plan"* is a chapter of the *Shang Shu* (*The Book of Documents*).

送唐先生南归序

唐鉴为湖南善化人，在京师做太常寺卿时，曾氏与一班志同道合的年轻人，拜唐鉴为师，研习理学，并践行于自我修身中。曾氏对唐鉴，有一种发自内心的敬佩之情。道光二十六年（1846），年近七十的唐鉴退休，离开京师准备南下回老家休养，曾氏写下这篇文章送给他。

文章以师道尊严开篇。接下来，作者回顾师道流传的大致过程。直到这时，才把唐先生抬出来，称赞他是真正的传道之师。最后，作者点出此文的写作目的。

这篇文章可视为曾氏所开创的“湘乡文派”的代表作。

古者道一化行，自卿大夫之弟子与凡民之秀，皆上之人置师以教之。于乡有州长、党正之俦，于国有师氏、保氏。天子既兼君师之任，其所择，大抵皆道、艺两优，教尊而礼严。弟子抠衣趋隅，进退必慎。内以有所惮而生其敬，外绢业以兴其材。故曰：

Foreword to *Bidding Goodbye to Master Tang on His Southward Journey Back Home*

Tang Jian was a native of Shanhua County (now part of Changsha City), Hunan Province. While Tang was Administrator of Imperial Sacrifices in Beijing, Zeng Guofan and a group of like-minded young people studied Neo-Confucianism and practiced self-cultivation under his direction as their mentor. Indeed, Zeng had the deepest esteem for Tang. In the 26th year of Emperor Daoguang's reign (1846), Tang retired just short of 70 and left Beijing for his hometown in the south. Zeng wrote this essay for him as a parting gift.

The essay begins with the noble profession of teaching. Next, the author reviews the way teachings are passed down from master to disciple. It is only then that Tang is singled out and commended for being a true teacher of Neo-Confucianism. Finally, the author explains the main purpose of his writing.

This essay may be regarded as the representative work of the Xiangxiang school initiated by Zeng Guofan.

Since ancient times, disciples who are senior officials and outstanding members of the public have had one path to education, namely, engaging teachers. In the countryside, they may be local officials; in the imperial government, they may be tutors and mentors for the imperial family. The emperor has the responsibility of both monarch and teacher. The people he selects generally excel in both the subject matter they teach and the methods they use to teach. The teachers are upright, and the disciples are so respectful that they adjust their clothes and hurry to sit in the corner, thus demonstrating a sense of propriety. From fear, they develop reverence and improve themselves through education. Therefore, it is said, "When the tradition of respecting teachers is established, vir-

“师道立而善人多。”此之谓也。

周衰，教泽不下流。仲尼干诸侯不见用，退而讲学于洙泗之间，从之游者如市。师门之盛，振古无俦。然自是人伦之中，别有所谓先生徒众者，非长民者所得与闻矣。仲尼既没，徒人分布四方，转相流衍。

吾家宗圣公传之子思、孟子，号为正宗。其他或离道而专趋于艺，商瞿授《易》于馯臂子弓，五传而为汉之田何。子夏之《诗》，五传而至孙卿，其后为鲁申培。左氏受《春秋》，八传而

tuous people will abound." That is truly the case.

With the decline of the Zhou Dynasty, the influence of education receded. When feudal princes failed to see his value, Confucius returned to the Zhu and Si rivers [1] to give lectures. People came in droves to learn from Confucius. The school was more prosperous than it had ever been. Afterward, however, there were other so-called teachers who had multiple disciples, but local officials could not reach them. After the death of Confucius, his disciples scattered to the four winds, spreading his teachings as they went.

The teachings of Confucius were passed down to Kong Ji [2](courtesy name Zisi) and Mencius, both of whose interpretations are considered the orthodox school of Confucianism. Other disciples of Confucius either strayed from the Confucianist way or turned to research on Confucianist texts. For instance, over the span of five generations, Shang Qu [3] was responsible for the transmission of the *Zhou Book of Change* down to Han Bi [4] (courtesy name Zigong) of the Warring States period and Tian He [5] (courtesy name Zizhuang) of the Western Han Dynasty. Over the span of five generations, Bu Shang [6] (courtesy name Zixia) was responsible for the transmission of the *Book of Poetry* down to Xun Kuang (better known as Xunzi) and then Shen Pei [7] of the Western Han Dynasty. And over the span of eight generations, Zuo Qiuming [8] was responsible for the transmission of the *Spring and Autumn Annals* down to Zhang Cang [9] of the Western Han Dynasty. Indeed, Han Dynasty

1 Confucius used to teach in an area between the Zhu and Si Rivers in the State of Lu.

2 Kong Ji (483-402 BC) was a grandson of Confucius.

3 Shang Qu (522-? BC) was a native of the State of Lu, a disciple of Confucius.

4 Han Bi (?-?) was a native of the State of Chu and a student of Shang Qu.

5 Tian He (?-?) was a famous Confucian scholar in the Western Han Dynasty.

6 Bu Shang (507-400 BC), also known as Buzi, was a native of the State of Jin and a disciple of Confucius.

7 Shen Pei (c. 219-135 BC), born in the State of Lu in the Warring States period, was a famous Confucian scholar in the early Western Han Dynasty.

8 Zuo Qiuming (556-452 BC), a native of the State of Xiaozhu, was a famous historiographer in the Spring and Autumn period.

9 Zhang Cang (253-152 BC) was a disciple of Xunzi and a master of the calendar in the early Western Han Dynasty.

至张苍。是以两汉经生，各有渊源。源远流歧，所得渐纤，道亦少裂焉。有宋程子、朱子出，绍孔氏之绝学，门徒之繁拟于邹鲁。反之躬行实践，以究群经要旨，博求万物之理，以尊闻而行知，数百千人，粲乎彬彬。故言艺则汉师为勤，言道则宋师为大，其说允已。

元明及我朝之初，流风未坠。每一先生出，则有徒党景附，虽不必束脩自上，亦循循隅坐，应唯敬对。若金、许、薛、胡、陆稼书、张念芝之俦，论乎其德则暗然，讽乎其言则犁然而当理，考乎其从游之徒，则践规蹈矩，仪型乡国。盖先王之教泽得以仅仅不斩，顽夫有所忌而发其廉耻者，未始非诸先生讲学与群从附和之力也。《诗》曰："风雨如晦，鸡鸣不已。"诚珍之也。今之

scholars of the Confucian classics derived those classics from various academic sources. These sources later became problematic as written texts became scarce and discrepancies arose. The Song Dynasty's Cheng Hao, Cheng Yi, and Zhu Xi continued the nearly lost teachings of Confucianism; their disciples were as numerous as those of Confucius and Mencius. They implemented the principles found in Confucian teachings to understand the essence of the Confucian classics. They respected what they heard and applied what they learned in order to seek the truth in all things in the universe. Hundreds of scholars such as these served as shining stars during the Song dynasties. Therefore, Han Dynasty scholars were most diligent about research on Confucianist texts, whereas Song Dynasty scholars made the most contributions to the Confucianist way.

During the Yuan, Ming, and early Qing dynasties, these traditions continued unabated. Whenever a master appeared, a band of followers attached to him like shadows; no remuneration was given, yet disciples followed the rules, humbly sat in their places, and responded respectfully. People such as Ruojin,[1] Lu Jiashu,[2] and Zhang Nianzhi may not have stood out for their virtue, but their language was correct and reasonable. Their disciples served as fine role models in the countryside. Indeed, the great tradition of teaching had survived since ancient times, and envious men answered to their sense of shame, perhaps because of the teachings of the masters and the influence of other disciples. According to *The Book of Songs*, "The wind and rain darken the sky; roosters crow without end."[3] This is a precious observation. Nowadays, the

1 Liu Ruojin (1586-1665), jinshi during Ming Emperor Tianqi's reign, became Minister of Punishmenst by the end of Emperor Chongzhen's reign.

2 Lu Longqi (1630-1692), also known as Shibiao and curtesy name Jiashu, was a native of Pinghu of Zhejiang Province and a famous Confucian scholar in the Qing Dynasty.

3 This verse symbolizes the phenomenon of learned people speaking out against social darkness.

世，自乡试、礼部试举主而外，无复所谓师者。间有一二高才之士，钩稽故训，动称汉京，闻老成倡为义理之学者，则骂讥唾侮。后生欲从事于此，进无师友之援，退犯万众之嘲，亦遂却焉。

吾乡善化唐先生，三十而志洛闽之学，特立独行，诟讥而不悔。岁庚子，以方伯内召为太常卿。吾党之士三数人者，日就而考德问业。虽以国藩之不才，亦且为义理所熏蒸，而确然知大闲之不可逾。未知于古之求益者何如，然以视夫世之貌敬举主与厌薄老成而沾沾一得自矜者，吾知免矣。

丙午二月，先生致仕得请，将归老于湖湘之间。故作师说一首，以识年来向道之由，且以告吾乡之人：苟有志于强立，未有不严于事长之礼，而可以成德者也。

only so-called teachers are patrons of the local and national imperial examinations. Occasionally, one or two gifted scholars explore the old precepts and discuss the imperial government. Upon hearing some elders advocate for a revival of the Confucian way, they answered with scorn, ridicule, and insults. If the youth of today want to continue the same advocacy, they must do so without the support of teachers or friends; they retreat from the ridicule of thousands and eventually abandon their efforts.

Master Tang, a native of Shanhua County in Hunan, my homeland, committed himself to Neo-Confucianism at the age of thirty. He is independent in thought and deed and stands unwavering in the face of ridicule. In 1840, when Master Tang was just a local official, the emperor appointed him Administrator of Imperial Sacrifices. Being one of a handful of scholars from my homeland, I consulted him daily. Although I have no talent, I am still influenced by the Confucian way and understand that the basic code of conduct cannot be overstepped. I do not know what a diligent student looked like in ancient times; however, I do know what to avoid when I see someone who superficially respects his master and despises elders who have virtue and talent, someone who becomes complacent and boastful despite achieving little.

In the second month of 1846, Master Tang resigned from his official post to retire in his hometown in Hunan. Therefore, I wrote the essay "On Teachers" to explain the reason for my recent pursuit of the true meaning of Confucianism and also to tell those in my native town that if they are committed to self-improvement and independence and respectfully serve their elders, then they may become people of great moral integrity.

原才

这篇文章写于道光二十六年（1846）。曾氏一向对人才极为重视，并以识人用人闻名于当世。这篇《原才》是他人才思想的理论文章。

从这篇文章中，我们可以看出曾氏对“一二人”特别重视。所谓“一二人”，即全国范畴内的领袖人物。这“一二人”因为处于非常崇高的位置，故而对于全国的士风民风有着巨大的影响，起着引导、示范的作用。

文章最后指出，不仅“一二人”，即便是很基层的管理者，也负有转移习俗、陶铸世风的责任。由此可知，这篇文章的落脚点是在阐述国家各级部门管理者的榜样作用以及对人才的导引力。

风俗之厚薄奚自乎？自乎一二人之心之所向而已。民之生，庸弱者，戢戢皆是也。有一二贤且智者，则众人君之而受命焉，尤智者所君尤众焉。此一二人者之心向义，则众人与之赴义；一二人者之心向利，则众人与之赴利。众人所趋，势之所归，虽有大力，莫之敢逆。故曰：“挠万物者莫疾乎风。”风俗之于人之心，始乎微，而终乎不可御者也。

On Discovering Talented People

This essay was written in the 26th year of Emperor Daoguang's reign (1846). Always one to prize talented people, Zeng Guofan is well-known for his ability to recognize and make the most of them. This is a theoretical work that explains his thoughts on talented people.

This essay confirms the degree to which Zeng valued the best and brightest who served as leaders at the national level. Their positions in the highest echelons afforded them opportunities to influence, guide, and model the national ethos.

Zeng ends the essay by pointing out that even administrators at the grass-roots level should shoulder responsibility for changing social customs and establishing good public morals. We can conclude that the purpose of this essay is to elaborate how administrators at all levels may serve as role models and attract talented people.

What determines which social customs become ingrained? The inclination of merely one or two individuals. Among the people, the mediocre and weak-minded abound. If one or two individuals are virtuous and wise, everyone will support and follow them, and wiser people will attract even larger crowds. If the same one or two individuals are inclined toward righteousness, then everyone will join their pursuit of righteousness; if the same one or two individuals are inclined toward self-interest, then everyone will join their pursuit of self-interest. When the actions of many converge, they create a driving force that even the powerful dare not disobey. As the saying goes, "Nothing bends the world faster than the wind." The impact of social customs may appear subtle at first, but eventually it becomes irresistible.

先王之治天下，使贤者皆当路在势，其风民也皆以义，故道一而俗同。世教既衰，所谓一二人者，不尽在位，彼其心之所向，势不能不腾为口说，而播为声气。而众人者，势不能不听命，而蒸为习尚。于是乎徒党蔚起，而一时之人才出焉。有以仁义倡者，其徒党亦死仁义而不顾；有以功利倡者，其徒党亦死功利而不返。水流湿，火就燥，无感不雠，所从来久矣。

今之君子之在势者，辄曰："天下无才。"彼自尸于高明之地，不克以己之所向，转移习俗，而陶铸一世之人，而翻谢曰无才，谓之不诬，可乎？否也。十室之邑，有好义之士，其智足以移十人者，必能拔十人中之尤者而材之。其智足以移百人者，必能拔百人中之尤者而材之。

In ancient times, emperors entrusted virtuous people to help steer the government; they educated the people using righteousness, thus establishing unified social norms and customs. After civilization declined, the one or two aforementioned individuals rarely served in important positions, thus they had to vigorously promote their aspirations to create social momentum. People would then respond by following them, and common practices developed. In this way, as more people joined their ranks, new talented people emerged. The followers of those who advocate benevolence and righteousness are more than willing to sacrifice themselves for the cause; the followers of those who advocate material gain are also more than willing to sacrifice themselves for the cause. As written in *The Book of Changes*, "Water flows toward wetness; fire burns toward dryness." No inspiration exists that cannot draw a response. It has been this way for ages.

Nowadays, those who wield power often lament, "There are no talented people in the world." Despite their distinguished status, they are unable to use their ideals to shift prevailing customs and nurture people of talent. Instead, they excuse themselves with the refrain, "There are no talented people." Is this argument valid? Not at all! In a small town of ten households, if an individual who advocates benevolence and righteousness has the intelligence to influence ten people, he will surely be capable of selecting the most outstanding of the ten and then cultivating his talents; if the same individual has the intelligence to influence one hundred people, he will surely be capable of selecting the most outstanding of the one hundred and then cultivating their talents.

然则转移习俗而陶铸一世之人，非特处高明之地者然也。凡一命以上，皆与有责焉者也。有国家者，得吾说而存之，则将慎择与共天位之人；士大夫得吾说而存之，则将惴惴乎谨其心之所向，恐一不当，而坏风俗，而贼人才。循是为之，数十年之后，万有一收其效者乎，非所逆睹已。

However, changing social traditions and nurturing a generation of talented people are the responsibility not only of distinguished people but also of those who hold minor positions within a government. If the person who governs a country adopts my ideas and carries them out, he will select talented people who can work together to safeguard the throne; if a scholar adopts and carries out my ideas, he will be cautious about his aspirations and be afraid that his ideas may be inappropriate, thus corrupting prevailing customs and harming talented people. If we do things this way, the day might come several decades from now when these ideas come to fruition, which is beyond my ability to foresee.

君子慎独论

这篇文章作于道光二十七年（1847）。这一年又逢翰林院、詹事府官员的大考，文章即作于考场中。曾氏在这场考试中排名第九，随即一夜间连升四级，由从四品中级官员一跃而为从二品的高级官员。由此可见此文在主考官眼中的分量。

《大学》《中庸》多次提到“君子慎独”。所谓慎独，指的是以谨慎之心对待独处，这是修身自律的关键。如果不能慎独，就谈不上真正的发自内心的修身。作者以简短而有力的文字，将慎独之要及如何做到慎独，说得实在而具操作性。

曾氏将慎独落实在自己的言行中，在朝中口碑甚好。这很可能是此文获得高分的重要原因。

尝谓独也者，君子与小人共焉者也。小人以其为独而生一念之妄，积妄生肆，而欺人之事成。君子懔其为独而生一念之诚，积诚为慎，而自慊之功密。其间离合幾微之端，可得而论矣。

盖《大学》自格致以后，前言往行，既资其扩充；日用细故，亦深其阅历。心之际乎事者，已能剖晰乎公私；心之丽于理者，

On Exercising Caution in Solitude

This essay was written in the 27th year of Emperor Daoguang's reign (1847) as part of another imperial examination given to officials at Hanlin Academy and Zhanshi House. With this essay, Zeng Guofan achieved the ninth place on the examination and was promoted four ranks overnight, from a mid-level official of the fourth rank to a senior official of the associate second rank. Clearly, the examiner thought very highly of Zeng's essay.

The *Great Learning* and the *Doctrine of the Mean* repeatedly mention that "the superior man should exercise caution in solitude." This refers to remaining cautious of one's thoughts and behavior even when others are not around, which is the key to self-discipline. Without being cautious in solitude, it would be impossible to genuinely cultivate one's moral character. In short but powerful writing, the author offers a practical explanation of its importance and how best to achieve it.

Zeng subscribed to this practice in his own private life, which formed the basis for his good reputation in the imperial government. This may be the reason that this essay received such a high score.

Both a superior man and a petty man have moments of solitude. A petty man in solitude harbors a false idea that accumulates into presumptuousness and ends up in deception. A superior man in solitude harbors a true idea of honesty that accumulates into caution and achieves self-satisfaction. The reasoning that separates the two mindsets can be found through discussion.

After the study of natural phenomena began with *The Great Learning*, the speech and behavior of past sages have broadened our views and enriched our minds; trivial matters in everyday life have also deepened our experiences. The broad-minded can

又足精研其得失。则夫善之当为，不善之宜去，早画然其灼见矣。而彼小人者，乃不能实有所见，而行其所知。于是一善当前，幸人之莫我察也，则趋焉而不决。一不善当前，幸人之莫或伺也，则去之而不力。幽独之中，情伪斯出，所谓欺也。惟夫君子者，惧一善之不力，则冥冥者有堕行；一不善之不去，则涓涓者无已时。屋漏而懔如帝天，方寸而坚如金石。独知之地，慎之又慎。此圣经之要领，而后贤所切究者也。

自世儒以格致为外求，而专力于知善知恶，则慎独之旨晦。自世儒以独体为内照，而反昧乎即事即理，则慎独之旨愈晦。要之，明宜先乎诚，非格致则慎亦失当。心必丽于实，非事物则独将失守。此入德之方，不可不辨者也。

differentiate between public and private affairs; the rational can distinguish between gains and losses. A superior man understands that what is good should be done and what is bad should be eliminated. A petty man lacks the necessary knowledge to do the things he knows he should. Hence, a petty man is hesitant about doing good because he fears that others will not know about it; he is half-hearted about correcting a bad habit because he trusts to luck that others will not discover it. In solitude, false illusions naturally emerge; this is deception. A superior man is afraid of slipping into degeneration if he fails to complete one good deed to his satisfaction and is afraid of forever making mistakes if he fails to eliminate one bad habit. In his private dark chamber, he behaves solemnly as though facing a god, and his backbone is as firm as a rock. When conducting business in solitude, we cannot be too cautious. These are the key principles that the ancient sages have followed and the issues that later generations of sages should explore.

The meaning of "exercising caution in solitude" has been obscured by scholars who believe that the study of natural phenomena is an external pursuit and therefore shift their focus to understanding good and evil. The concept of "exercising caution in solitude" has been further obscured by contemporary Confucian scholars who identified the condition of solitude as the foundation for understanding all natural phenomena. In summary, a clear understanding of reason precedes honesty, as without a deep exploration of natural phenomena, caution can easily become inappropriate; thinking must be based on reason, as without, reason it is impossible to exercise caution in solitude. This is the way to improve virtue and refine achievements; thus we cannot afford to not give it serious consideration.

欧阳生文集序

欧阳生名勋，字子和，湘潭人，他的父亲欧阳兆熊，是曾氏一生中全始全终的一位重要朋友。道光二十年（1840），曾氏一人进京参加散馆考试，在旅馆里生重病，几于不治，全靠欧阳兆熊延医照料度过危难，两人由此结下深厚情谊。欧阳兆熊是一位刻书藏书专家，晚年主持金陵书局，刻印王船山遗书。

咸丰五年（1855），他的年仅二十余岁的儿子欧阳勋去世。欧阳勋年纪虽轻，然诗文俱佳。他的英年早逝令欧阳兆熊非常悲痛，也令曾氏十分惋惜。咸丰八年，欧阳兆熊将儿子的文章结集刻印，曾氏怀着安慰好友、怜恤后生之心，为文集写下这篇序言。

序言中，他将欧阳勋列为桐城派在湖南的传人，这是对年轻的欧阳勋很高的评价。

乾隆之末，桐城姚姬传先生鼐，善为古文辞，慕效其乡先辈方望溪侍郎之所为，而受法于刘君大櫆及其世父编修君范。三子

Foreword to the *Collected Works of Ouyang Sheng*

Ouyang Sheng, who was born in Xiangtan County, Hunan Province, had the given name "Xun" and was also known by his courtesy name "Zihe." His father, Ouyang Zhaoxiong, was an important lifelong friend of Zeng Guofan. In the 20th year of Emperor Daoguang's reign (1840), Zeng traveled alone to Beijing to participate in an examination held by Hanlin Academy to select imperial historiographers. While in the capital, he became gravely ill at his hotel and almost died. Fortunately, Ouyang Zhaoxiong sent for a doctor and tended to Zeng until he recovered. This experience cemented a deep bond between the two. Ouyang Zhaoxiong specialized in printing and collecting books. In his later years, he directed Jinling Publishing House and printed Wang Chuanshan's posthumous books.

In the fifth year of Emperor Xianfeng's reign (1855), his son, Ouyang Xun, passed away while still only in his twenties. Despite his youth, Ouyang Xun had been a talented writer of poetry and prose, which made his early death all the more poignant for his father and Zeng. In the eighth year of Emperor Xianfeng's reign (1858), Ouyang Zhaoxiong collected and published his son's writings, and Zeng expressed empathy for his good friend by writing this foreword to his son's collected works.

In the foreword, Zeng lauds Ouyang Xun as one of the new generation of writers from the Tongcheng school in Hunan. This was an extraordinary recommendation for one so young.

Toward the end of Emperor Qianlong's reign lived Yao Nai (courtesy name Jichuan), a native of Tongcheng in Anhui Province and a skilled writer of classical prose. He admired and emulated the prose written by Fang Bao (courtesy name Wangxi) and learned writing skills from Liu Dakui and his uncle, Yao Fan. All

既通儒硕望，姚先生治其术益精。历城周书昌永年为之语曰：“天下之文章，其在桐城乎！”由是学者多归向桐城，号“桐城派”，犹前世所称江西诗派者也。

姚先生晚而主钟山书院讲席，门下著籍者，上元有管同异之、梅曾亮伯言，桐城有方东树植之、姚莹石甫。四人者，称为高第弟子。各以所得，传授徒友，往往不绝。在桐城者，有戴钧衡存庄，事植之久，尤精力过绝人。自以为守其邑先正之法，禫之后进，义无所让也。其不列弟子籍，同时服膺，有新城鲁仕骥絜非、宜兴吴德旋仲伦。絜非之甥为陈用光硕士。硕士既师其舅，又亲受业姚先生之门。乡人化之，多好文章。硕士之群从，有陈学受

three highly esteemed scholars were natives of Tongcheng who were famed for their knowledge, but Yao Nai's writing was even more exquisite than the scholars he admired. Zhou Yongnian (courtesy name Shuchang), a native of Licheng in Shandong Province, once remarked, "The quintessence of the essay can be found in Tongcheng!" Consequently, most scholars converted to Tongcheng scholars, thus forming the Tongcheng school, which was similar to the Jiangxi poetry school of previous generations.

In his later years, Yao Nai lectured at Zhongshan Academy in Nanjing. Among his disciples were Guan Tong (courtesy name Yizhi) and Mei Zengliang (courtesy Boyan) from Shangyuan County, and Fang Dongshu (courtesy name Zhizhi) and Yao Ying (courtesy name Shifu) from Tongcheng County. These four were considered outstanding disciples of Yao Nai. They imparted all they had learned from Yao Nai to their students and friends, ensuring that this knowledge would be passed down wherever they went. In Tongcheng, Dai Junheng (courtesy name Cunzhuang), who had spent much time studying with Fang Dongshu, was exceptionally diligent. He strongly believed that the teachings of Tongcheng's older generations should be passed down to younger ones; he saw no need for modesty when it came to the issue of morality. Those not listed as disciples but who claimed to be out of respect for Yao Nai included Lu Shiji (courtesy name Jiefei) of Xincheng County in Jiangxi and Wu Dexuan (courtesy name Zhonglun) of Yixing County in Jiangsu. Lu Shiji had a nephew named Chen Yongguang who was a scholar; he was a student not only of his uncle but also of Yao Nai. The people from his hometown felt his influence through education and learned to enjoy his writings. Local scholars flocked to learn from Chen Yongguang, including Chen Xueshou (courtesy name Yishu) and Chen Pu (courtesy name Guangfu) of Xincheng County and Wu Jiabin (courtesy name Zixu) of Nanfeng County.

艺叔、陈溥广敷，而南丰又有吴嘉宾子序，皆承絜非之风，私淑于姚先生。由是江西建昌有桐城之学。

仲伦与永福吕璜月沧交友，月沧之乡人有临桂朱琦伯韩、龙启瑞翰臣、马平王锡振定甫，皆步趋吴氏、吕氏，而益求广其术于梅伯言。由是桐城宗派流衍于广西矣。

昔者，国藩尝怪姚先生典试湖南，而吾乡出其门者，未闻相从以学文为事。既而得巴陵吴敏树南屏称述其术，笃好而不厌。而武（凌）〔陵〕杨彝珍性农、善化孙鼎臣芝房、湘阴郭嵩焘伯琛、（淑）〔溆〕浦舒焘伯鲁，亦以姚氏文家正轨，违此则又何求？最后得湘潭欧阳生。生，吾友欧阳兆熊小岑之子，而受法于巴陵吴君、湘阴郭君，亦师事新城二陈。其渐染者多，其志趋嗜好，举天下之美，无以易乎桐城姚氏者也。

They all inherited Lu Shiji's style of writing, which in turn came from Yao Nai. Consequently, the Tongcheng school was established in Jiangxi's Jianchang County.

Wu Dexuan befriended Lü Huang (courtesy name Yuecang) of Yongfu County in Guangxi. People from that area, including Zhu Qi (courtesy name Bohan) and Long Qirui (courtesy name Hanchen) of Lingui County and Wang Xizhen (courtesy name Dingfu) of Maping County, became followers of Wu Dexuan and Lü Huang and even sought to learn from Mei Zengliang (courtesy name Boyan). Consequently, the Tongcheng school developed in Guangxi.

Previously, I wondered why despite Yao Nai presiding over the imperial examinations in Hunan, none of the scholars from my hometown who studied under him followed his example to choose writing as a profession. Soon after, I learned that Wu Minshu (courtesy name Nanping) of Baling County (present-day Yueyang City) praised Yao Nai's academic achievements and expressed deep admiration for Yao Nai. Yang Yizhen (courtesy name Xingnong) of Wuling County, Sun Dingchen (courtesy name Zhifang) of Shanhua County, Guo Songtao (courtesy name Bochen) of Xiangyin County, and Shu Tao (courtesy name Bolu) of Xupu County also believed that Yao Nai established a standard for literary writing. Where would they turn if not to Yao Nai's way of writing? At last, I learned that Ouyang Xun of Xiangtan County was also a follower of Yao Nai. Ouyang Xun was the son of my friend Ouyang Zhaoxiong (courtesy name Xiaocen). He followed Wu of Baling and Guo of Xiangyin to study writing under Chen Xueshou and Chen Pu of Xincheng County. Many people have been deeply influenced by the Tongcheng school. They share a common belief that not even the most beautiful things in the world can measure up to their admiration for the Tongcheng school's Yao Nai.

当乾隆中叶，海内魁儒畸士崇尚鸿博，繁称旁证，考核一字，累数千言不能休。别立帜志，名曰“汉学”。深摈有宋诸子义理之说，以为不足复存，其为文尤芜杂寡要。姚先生独排众议，以为义理、考据、词章三者不可偏废。必义理为质，而后文有所附，考据有所归。一编之内，惟此尤兢兢。当时孤立无助，传之五六十年。近世学子稍稍诵其文，承用其说。道之兴废，亦各有时，其命也欤哉！自洪、杨倡乱，东南荼毒。钟山石城，昔时姚先生撰杖都讲之所，今为犬羊窟宅，深固而不可拔。桐城沦为异域，既克而复失。戴钧衡全家殉难，身亦欧血死矣！

余来建昌，闻新城、南丰兵燹之余，百物荡尽，田荒不治，蓬蒿没人，一二文士转徙无所。而广西用兵九载，群盗犹汹汹，骤不可爬梳，龙君翰臣又物故。独吾乡少安，二三君子尚得优游

During the middle period of Emperor Qianlong's reign, famous Confucian scholars advocated greatness, erudition, and an ornate style of writing. They would employ thousands of words to conduct a study of just one character. For this, they founded a new school of learning called "sinology" and brushed aside the Confucian way advocated by Song Dynasty scholars. Essays written by these famous Confucian scholars were disorganized and pointless. Yao Nai alone ruled out discordant arguments and argued that the following deserved equal attention: the Confucian way, textual research, and literary composition. He argued that the Confucian way must serve as the foundation for writing so that diction can add cohesion and textual research can be properly conducted. He advised scholars to pay special attention to this theory when writing an essay. Despite a lack of support, Yao Nai advocated this theory for five to six decades. Some recent scholars have begun reading his essays and grown to accept his academic argument. There is a time for academic arguments to flourish and a time for them to fade. This is just fate! Since Hong Xiuquan and Yang Xiuqing led their rebellion, southeastern China has experienced great suffering. Zhongshan Stone Town, where Yao Nai once held a staff and taught at Zhongshan Academy, is now a stronghold of scoundrels and degenerates. Tongcheng has fallen into the hands of the rebels, retaken only to be lost again. Dai Junheng's entire family died during the rebellion, and Dai himself lost his life while vomiting blood!

When I arrived in Jianchang Prefecture in Jiangxi Province, I heard that warfare had desolated Xincheng and Nanfeng Counties: everything was in havoc, and the fields lay in waste. A few men of letters survived only to become homeless and adrift. In Guangxi, bandits still ran rampant after nine years of war, and I learned that Long Qirui (Hanchen) passed away. Only my hometown was relatively untouched. Some scholars were still able to study litera-

文学，曲折以求合桐城之辙。而舒涛前卒，欧阳生亦以瘵死。老者牵于人事，或遭乱不得竟其学；少者或中道夭殂。四方多故，求如姚先生之聪明早达，太平寿考，从容以跻于古之作者，卒不可得。然则业之成否，又得谓之非命也耶？

欧阳生名勋，字子和，没于咸丰五年三月，年二十有几。其文若诗清缜喜往复，亦时有乱离之慨。庄周云："逃空虚者，闻人足音跫然而喜。"而况昆弟亲戚之謦咳其侧者乎？余之不闻桐城诸老之謦咳也久矣！观生之为，则岂直足音而已！故为之序，以塞小岑之悲，亦以见文章与世变相因，俾后之人得以考览焉。

咸丰八年十二月曾国藩叙

ture at a leisurely pace, carrying on the tradition of the Tongcheng school. Shu Tao passed away prior to this, and Ouyang Xun died of illness. Elderly scholars were either preoccupied with personal matters or forced to suspend their studies due to the rebellion; some young scholars lost their lives while still at their studies. With troubles everywhere, now it was impossible to find a scholar like Yao Nai, who was not only intelligent, but had established himself at an early age, created a place for himself among the classic authors of Chinese literature, and died of old age. Thus, is it destiny that dictates whose academic pursuits succeed?

Ouyang Sheng, whose given name was Xun and courtesy name was Zihe, passed away in his twenties in March of the fifth year of Emperor Xianfeng's reign (1855). His essays and poems were refreshing and meticulous. He enjoyed responding to others with a poem and singing in harmony, and he often expressed his sorrow for the turbulent times. Zhuangzi said, "Those who walk along a deserted area are glad to hear the sound of footsteps." What about the sound of brothers and relatives talking and laughing around me? It has been a long time since I have heard the old masters of the Tongcheng school talking and laughing. Could it be that reading Ouyang Sheng's literary works is the same as hearing footsteps? Therefore, I have written him this foreword to honor the grief of his father Ouyang Zhaoxiong. I have also identified the connection between writings and the changes in our times, so later generations will be able to explore them further.

Zeng Guofan, in the 12th month of the eighth year of Emperor Xianfeng's reign (1858)

圣哲画像记

此文作于咸丰九年（1859），是曾氏一生文章中很重要的一篇。

他在三千年的中国历史中，挑出三十二人（实际上是三十四人，程颐、程颢两兄弟并称“二程”而为一，王念孙、王引之并称“王氏父子”而为一）作为圣哲的代表人物，分为八组，并一一加以概括性的说明。

周文王、周公、孔子、孟子是圣人，庄子、左丘明、司马迁、班固是长于著述之才，诸葛亮、陆贽、范仲淹、司马光是治理之才，周敦颐、二程、朱熹、张载是理学大师，韩愈、柳宗元、欧阳修、曾巩是文章高手，李白、杜甫、苏轼、黄庭坚是诗中大家，许慎、郑玄、杜预、马端临为考订专家，顾炎武、秦蕙田、姚鼐、王氏父子则为学问大成者。

曾氏认为，这三十多人都是中华民族的圣哲，好好地研究他们中的任何一人，读通他们所著的任何一本书，都能终生受益无穷。

国藩志学不早，中岁侧身朝列，窃窥陈编，稍涉先圣昔贤魁儒长者之绪。驽缓多病，百无一成；军旅驰驱，益以芜废。丧乱

Portraits of Sages

This essay from the ninth year of Emperor Xianfeng's reign (1859) stands out among Zeng Guofan's writings.

He selected 32 people [1] from China's 3,000-year history to be held up as embodiments of all the sages in China. He then categorized them into eight groups and provided a general account of each sage.

King Wen of Zhou, the Duke of Zhou (a son of King Wen of Zhou), Confucius, and Mencius were great sages. Zhuangzi, Zuo Qiuming, Sima Qian, and Ban Gu were exceptional writers. Zhuge Liang, Lu Zhi, Fan Zhongyan, and Sima Guang were statesmen. Zhou Dunyi, the Cheng brothers, Zhu Xi, and Zhang Zai were masters of Neo-Confucianism. Han Yu, Liu Zongyuan, Ouyang Xiu, and Zeng Gong were gifted essayists. Li Bai, Du Fu, Su Shi, and Huang Tingjian were influential poets. Xu Shen, Zheng Xuan, Du Yu, and Ma Duanlin were experts in textual research. Gu Yanwu, Qin Huitian, Yao Nai, and the Wang father and son were venerated scholars.

Zeng revered the figures above as sages of the Chinese tradition and believed that studying any one of them and reading any of their works would bring lifelong benefits.

I did not resolve to pursue my studies at an early age. It was not until I reached middle age and joined the ranks of officials at the imperial court that I began reading ancient writings, thus catching a glimpse of the work done by the ancient sages. Being slow-minded and in poor health, I have accomplished nothing. Being in the military fighting on all fronts has meant that I have neglected my

1 Zeng actually selected 34 people. He considered Cheng Yi and Cheng Hao, who were known as the Cheng brothers, as one person and considered Wang Niansun and Wang Yinzhi, who were father and son, as one person as well.

未平，而吾年将五十矣。往者吾读班固《艺文志》及马氏《经籍考》，见其所列书目，丛杂猥多，作者姓氏，至于不可胜数，或昭昭于日月，或湮没而无闻。及为文渊阁直阁校理，每岁二月侍从宣宗皇帝入阁，得观《四库全书》，其富过于前代所藏远甚，而存目之书数十万卷，尚不在此列。

呜呼！何其多也！虽有生知之资，累世不能竟其业，况其下焉者乎！故书籍之浩浩，著述者之众，若江海然，非一人之腹所能尽饮也，要在慎择焉而已。余既自度其不逮，乃择古今圣哲三十余人，命儿子纪泽图其遗像，都为一卷，藏之家塾。后嗣有志读书，取足于此，不必广心博骛，而斯文之传，莫大乎是矣。昔在汉世，若武梁祠、鲁灵光殿，皆图画伟人事迹，而《列女传》

education. While death and disorder continue unabated, I am approaching 50 years of age. In the past, when I read classics such as Ban Gu's "Treatise on Literature (*Yi Wen Zhi*)" from the *Book of Han* and Ma Duanlin's "Verifying Confucian Classics (*Jing Ji Kao*)" from *A General Record of Documents* (*Wen Xian Tong Kao*), I discovered that there were a vast number of catalogued books and countless authors, some of whom are as bright as the sun and the moon and others who have faded into obscurity. When I was working as a reviser at the Belvedere of Literary Profundity, I accompanied Emperor Daoguang and thus had access to *The Complete Library in the Four Branches of Literature*, also known as *Si Ku Quan Shu*, which included far more books than had been collected in previous dynasties. Moreover, tens of thousands of books that are catalogued in the imperial pavilion are not included in *the Complete Library in the Four Branches of Literature*.

Alas! How can there be so many books! Even someone with the wisdom of a sage could not finish reading that many over multiple lifetimes, never mind someone who is slow-minded. Clearly, the number of books and authors is as vast as the water in the rivers and seas; it is impossible for one stomach to drink it all in. The key is carefully choosing what to read. Recognizing my limitations, I have chosen more than thirty sages, both ancient and contemporary, and asked my son Jize to draw a portrait for each one, to be collected and bound into one volume for the collection in my family library. Later generations who want an education can simply read the works of the selected sages. There is no need to spend time reading extensively because the academic tradition has not surpassed their works. As early as the Han Dynasty, places such as Wuliang Shrine and Lulingguang Hall included depictions of the achievements of great men, and *Biographies of Exemplary Women* also featured illustrations. Such portraits and illustrations have

亦有画像，感发兴起，由来已旧。习其器矣，进而索其神，通其微，合其莫，心诚求之，仁远乎哉？

国藩记

尧舜禹汤，史臣记言而已。至文王拘幽，始立文字，演《周易》，忧勤惕厉之意，载与俱出。周孔代兴，六经炳著，师道备矣。秦汉以来，孟子盖与庄、荀并称。至唐，韩氏独尊异之。而宋之贤者，以为可跻之尼山之次，崇其书以配《论语》。后之论者，莫之能易也。兹以亚于三圣人后云。

左氏传经，多述二周典礼，而好称引奇诞，文辞烂然，浮于质矣。太史公称庄子之书皆寓言，吾观子长所为《史记》，寓言亦

long inspired later generations to pursue their studies. Becoming familiar with the physical appearance of the sages and then exploring their minds may help to master their ideas and connect to them spiritually. As long as we embrace a sincere desire to study, how can the way of benevolence be far behind?

Zeng Guofan

Emperors Yao, Shun, Yu, and Tang left no works behind except for statements recorded by historiographers. It was not until King Wen of Zhou was imprisoned that the writings of a contemporary author appeared. In order to express his sorrow and vigilance, King Wen of Zhou wrote an essay, which was published and circulated, interpreting *The Book of Changes*. Thereafter, the writings of the Duke of Zhou and Confucius appeared, and the Six Classics were published, thus establishing methods of teaching. Since the Qin and Han dynasties, Mencius has been recognized as a sage alongside Zhuangzi and Xunzi. During the Tang Dynasty, however, Han Yu had great reverence for Mencius in particular. The sages of the Song Dynasty considered Mencius second only to Confucius and compared his book to *The Analects*. Later generations of scholars were unable to change this view. Therefore, I place Mencius behind the three sages: King Wen of Zhou, the Duke of Zhou, and Confucius.

Zuo Qiuming wrote the *Zuo Zhuan* as a commentary on the *Spring and Autumn Annals*. In his annotations, Zuo Qiuming mostly provided descriptions of the decrees, regulations, and code of conduct of the Eastern and Western Zhou dynasties. He was known for the flamboyant language he used to quote bizarre tales that added no substance. Sima Qian called the works of Zhuangzi all fables. In my opinion, fables account for sixty to seventy percent of Sima Qian's *Records of the Grand Historian*. Ban Gu lagged

居十之六七。班氏闳识孤怀，不逮子长远甚，然经世之典，六艺之旨，文字之源，幽明之情状，粲然大备，岂与夫斗筲者争得失于一先生之前，姝姝而自悦者哉！

诸葛公当扰攘之世，被服儒者，从容中道。陆敬舆事多疑之主，驭难驯之将，烛之以至明，将之以至诚，譬若御驽马登峻坂，纵横险阻，而不失其驰，何其神也！范希文、司马君实遭时差隆，然坚卓诚信，各有孤诣。其以道自持，蔚成风俗，意量亦远矣。昔刘向称董仲舒王佐之才，伊、吕无以加；管、晏之属，殆不能及。而刘歆以为董子师友所渐，曾不能几乎游、夏。以予观四贤者，虽未逮乎伊、吕，固将贤于董子。惜乎不得如刘向父子而论定耳。

自朱子表章周子、二程子、张子，以为上接孔孟之传，后世君相师儒笃守其说，莫之或易。乾隆中，闳儒辈起，训诂博辨，

far behind Sima Qian in talent and ambition, but he provided very clear and detailed descriptions of the decrees and regulations that govern the society, the substance of the Six Classics, the origins of texts, and spiritual and earthly matters. How is this comparable to those of limited ability who vie for success in the company of elders and feel pleased with themselves!

Zhuge Liang was born at a turbulent time, yet his Confucian beliefs helped him navigate the right way in the world. Lu Zhi (courtesy name Jingyu) served a suspicious monarch and ruled difficult generals; by illuminating the monarch's heart and commanding the generals with sincerity, he achieved a feat on par with charging an inferior horse over steep terrain while beset by danger on all sides – what a miracle! Living in slightly better times, Fan Zhongyan and Sima Guang each made unique contributions rooted in their determination and integrity. They followed the right way, which promoted positive social customs that have had far-reaching impact! A famed writer of the Western Han Dynasty, Liu Xiang believed that Dong Zhongshu had just the right capabilities for assisting a monarch, and Yi Yin and Lü Shang were deemed just about as capable, while Guan Zhong and Yan Ying fell far below that standard. However, Liu Xin, son of Liu Xiang, believed that the influence exerted by teachers and friends made him less capable than Ziyou and Zixia. While I do not consider the four (Zhuge Liang, Lu Jingyu, Fan Xiwen, and Sima Junshi) to be superior to Yi Yin or Lu Shang, I do hold them higher than Dong Zhongshu. It is unfortunate that I cannot offer definitive judgments on them as Liu Xiang and Liu Xin did.

Later generations of monarchs, prime ministers, teachers, and scholars alike had come to blindly accept the doctrines of Zhou Dunyi, Cheng Hao, Cheng Yi, and Zhang Zai as standard interpretations of Confucius and Mencius because Zhu Xi had highly

度越昔贤，别立徽志，号曰汉学。摈有宋五子之术，以谓不得独尊。而笃信五子者，亦屏弃汉学，以为破碎害道，断断焉而未有已。吾观五子立言，其大者多合于洙泗，何可议也？其训释诸经，小有不当，固当取近世经说以辅翼之，又可屏弃群言以自隘乎？斯二者亦俱讥焉。

西汉文章，如子云、相如之雄伟，此天地遒劲之气，得于阳与刚之美者也。此天地之义气也。刘向、匡衡之渊懿，此天地温厚之气，得于阴与柔之美者也。此天地之仁气也。东汉以还，淹雅无惭于古，而风骨少隤矣。韩、柳有作，尽取扬、马之雄奇万

regarded them. During Emperor Qianlong's reign, famous Confucian scholars emerged in large numbers. They were engaged in expositions of Confucian classics and detailed textual research on a greater scale than their predecessors. They even established a new school of studies called "Sinology." These Confucianists from the Qing Dynasty rejected the Neo-Confucianism of Zhou Dunyi, Cheng Hao, Cheng Yi, Zhang Zi, and Zhu Xi, arguing that the Neo-Confucianists from the Song dynasties should not be the only ones that are venerated. On the other hand, those who sincerely believed in the Neo-Confucianism of the Song Dynasty's Zhou Dunyi, Cheng Hao, Cheng Yi, Zhang Zi, and Zhu Xi rejected Sinology, arguing that it was fragmented and harmful to the way of Confucianism. The debate between these two groups of scholars still continues. In my opinion, the theories established by the five Neo-Confucianists named above are generally consistent with the teachings of Confucius. What is there to reproach? Meanwhile, the school of Sinology has some slightly improper areas in its interpretation of Confucian classics; they should consider using the most recent interpretation of Confucian classics as an aid. How can they exclude other opinions and limit themselves? These two groups of scholars are equally ridiculous.

The greatness of essays written in the Western Han Dynasty by writers such as Yang Xiong and Sima Xiangru originates from the powerful *qi* that exists between heaven and earth and imbues the writing with a striking masculinity; this constitutes the sense of righteousness in the world. The profound beauty of writings by Liu Xiang and Kuang Heng originates from the gentle qi that exists between heaven and earth and instills a feminine beauty into the writing; this constitutes the benevolence in the world. Essays written after the Eastern Han Dynasty were no less erudite than those composed in ancient times, but they were stylistically weaker. Han Yu and then Liu Zongyuan channeled Yang Xiong and Sima Xian-

变，而内之于薄物小篇之中，岂不诡哉！欧阳氏、曾氏皆法韩公，而体质于匡、刘为近。文章之变，莫可穷诘，要之不出此二途，虽百世可知也。

余钞古今诗，自魏晋至国朝，得十九家。盖诗之为道广矣，嗜好趋向，各视其性之所近，犹庶羞百味，罗列鼎俎，但取适吾口者，哜之得饱而已。必穷尽天下之佳肴，辩尝而后供一馔，是大惑也；必强天下之舌，尽效吾之所嗜，是大愚也。庄子有言："大惑者，终身不解；大愚者，终身不灵。"余于十九家中，又笃守夫四人者焉。唐之李、杜，宋之苏、黄，好之者十而七八，非之者亦且二三。余惧蹈庄子不解不灵之讥，则取足于是终身焉已耳。

司马子长网罗旧闻，贯串三古，而八书颇病其略；班氏《志》较详矣，而断代为书，无以观其会通。欲周览经世之大法，必自

gru by applying their magnificent changes to essays on less-than-magnificent topics – it is just extraordinary! Ouyang Xiu and Zeng Gong attempted to pattern their essays after those of Han Yu, but their essays were structurally more similar to those of Kuang Heng and Liu Xiang. Therefore, it is impossible to thoroughly study the evolution of the essay. The essay only has two paths for change: the two polarities of masculinity and femininity. One hundred generations hence, this will still be the same.

I have selected 19 poets [1] from the Wei-Jin period to the reigning Dynasty. Generally speaking, the study of poetry is an immense undertaking. Individual preferences are determined by one's temperament. For example, when presented with a table loaded with countless plates of delicious food, we eat our fill with food that suits our tastes. It would be confusing to insist on tasting all of the delicacies the world has to offer before starting our meal; it would be ignorant to force everyone in the world to adopt our personal preferences. Zhuangzi once said, "A confused man will never think with clarity; an ignorant man will never understand." I have given careful attention to four of the nineteen poets, namely, the Tang Dynasty's Li Bai and Du Fu and the Song Dynasty's Su Shi and Huang Tingjian. Perhaps eight of every ten people are fond of these four poets. So as not to be ridiculed by Zhuangzi as confused or ignorant, I have selected works by the authors below to study throughout my life.

Sima Qian's *Records of the Grand Historian* compiles ancient knowledge and historical accounts from three ancient time periods, but his "Eight Treatises" is less than thorough. Although the "Ten Treatises" in Ban Gu's *Book of Han* are more detailed, they

1 Zeng Guofan compiled an Anthology of Poems by Eighteen Poets from the Wei-Jin period to the Song-Jin period, including Cao Zhi, Ruan Ji, Tao Yuanming, Xie Lingyun, Bao Zhao, Xie Tiao, Wang Wei, Meng Haoran, Li Bai, Du Fu, Han Yu, Bai Juyi, Li Shangyin, Du Mu, Su Shi, Huang Tingjian, Lu You, and Yuan Haowen.

杜氏《通典》始矣。马端临《通考》，杜氏伯仲之间，郑《志》非其伦也。百年以来，学者讲求形声、故训，专治《说文》，多宗许、郑，少谈杜、马。吾以许、郑考先王制作之源，杜、马辨后世因革之要，其于实事求是一也。

先王之道，所谓修己治人、经纬万汇者，何归乎？亦曰礼而已矣。秦焚书籍，汉代诸儒之所掇拾，郑康成之所以卓绝，皆以礼也。杜君卿《通典》，言礼者十居其六，其识已跨越八代矣！有宋张子、朱子之所讨论，马贵与、王伯厚之所纂辑，莫不以礼为兢兢。我朝学者，以顾亭林为宗，国史《儒林传》褎然冠首。吾

only provide an account of the laws and institutions of one dynasty, thus they are inadequate for an accurate study of institutions across multiple dynasties. For a broad perspective on government in China, we must start with *Comprehensive Institutions* (*Tong Dian*) by Du You (courtesy name Junqing). *A General Record of Documents* (*Wen Xian Tong Kao*) by Ma Duanlin (courtesy name Guiyu) is comparable to Du You's *Tong Dian*, whereas *General Treatises* by Zheng Qiao (courtesy name Yuzhong) is not. For almost a century, scholars have focused on the pictophonetic exegesis of Chinese characters and the annotations to *Etymology of Chinese Characters* (*Shuo Wen Jie Zi*). While most scholars hold Xu Shen (courtesy name Shuzhong) and Zheng Xuan (courtesy name Kangcheng) in high esteem, few ever mention Du You and Ma Duanlin. In my opinion, Xu Shen and Zheng Xuan conduct textual criticism on the origin of works by former sages, whereas Du You and Ma Duanlin analyze the evolution of later periods. However, they all attempt to seek the truth from facts.

What guided the ancient emperors to practice self-cultivation, to govern the people, and to organize all things? The answer is rites. They are the reason that the Qin Dynasty burned books, the subject that Han Dynasty scholars sought to explore, and the source of Zheng Xuan's extraordinary abilities. Six tenths of Du You's *Tong Dian* is about rites, with information covering more than eight dynasties![1] During the Song and Yuan dynasties, rites were the focus of Zhang Zai, Zhu Xi, Ma Duanlin (courtesy name Guiyu), and Wang Yinglin (courtesy name Bohou). Our great Qing Dynasty scholar Gu Yanwu, who wrote under the pseudonym Tinglin, was prominently listed in the *Book of Han's Biographies of Confucian Scholars* (*Ru Lin Zhuan*). When I read the section of his book on the cultivation of etiquette and customs, I was struck by

1 The eight dynasties refer to the Han, Wei, Jin, Song, Qi, Liang, Chen, and Sui dynasties.

读其书，言及礼俗教化，则毅然有守先待后，舍我其谁之志，何其壮也！厥后张蒿庵作《中庸论》，及江慎修、戴东原辈，尤以礼为先务。而秦尚书蕙田遂纂《五礼通考》，举天下古今幽明万事，而一经之以礼，可谓体大而思精矣。吾图画国朝先正遗像，首顾先生，次秦文恭公，亦岂无微旨哉！桐城姚鼐姬传、高邮王念孙怀祖，其学皆不纯于礼。然姚先生持论闳通，国藩之粗解文章，由姚先生启之也。王氏父子集小学训诂之大成，夐乎不可几已。故以殿焉。

姚姬传氏言学问之途有三：曰义理，曰词章，曰考据。戴东原氏亦以为言。如文、周、孔、孟之圣，左、庄、马、班之才，诚不可以一方体论矣。至若葛、陆、范、马，在圣门则以德行而兼政事也。周、程、张、朱，在圣门则德行之科也，皆义理也。

his determination to pass down traditions to future generations. How magnificent! Later, Zhang Erqi (courtesy name Jiruo, pseudonym Hao'an) wrote *Annotations on the Doctrine of the Golden Mean* (*Zhong Yong Lun*). He and subsequent scholars, such as Jiang Yong (courtesy name Shenxiu) and Dai Zhen (courtesy name Dongyuan), prioritized the study of rites. Qin Huitian (courtesy name Shufeng, pseudonym Weijing) used the concept of rites to organize everything that happened between men and gods in ancient and modern times in his exhaustive yet accurate book A *Comprehensive Examination of the Five Rites* (*Wu Li Tong Kao*). Therefore, my portraits of Qing Dynasty sages begin with Gu Yanwu and Qin Huitian. The order of the portraits is not random! Yao Nai and Wang Niansun did not focus solely on rites in their scholarly discussions. However, Yao Nai's essays are erudite and clearly presented and have served as a guide when I attempt to compose rough essays of my own. Wang Niansun and his son Wang Yinzhi epitomized the development of philology and exegesis, and their talents were unparalleled, so I have concluded my list of prominent scholars with them.

According to Yao Nai, there are three paths to learning: the Confucian way, literary composition, and textual research. This theory has also been put forward by Dai Zhen. The virtues of the sages (King Wen of Zhou, the Duke of Zhou, Confucius, and Mencius) and the talents of the exceptional writers (Zuo Qiuming, Zhuang Zhou, also known as Zhuangzi, Sima Qian, and Ban Gu) cannot be categorized together under any one of the four disciplines of learning in Confucianism. As for the statesmen (Zhuge Liang, Lu Zhi, Fan Zhongyan, and Sima Guang), they may be grouped together under virtuous conduct and political achievement. The masters of Neo-Confucianism (Zhou Dunyi, Cheng Hao, Cheng Yi, Zhang Zai, and Zhu Xi) engaged in argumentation and fall into the category of virtuous conduct, or to be specific,

韩、柳、欧、曾、李、杜、苏、黄，在圣门则言语之科也，所谓词章者也。许、郑、杜、马、顾、秦、姚、王，在圣门则文学之科也。顾、秦于杜、马为近，姚、王于许、郑为近，皆考据也。此三十二子者，师其一人，读其一书，终身用之，有不能尽。若又有陋于此，而求益于外，譬若掘井九仞而不及泉，则以一井为隘，而必广掘数十百井，身老力疲，而卒无见泉之一日。其庸有当乎？

自浮屠氏言因果祸福而为善获报之说，深中于人心，牢固而不可破。士方其占毕咿唔，则期报于科第禄仕；或少读古书，窥著作之林，则责报于遐迩之誉，后世之名；纂述未及终编，辄冀得一二有力之口，腾播人人之耳，以偿吾劳也。朝耕而暮获，一施而十报，譬若沽酒市脯，喧聒以责之贷者，又取倍称之息焉。

the Confucian way. The gifted essayists (Han Yu, Liu Zongyuan, Ouyang Xiu, Zeng Gong, Li Bai, Du Fu, Su Shi, and Huang Tingjian) may be grouped together under language, or to be specific, under literary composition. The textual researchers (Xu Shen, Zheng Xuan, Du You, Ma Duanlin, Gu Yanwu, Qin Huitian, Yao Nai, and Wang Niansun and his son Wang Yinzhi) may be categorized under literature. Gu Yanwu and Qin Huitian are more similar to Du You and Ma Duanlin, whereas Yao Nai and Wang Niansun and his son Wang Yinzhi are more similar to Xu Shen and Zheng Xuan. If we were to follow the example of any one of these thirty-two sages and read any one of their books, we would have more than a lifetime of material to digest. Any attempt to find deeper books elsewhere is bound to be disappointing. It would be like digging a well nine *ren* [1] (more than 20 meters deep) without finding a spring. Thinking the well is too narrow, we dig dozens and dozens of wells until we are old and weary without ever finding water. Is that not all for nothing?

Since Buddhist disciples first began talking about karma, the concept of rewards for good deeds has become permanently ingrained in people's minds. Having barely picked up a book, scholars expect to become high-ranking officials with big salaries. After reading a few of the ancient classics for just a glimpse into that wealth of knowledge, some people think they deserve widespread praise and lasting fame. Even before they finish writing it, some people hope that one or two influential people will publicize their book to repay them for their hard work. They sow the land in the morning and expect to harvest crops by nightfall; they exert minimal effort but want ten times the reward. This is just like those who haggle over the price when buying wine and meat but double their profits when selling them. Those who fail to acquire wealth

1 In ancient Chinese measurement, one *ren* is equal to 7 or 8 *chi*, roughly 2.5 meters.

禄利之不遂，则徼幸于没世不可知之名。甚者至谓孔子生不得位，没而俎豆之报隆于尧舜。郁郁者以相证慰，何其陋欤！

今夫三家之市，利析锱铢，或百钱逋负，怨及孙子；若通阛贸易，瑰货山积，动逾千金，则百钱之有无，有不暇计较者矣；商富大贾黄金百万，公私流衍，则数十百缗之费，有不暇计较者矣。均是人也，所操者大，犹有不暇计其小者；况天之所操尤大，而于世人毫末之善，口耳分寸之学，而一一谋所以报之，不亦劳哉！商之货殖同、时同，而或赢或绌；射策者之所业同，而或中或罢；为学著书之深浅同，而或传或否，或名或不名，亦皆有命焉，非可强而几也。

古之君子，盖无日不忧，无日不乐。道之不明，己之不免为乡人一息之或懈，忧也；居易以俟命，下学而上达，仰不愧而俯

and rank hope to gain a good reputation posthumously. They even point out that, despite never serving as an official, Confucius has been rewarded with more sacrifices than Emperors Yao and Shun. How superficial it is to point to Confucius as proof for consolation after one's own failures!

In a tiny market of only three families, everybody haggles over the slightest profit; a debt of one hundred cents will be resented for generations. In a city-wide market, precious goods pile up like mountains, and trade volume easily exceeds a thousand pieces of gold; people have little time to haggle over one hundred coppers. As for a big tycoon who manages a million taels of gold that circulate and multiply in the public and private sectors, he has little time to haggle over a hundred strings of coppers worth of expenses. The same is true of mankind. When we have a fortune, we are not preoccupied with pittances. Then what about the gods, who manage much grander things? Would it not be too much work for the gods to repay the slightest kindness or the most superficial bit of knowledge gained every time? Despite having identical goods and operating hours, some merchants make money, and others lose money; likewise, despite answering the same examination questions, some candidates pass, and others fail; and despite being equally skilled writers, some scholars are able to pass down their writings to later generations, and others are not; some scholars become famous, and others do not. This all depends on fate and cannot be bent to our will.

In ancient times, not a day passed when the superior man did not feel both anxiety and happiness. When he considered himself a despicable person for failing to thoroughly understand the way of the sages, or when he experienced a moment of laziness, these were times he should have felt anxiety. When he felt at ease and awaited destiny, felt confident about studying spiritual and

不怍，乐也。自文王、周、孔三圣人以下，至于王氏，莫不忧以终身，乐以终身，无所于祈，何所为报？己则自晦，何有于名？惟庄周、司马迁、柳宗元三人者，伤悼不遇，怨悱形于简册，其于圣贤自得之乐，稍违异矣。然彼自惜不世之才，非夫无实而汲汲时名者比也。苟汲汲于名，则去三十二子也远矣。将适燕晋而南其辕，其于术不益疏哉？

文周孔孟，班马左庄，葛陆范马，周程朱张，韩柳欧曾，李杜苏黄，许郑杜马，顾秦姚王，三十二人，俎豆馨香。临之在上，质之在旁。

earthly matters, or felt no shame before gods or man, these were times he should have felt happy. Ancient sages, from King Wen of Zhou, the Duke of Zhou, and Confucius, all the way to Wang Niansun and his son Wang Yinzhi, experienced anxiety and happiness throughout their lives. They asked for nothing, so what would they want in return? They strived to maintain their privacy, so what kind of fame would they want? Only Zhuang Zhou (Zhuangzi), Sima Qian, and Liu Zongyuan lamented in their writings about living in the wrong time, which is slightly at odds with the concept of sages being content with their own lot. However, they were simply expressing regret about their talents being unrecognized and being compared to people with no genuine talent. Those who seek fame are far from the ranks of the 32 sages presented here. If a person bound for Hebei and Shanxi points his carriage south, would he not be straying far off course?

Here are the 32 sages: King Wen of Zhou, the Duke of Zhou, Confucius, Mencius, Ban Gu, Sima Qian, Zuo Qiuming, Zhuangzi, Zhuge Liang, Lu Zhi, Fan Zhongyan, Sima Guang, Zhou Dunyi, Cheng brothers, Zhu Xi, Zhang Zai, Han Yu, Liu Zongyuan, Ouyang Xiu, Zeng Gong, Li Bai, Du Fu, Su Shi, Huang Tingjian, Xu Shen, Zheng Xuan, Du You, Ma Duanlin, Gu Yanwu, Qin Huitian, Yao Nai, and the Wang father and son. They have been offered sacrifices and incense. One could say they are supervising us from above or walking beside us offering instructions.

英雄诫子弟

曾氏读史，看到历史上一个带有普遍性的现象：古时许多英雄豪杰，他们本人气度恢阔，谋划宏远，但他们教育子弟，则往往重在谦恭谨慎、收敛退抑这些方面。曾氏在文章中举了刘备、李暠、刘义隆、马援四人为例。

这是为什么？原来，那些成就大业的英雄豪杰，人们看到的只是他们的光彩与伟岸，至于他们平时点点滴滴的积累，则被忽视了。而他们自己则非常清醒地知道，正是平时那些不起眼的点点滴滴，才成就了别人眼中的光彩与伟岸。他们要把真实情况告诉子弟，让他们懂得由近致远、自卑向高的人生真谛。这其实也是曾氏自己的阅历。

这篇读史笔记，传忠书局刻本《曾文正公全集》将它编在咸丰九年(1859)。

古之英雄，意量恢拓，规模宏远，而其训诫子弟，恒有恭谨敛退之象。

刘先主临终敕太子曰："勉之！勉之！勿以恶小而为之，勿以善小而不为。惟贤惟德，可以服人。汝父德薄，不足效也。汝与丞相从事，事之如父！"

西凉李暠手令戒诸子，以为"从政者，当审慎赏罚，勿任爱

Outstanding Figures on Educating Their Children

Zeng Guofan recognized a common thread among the historical books that he read: many outstanding figures from antiquity displayed great comportment and conceived magnificent plans, but they often focused on modesty, prudence, and restraint when educating their children. In this essay, Zeng cites Liu Bei, Li Hao, Liu Yilong, and Ma Yuan as examples.

What is the reason behind this? These outstanding figures who achieved great things are famous for their glory and success, yet the buildup of painstaking effort that went into these achievements is usually overlooked. However, they themselves understood the vital role that this ordinary work played. Indeed, they expressed as much to their children so that they might understand the true meaning of life and the work required to be successful. This also conforms to Zeng Guofan's own experiences.

The historical note below was compiled in *The Complete Writings of Zeng Guofan* by Chuanzhong Publishing House in the ninth year of Emperor Xianfeng's reign (1859).

Outstanding figures from ancient times were magnanimous visionaries, yet they always maintained an attitude of modesty, prudence, thrift, and gentleness when educating their children.

On his deathbed, Liu Bei of the Three Kingdoms period commanded his son, "Pay attention! Neither commit evil nor refrain from doing good just because you deem it trivial. Without wisdom and virtue, you will never be convincing. I am not virtuous enough, so I am not a good example for you. Work with the prime minister and serve him as you would your father!"

During the Southern and Northern dynasties period, King

憎。近忠正，远佞谀，勿使左右窃弄威福。毁誉之来，当研核真伪。听讼折狱，必和颜任理，慎勿逆诈亿，必轻加声色，务广咨询，勿自专用。吾莅事五年，虽未能息民，然含垢匿瑕，朝为寇仇，夕委心膂，粗无负于新旧。事任公平，坦然无类，初不容怀有所损益。计近则如不足，经远乃为有余。庶亦无愧前人也”。

宋文帝以弟江夏王义恭都督荆湘等八州诸军事，为书诫之曰：“天下艰难，国家事重，虽曰守成，实亦未易。隆替安危，在吾曹耳！岂可不感寻王业，大惧负荷！汝性褊急，志之所滞，其欲必

Li Hao of the Western Liang admonished his sons, "A politician should treat rewards and punishments with caution. He cannot allow his likes and dislikes to dictate his decisions. He should become closer to those who are loyal and upright and distance himself from those who fawn and flatter. He should never allow those around him to steal his authority. He must discern the truth from praise and criticism. When settling a lawsuit, he should maintain a benign countenance and align himself with reason; he should not prejudge without evidence. He must speak softly in a neutral tone and refrain from throwing his weight around; he must pool wisdom and refrain from acting arbitrarily. I have been king for five years. Although unable to bring peace to the people, I have remained broad-minded; a foe in the morning may become a trusted subordinate by the evening, and I treat friends new and old alike. Matters should be handled fairly, with everyone treated equally and without discrimination. There will be losses in the beginning, but things will work out well in the end. This is how I have managed state affairs. If you follow my advice, then you can hold your head up high before our ancestors."

Emperor Wen of Song (personal name Liu Yilong) was the emperor of the Liu Song Dynasty during the Southern and Northern dynasties period. He appointed his brother Liu Yigong the King of Jiangxia and made him responsible for military affairs in eight prefectures, including Jingzhou and Xiangzhou. He wrote to his younger brother, "The world is at a difficult time, and the responsibility for governing the kingdom rests heavy. Although we are just maintaining what our father achieved, it is still no easy task. It is up to us brothers to ensure that our kingdom prospers and remains stable instead of declining into chaos! How could we not take on the weighty responsibility our father passed down to us? You are too impatient when you want to do something. When you

行；意所不存，从物回改，此最弊事！宜念裁抑。卫青遇士大夫以礼，与小人有恩，西门安于矫性齐美。关羽、张飞，任偏同弊。行己举事，深宜鉴此！若事异今日，嗣子幼蒙，司徒当周公之事，汝不可不尽祗顺之理。尔时天下安危，决汝二人耳！汝一月自用钱，不可过三十万。若能省此益美。西楚府舍，略所谙究，计当不须改作，日求新异。凡讯狱多决，当时难可逆虑，此实为难。至讯日，虚怀博尽，慎无以喜怒加人！能择善者而从之，美自归已；不可专意自决，以矜独断之明也。名器深宜慎惜，不可妄以假人，昵近爵赐，尤应裁量。吾于左右，虽为少恩，如闻外论，不以为非也。以贵凌物，物不服；以威加人，人不厌。此易达事

lose interest, you change your mind under the influence of the outside world. These are the most harmful things one can do, so you must find a way to keep these behaviors in check. Wei Qing of the Western Han Dynasty used etiquette to appeal to intellectuals and was gracious towards the common people. Both Ximen Bao of the Warring States period and Dong Anyu of the Spring and Autumn period were widely praised for correcting their respective temperaments. Famed warriors Guan Yu and Zhang Fei of the Three Kingdoms period exhibited the same shortcoming of going to extremes. Learn from their examples and take responsibility for your own behavior! If the political climate changes in the days to come, my heir, your nephew, who is still young and unseasoned, will assume the throne. You must follow the example of the Duke of Zhou by serving the new king with respect and obedience. Whether the land is safe or in jeopardy depends on the two of you. Do not spend more than 300,000 taels of silver a month. Indeed, it would be better if you spent even less. As for your residence in West Chu, modify it somewhat, but do not make constant renovations. Give judicial cases due consideration and avoid acting rashly. Indeed, making the right decision on the spot is difficult. On the day of the trial, remain open-minded and solicit a wide range of opinions. Allowing your own emotions to color your decision should be avoided at all costs. Choose the right course and act on it regardless of any benefit to oneself. Do not act arbitrarily or flaunt your power. Exercise caution when offering official posts; do not appoint anyone too easily and give extra scrutiny to recommendations from those close to you. I seldom grant favors to those around me. Although I have heard others complain about this, I do not think that my choices have been wrong. It is easy to understand that nobody willingly submits to anyone who uses their status to override them or uses their power to impose on them.

耳。声乐嬉游，不宜令过。蒱酒渔猎，一切勿为。供用奉身，皆有节度。奇服异器，不宜兴长。又宜数引见佐史。相见不数，则彼我不亲。不亲，无因得尽人情；人情不尽，复何由知众事也？”

数君者，皆雄才大略，有经营四海之志，而其教诫子弟，则约旨卑思，敛抑已甚。

伏波将军马援，亦旷代英杰。而其诫兄子书曰：“吾欲汝曹闻人过失，如闻父母之名。耳可得闻，口不可得言也。好议论人长短，妄是非政法，此吾所大恶也，宁死不愿子孙有此行也！龙伯高敦厚周慎，口无择言，谦约节俭，廉公有威。吾爱之重之！愿汝曹效之！杜季良豪侠好义，忧人之忧，乐人之乐，父丧致客，数郡毕至。吾爱之重之！不愿汝曹效也！效伯高不得，犹为谨敕

Do not overindulge in women, music, and entertainment, and refrain from taking part in gambling, drinking, fishing, and hunting. Practice moderation in your personal life and avoid outlandish clothing and curiosities that only draw attention. Meet frequently with your subordinates to avoid mutual feelings of indifference. Otherwise, how will you assess their temperament and learn what is happening around you?"

These were gifted monarchs who had great ambitions, yet they were succinct, humble, and restrained in writings to educate their children.

Ma Yuan of the Eastern Han Dynasty was considered an unrivaled hero who was known as the general who calmed the waves. However, in a letter to his nephews, he urged, "I hope that you will react to others' mistakes the same as you would to your parents' names: with your ears open and your mouth closed.[1] In particular, I abhor the practice of judging the merits and flaws of others and arbitrarily commenting on governmental laws and decrees. Death would be preferable to having descendants who behaved in such a way. Long Bogao[2] is an honest and sincere man who handles matters cautiously and follows etiquette when he speaks. There is nothing improper about him. He is unassuming and lives frugally. He is honest in performing his duties and acts dignified. I like and respect him and would like you to follow his example. Du Jiliang[3] is forthright and just. He feels other people's sorrows and joys as his own. When his father died, people from different prefectures came to express their condolences. I like and respect him, but I do not want you to follow his example. People who model themselves on Long Bogao but fail to live up to his example may still become

1 According to Chinese tradition, calling parents and elders by their names is considered bad manners and thus is avoided.

2 Long Bogao (1 BC-AD 88) was the head of Shandu County in Hubei and later served as the head of Lingling Prefecture in Hunan during the Eastern Han Dynasty.

3 Du Jiliang (?-?) was a cavalry marshal of the Eastern Han Dynasty.

之士，所谓刻鹄不成尚类鹜者也。效季良不得，陷为天下轻薄子，所谓画虎不成反类狗者也。”此亦谦谨自将，敛其高远之怀，即于卑迩之道。盖不如是，则不足以自致于久大。藏之不密，则放之不准。苏轼诗“始知真放本精微”，即此义也。

cautious people. As the saying goes, 'If one fails to whittle a swan, one may still whittle a duck.' People who model themselves on Du Jiliang but fail to live up to his example will sink into frivolity. As another saying goes, 'One attempts to draw a tiger, but instead draws a dog.'" General Ma Yuan held himself to a high standard of modesty and prudence and restrained lofty ambitions in favor of simplicity. Otherwise, he would never have had the strength to achieve what he did. The failure to conceal an object thoroughly means one cannot accurately expose it. Su Shi captured this concept in the following verse, "Now I understand that subtlety is the basis for magnanimity."

箴言书院记

咸丰十一年（1861）六月下旬，得知胡林翼病危，曾氏冒着酷暑写下这篇文章。

胡林翼，湖南益阳人，翰林出身，是曾氏的亲密战友，官居湖北巡抚。为使家乡子弟能得到好的教育，他在益阳创办箴言书院，并嘱托曾氏为此事写一篇文章。这便是此文写作的背景。

这篇文章借箴言书院的创办，阐述教育对人之成长的重大作用，再次彰显作者本人重视人才、重视教育的一贯思想。

国藩以道光戊戌通籍于朝，湘人官京师者，多同时辈流。其射策先朝，耆年宿望，凋散略尽。而少詹事益阳胡云阁先生，独为老师祭酒。乡之人，就而考德稽疑，如幽得烛，众以无陨，而哲嗣润之，亦以编修趾美名父，回翔馆阁。今兵部侍郎、湖北巡抚，海内称为宫保胡公者是也。

A Note to Zhenyan Academy

Late in the sixth month of the 11th year of Emperor Xianfeng's reign (1861), Zeng Guofan ignored the intense summer heat to write this essay upon learning that Hu Linyi was critically ill.

Hu Linyi was a native of Yiyang in Hunan Province. A graduate of Hanlin Academy and former governor of Hubei Province, he and Zeng Guofan were close friends and comrades-in-arms. In an effort to help children in his hometown receive a proper education, Hu Linyi founded Zhenyan Academy and asked Zeng Guofan to write an essay for the school.

Zeng Guofan took the founding of Zhenyan Academy as an opportunity to expound on the importance of education in people's growth, once again highlighting his belief that talented people and education should be promoted.

I secured an official position in the imperial government in the 18th year of Emperor Daoguang's reign (1838). Most of the Hunan natives who served as officials in the capital were of my generation. Those who passed the imperial examination during the previous emperor's reign had either passed away or dispersed to other areas, of whom Hu Yunge remained as the Vice Minister of Zhanshi House. People from his hometown approached him to study morality, and he enlightened them just as a candle in the darkness. After his passing, his son Hu Linyi (courtesy name Runzhi) continued in the fine tradition of his father and was highly regarded in academic circles. Currently, Hu Linyi serves as the Vice Minister of War and the Governor of Hubei. He is known throughout the country by his honorary title "Grand Tutor Hu".

少詹君晚而纂《弟子箴言》十四卷，国藩实尝受而读之。自洒扫应对，以暨天地经纶，百家学术，靡不毕具。甄录古人嘉言，衷以己意，辞浅而指深，要使学者自幼而端所习，随其材之小大，董劝渐摩，徐底于成而已。

窃尝究观夫天之生斯人也，上智者不常，下愚者亦不常，扰扰万众，大率皆中材耳。中材者，导之东而东，导之西而西；习于善而善，习于恶而恶。其始瞳焉无所知识，未几而骋耆欲，逐众好。渐长渐贯，而成自然。由一二人以达于通都，渐流渐广，而成风俗。风之为物，控之若无有，鳍之若易靡；及其既成，发大木，拔大屋，一动而万里应，穷天人之力，而莫之能御。先王鉴于此，欲民生蚤慎所习，于是设为学校以教之：琴瑟鼓钟以习其耳，俎豆登降以习其目，诗书讽诵以习其口，射御投壶以习其筋力，书升以作其能，而郊遂以作其耻。故其高材，则道足济天下，而智周万汇。其次亦不失为圭璧自饬之士。贾生有言："习与

In his twilight years, Hu Yunge compiled the book *Maxims for Disciples* in 14 volumes. I have received and read a copy. The book offers a comprehensive treatment on subjects ranging from personal conduct to treatises on heaven and earth. Employing copious quotations from ancient scholars to support his own arguments, Hu uses simple language to express profound ideas and teaches disciples to study correctly from a young age. It guides and encourages disciples according to their ability to study until they attain academic excellence.

From my personal observations, very few either brilliant or ignorant people are born into this world. Instead, most people are born with average intelligence. They are guided by others and acquire knowledge of good and evil from their environments. They start out rather ignorant; however, before long, they follow their desire to engage in activities they find enjoyable. These develop into habits that become second nature. From one or two individuals, these habits spread out across wide areas and evolve into customs. A custom is just like the wind. It vanishes when manipulated and dissipates when clutched. Once formed, it can uproot giant trees and topple tall buildings. When it moves, all things respond; nothing in the world can stop it. Understanding this, ancient sovereigns established schools to educate their people and prevent them from developing bad habits. Musical instruments were made to train their ears; sacrificial rites were formed to train their eyes; poetry and prose were created to train their speech; archery, riding, and other games were performed to train their physical strength; books were published to train their capabilities; and people were sent to remote regions to reinforce their sense of shame. As a result, the wise have enough wisdom to govern and enough intelligence to manage all things on earth. Those who are less wise may find motivation to better themselves. Jia Yi of the

正人居之，不能毋正。犹生长于齐，不能不齐言也。”其不然欤？

侍郎自开府湖北以来，即以移风易俗为己任。自部曲之长，郡县之吏，暨百执事，片善微长，不敢自襮，而褒许随之。曰：“尔之发见者微，而善端宏大，不可量也。”或有过差，方图盖覆，谴亦及之。曰：“此犹小眚，过是，诛罚重矣。”与其新，不苛其旧；表其独，不遗其同。上下兢兢，日有课，月有举。当世推湖北人才极盛。侍郎则曰：“吾先人箴言中，育才之法如此。吾讵能继述直什一耳？”咸丰十年，侍郎治鄂六载矣，功成而化洽。又以一湖之隔，吾教成于北，而反遗吾父母之邦，其谓我何？于是建箴言书院，将萃益阳之士而大淑之。置良田以廪生徒，储典籍以馈孤陋。宽其涂辙，而严其教条。崇实而黜华，贱通而尚介。循是不废，岂惟一邑之幸！即汉之十三家法，宋之洛闽渊源，于

Western Han Dynasty once said, "One who resides with upright people will not go astray, just as one who grows up in the State of Qi will surely speak the Qi dialect." Is that not so?

After becoming governor of Hubei, Hu Linyi embarked on a mission to transform existing social traditions. From the heads of militias to government clerks and officials, Hu would praise them for the slightest worthy behavior, saying, "What you have done may seem small, but it is profound beyond measure." He would criticize them for trying to hide a mistake, saying, "This may seem like a small mistake, but even a slightly bigger one will be dealt with harshly." Hu would praise any new improvements rather than bring up old mistakes. He would recognize a different opinion without abandoning a similar one. People who worked with him exercised caution as he conducted daily inspections and monthly reviews. People claim that Hubei is a bastion for talent, but Hu Linyi said, "Our education is based on the maxims of my ancestors; how could I pass down even one tenth of what they taught us?" By the tenth year of Emperor Xianfeng's reign (1860), Hu Linyi had been governing Hubei for six successful years. Having accomplished much in Hubei, which is north of Hunan across Dongting Lake, he thought, "What will people think of me if I contribute nothing to education in my own hometown?" Consequently, he established Zhenyan Academy in Yiyang as a place for local scholars to gather and study. He cultivated farmland to feed the scholars at his school and collected classic books to educate those who lacked a solid foundation. He widened the door to education but imposed strict rules on those who chose to enter. He revered substance and denounced luxury; he advocated uprightness but belittled tact. Carrying on these principles will benefit people from Yiyang and beyond! The thirteen schools of education from the Han dynasties and the academic traditions of the Song dynasties are now prac-

是乎在。

后有名世者出，观于胡氏父子仍世育才肫肫之意，与余小子慎其所习之说，可以兴矣。

ticed at Zhenyan Academy.

If emerging scholars of later generations are impressed both by Hu Linyi and his father's determination to nurture new talents and my ideas about teaching students to exercise caution when developing habits, Zhenyan Academy will flourish.

《王船山遗书》序

这篇文章写于同治五年（1866）。打下南京不久，曾氏兄弟在满目疮痍的古城创办金陵书局，并举全局之力刊印王船山的遗著。他本人在繁忙的事务之余，还抽空校阅了船山著作一百余卷，订正讹脱一百七十余处，并写下这篇序言。

序言说明自己为什么要来做这件事。为什么呢？因为古圣历来用仁与礼，以平息人们内心的情绪和外部的纷争。王船山的著作对于仁与礼议论深刻，可以让人明白人世间的道理，万事万物的运行规律，如此社会可避免祸乱，获得长久安宁。

王船山先生遗书，同治四年十月刻竣，凡三百二十二卷。国藩校阅者，《礼记章句》四十九卷，《张子正蒙注》九卷，《读通鉴论》三十卷，《宋论》十五卷，《四书》《易》《诗》《春秋》诸经

An Introduction to *Posthumous Works of Wang chuanshan*

This essay was written in the fifth year of Emperor Tongzhi's reign (1866). Not long after retaking Nanjing, the Zeng brothers established Jinling Publishing House in the devastated ancient city and published Wang Chuanshan's posthumous works. Despite his busy schedule, Zeng Guofan managed to review more than 100 volumes of Wang Chuanshan's works, correct more than 170 mistakes, and write an introduction.

In the introduction, Zeng Guofan includes his reasons for wanting to write it. What was his reasoning? Throughout the ages, the ancient sages used benevolence and propriety to pacify emotions and disputes. Wang Chuanshan's writings presented a profound discussion on benevolence and propriety. Zeng believed that this discussion could help people both understand the right way of the world and abide by the general laws of all things so as to prevent society from devolving into chaos and instead promote a long-lasting peace.

The posthumous works of Wang Chuanshan (actual name Wang Fuzhi) comprise 322 volumes that were printed in the tenth month of the fourth year of Emperor Tongzhi's reign (1865). The works I have edited include *A Textual Annotation of the Book of Rites* (*Li Ji Zhang Ju*, 49 volumes), *A Commentary on Zhang Zai's Rectifying Ignorance* (*Zhang Zi Zheng Meng Zhu*, 9 volumes), *A Commentary on Comprehensive Mirror for Aid in Government* (*Du Tong Jian Lun*, 30 volumes), *A Treatise on the Song Dynasty* (*Song Lun*, 15 volumes), and 14 collated volumes on *the Four Books*, *the Zhou Book of Change*, *the Book of Poetry*, and *the Spring and Autumn Annals*, as well as their anecdotes and annotations. I also corrected more than 170 mistakes and omissions. As I had little

稗疏考异十四卷，订正讹脱百七十余事。军中鲜暇，不克细细全编，乃为序曰：

昔仲尼好语求仁，而雅言执礼，孟氏亦仁礼并称，盖圣王所以平物我之情，而息天下之争，内之莫大于仁，外之莫急于礼。自孔孟在时，老庄已鄙弃礼教。杨墨之指不同，而同于贼仁。厥后众流歧出，载籍焚烧，微言中绝，人纪紊焉。汉儒掇拾遗经，小戴氏乃作记，以存礼于什一。又千余年，宋儒远承坠绪，横渠张氏乃作《正蒙》，以讨论为仁之方。船山先生注《正蒙》数万言，注《礼记》数十万言，幽以究民物之同原，显以纲维万事，弭世乱于未形。其于古昔明体达用、盈科后进之旨，往往近之。

先生名夫之，字而农，以崇祯十五年举于乡。目睹是时朝政

spare time in the army, I was unable to revise all of Wang Chuanshan's works. Here is the introduction.

Centuries ago, Confucius eloquently expounded on the meaning of benevolence and propriety, as did Mencius, who paid equal attention to both. The ancient sages pacified people's desires and settled disputes by means of benevolence from within and propriety in the outside world. Even in Confucius' and Mencius' times, teachings on propriety were rejected by Laozi and Zhuangzi. Although Yang Zhu's idea of "self-preservation" clashed with Mozi's idea of "universal love," they both contorted teachings on benevolence. Afterward, many schools of thought emerged in the wrong way, and books on ancient rites were reduced to ashes. Words of wisdom disappeared, and human relations were corrupted. During the Han Dynasty, Confucian scholars collected and edited surviving works. For example, Dai Sheng wrote *Ritual Records of Dai the Junior* (*Xiao Dai Li Ji*), which preserved one tenth of the rites. After more than a thousand years, Confucian scholars of the Song dynasties attempted to revive the study of Confucian texts. Zhang Zai of Hengqu in Shaanxi, for example, wrote *Rectifying Ignorance* (*Zheng Meng*) to discuss the practice of benevolence. Wang Chuanshan went on at great length to annotate *Rectifying Ignorance* (*Zheng Meng*) and *Ritual Records of Dai the Junior* (*Xiao Dai Li ji*). He traced the origins of various customs and connected them with prominent laws and regulations in an effort to eliminate social disasters before they broke out. His ideas conformed to the ancient sages' teachings that we should understand the essence of benevolence and propriety for social administration, thus laying a solid foundation for future progress.

Wang Chuanshan (given name Fuzhi, courtesy name Ernong) passed Hunan's provincial-level imperial examination in the 15th year of Emperor Chongzhen's reign (1642) during the Ming Dynas-

刻核无亲，而士大夫又驰骛声气，东林、复社之徒，树党伐仇，颓俗日蔽。故其书中黜申韩之术，嫉朋党之风，长言三叹而未有已。既一仕桂藩，为行人司，知事终不可为，乃匿迹永、郴、衡、邵之间，终老于湘西之石船山。

圣清大定，访求隐逸。鸿博之士，次第登进。虽顾亭林、李二曲辈之艰贞，征聘尚不绝于庐。独先生深闷固藏，邈焉无与。平生痛诋党人标谤之习，不欲身隐而文著，来反唇之讪笑。用是，其身长遁，其名寂寂，其学亦竟不显于世。荒山敝榻，终岁孳孳，以求所谓育物之仁，经邦之礼。穷探极论，千变而不离其宗；旷百世不见知，而无所于悔。先生没后，巨儒迭兴，或攻良知捷获

ty. At that time, government examinations and inspections were stricter. As scholars eagerly attempted to develop their reputations, followers of the Donglin and Fushe schools became fierce rivals who formed cliques and fought one another, pushing society to become more corrupt. Against this backdrop, Wang Chuanshan used his writings to denounce the legalist ideas represented by Shen Buhai and Han Fei and to condemn the atmosphere created by the cliques, whom he criticized at great length. He eventually served the King of Gui as a member of the Messenger Office. When he realized that resistance against the armies of the Qing Dynasty was futile, he fled to hide in Yongzhou, Chenzhou, Hengzhou (present-day Hengyang), and Shaozhou (present-day Shaoyang), eventually settling and living out his days at Mount Shichuan in western Hunan.

After gaining full control of China, the Qing government attempted to recruit intellectuals who had been reclusive and promoted those with extensive learning to serve in office. Although scholars such as Gu Yanwu (also known as Gu Tinglin) and Li Yong (also known as Li Erqu) remained loyal to the late Ming Dynasty, the imperial court repeatedly sent for them. Only Wang Chuanshan disappeared deep into the mountains, where the imperial government could not find him. Throughout his life, Wang Chuanshan reviled the evil practice of forming cliques to slander others. He avoided literary fame because it would have invited their ridicule. Consequently, he remained a recluse who was unknown to the rest of the world as either a thinker or an individual. On a worn-out couch in the barren mountains, Wang Chuanshan was unceasing in his efforts to develop a thorough understanding of benevolence, which is for the cultivation of individuals, and propriety, which is for administering state affairs. He carried out exhaustive and in-depth research in a variety of fields but never

之说，或辨《易》图之凿，或详考名物，训诂、音韵，正《诗集传》之疏，或修补三礼时享之仪，号为卓绝。先生皆已发之于前，与后贤若合符契。虽其著述大繁，醇驳互见，然固可谓博文约礼，命世独立之君子已。

道光十九年，先生裔孙世全始刊刻百五十卷。新化邓显鹤湘皋实主其事。湘潭欧阳兆熊晓晴赞成之。咸丰四年，寇犯湘潭，板毁于火。同治初元，吾弟国荃乃谋重刻，而增益百七十二卷，仍以欧阳君董其役。南汇张文虎啸山、仪征刘毓嵩伯山等分任校

strayed from his fundamental approach to scholarship. He also never bemoaned the possibility of forever remaining in obscurity. After his death, brilliant Confucian scholars emerged and contributed to scholarship by exploring a variety of subjects, such as recognizing the role of a good conscience in acquiring knowledge, defining the hexagrams found in *the Zhou Book of Change* (*Zhou Yi*), conducting etymological, exegetic, and phonetic studies of the classics, annotating *Poetry Anthology* (*Shi Ji Zhuan*), and reconstructing rituals described in the three great books on rites.[1] Wang Chuanshan was a pioneer in all these fields, and his research aligned with that of later scholars. His multitude of writings were noted for being both simple and complex. However, he was an independent and reclusive superior man who pursued knowledge and abided by etiquette and law.

In the 19th year of Emperor Daoguang's reign (1839), one of Wang Chuanshan's descendants, Wang Shiquan, began publishing 150 volumes of his posthumous works. The actual printing was presided over by Deng Xianhe (courtesy name Xianggao) of Xinhua County, Hunan Province, and was approved by Ouyang Zhaoxiong (courtesy name Xiaoqing) of Xiangtan County. In the fourth year of Emperor Xianfeng's reign (1854), Taiping rebels invaded Xiangtan, and the printing plates were destroyed by fire. Early in Emperor Tongzhi's reign, one of my younger brothers, Zeng Guoquan, planned to reprint Wang Chuanshan's works with an additional 172 volumes. The printing was still funded by Ouyang Zhaoxiong, and the collation was conducted by Zhang Wenhu (courtesy name Xiaoshan) of Nanhui, Liu Yusong (courtesy name Boshan) of Yizheng, and others. Preparations began in Anqing and were finally completed in Jinling (present-day Nanjing). Consequently,

1 The three great books on rites are *The Zhou Book of Rites*, *The Book of Etiquette and Ceremonial*, and *Ritual Records of Dai the Junior*.

雠。庀局于安庆，蒇事于金陵。先生之书，于是粗备。后之学者，有能秉心敬恕，综贯本末，将亦不释乎此也。

most of Wang Chuanshan's works are now in print. With sincerity and diligence, this anthology will serve as an indispensable tool to future scholars who wish to conduct comprehensive studies on his writings.

书赠仲弟六则

此文作于同治七年（1868）十月二十四、二十五日。

这年九月二十八日，曾氏四弟国潢从湖南老家来到南京。自从咸丰八年六月复出后，两兄弟有十一年没有见面了。此时曾氏五十八岁，国潢也快五十。在那个时代，可以算得上老年兄弟。曾氏在文章后面的跋语中说“老年昆弟，乱后相聚，其乐可知”。早在这年七月下旬，曾氏便接到调任直隶总督的上谕，即将北上赴任。国潢这个时候来，既是看望，也是送行。

兄弟分手之时，曾氏写下这篇文章相送。

清

《记》曰：“清明在躬。”吾人身心之间，须有一种清气。使子弟饮其和，乡党熏其德，庶几积善可以致祥。饮酒太多，则气必昏浊；说话太多，则神必躁扰。弟于此二弊，皆不能免。欲葆清气，首贵饮酒有节，次贵说话不苟。

Six Notes to My Brother Guohuang

These six notes were written between the 24th and 25th days of the tenth month in the seventh year of Emperor Tongzhi's reign (1868).

Earlier that year, on the 28th day of the ninth month, one of Zeng Guofan's younger brothers, Zeng Guohuang, came to Nanjing from their hometown in Hunan. Since Zeng Guofan returned to officialdom in June of the eighth year of Emperor Xianfeng's reign (1858), the two brothers had been apart for 11 years. With Zeng Guofan, 58, and Zeng Guohuang approaching 50, the pair could have been described as elderly siblings. In the postscript to the notes, Zeng even remarked, "It was such a joy for us old brothers to meet." Prior to this, late in the seventh month, Zeng Guofan had been appointed governor of Zhili and was preparing to travel north to assume his post. Zeng Guohuang intended to meet him on this visit and see him off.

Zeng Guofan wrote this essay for his younger brother on their parting.

On Clarity

According to the *Book of Rites*, "Clarity is reflected in oneself." Our bodies and minds must be instilled with an air of clarity, thereby creating a harmonious atmosphere for younger family members and influencing neighbors and friends with moral excellence; perhaps good deeds bring good fortune. Drinking too much alcohol will muddle one's state of mind; talking too much will make one restless. You are not exempt from these two maladies. To retain clarity, you should discipline yourself to drink moderately and speak discreetly.

俭

凡多欲者不能俭，好动者不能俭。多欲如好衣、好食、好声色、好书画古玩之类，皆可浪费破家。弟向无癖嗜之好，而颇有好动之弊。今日思作某事，明日思访某客，所费日增而不觉。此后讲求俭约，首戒好动。不轻出门，不轻举事。不特不作无益之事，即修理桥梁、道路、寺观、善堂，亦不可轻作。举动多则私费大矣。其次则仆从宜少，所谓食之者寡也。其次则送情宜减，所谓用之者舒也。否则今日不俭，异日必多欠债。既负累于亲友，亦贻累于子孙。

明

三达德之首曰智，智即明也。古来豪杰，动称英雄。英即明也。明有二端：人见其近，吾见其远，曰高明；人见其粗，吾见其细，曰精明。高明者，譬如室中所见有限，登楼则所见远矣，登山则所见更远矣。精明者，譬如至微之物，以显微镜照之，则

On Frugality

Generally speaking, neither those with excessive desires nor those who are overactive can be frugal. The former may ruin their families by squandering money on desires for clothing, food, drink, carnal pleasures, calligraphy, paintings, and antiques. You have never had a special hobby, but you are restless. As you plan to do one thing today and visit someone tomorrow, your expenditures increase daily without you even realizing. Going forward, you must prioritize frugality. First, you should learn to be less restless. Do not be rash about leaving home or undertaking activities. You should refrain from taking part in unprofitable projects, even if they involve building bridges, roads, temples, or charitable institutions. Participating in many activities leads to increased expenditures. Next, you should keep as few servants as possible. According to the *Great Learning*, "Let the number of consumers be few." Additionally, you should cut back on gifts, for as the *Great Learning* also says, "Lower expenditures so you may rest at ease." Otherwise, you will be trapped in debt, thus burdening not only your family and friends, but also your descendants.

On Brilliance

The first of the three major virtues is wisdom, which may also be called brilliance. Since ancient times, people of exceptional ability have tended to be called heroes and have been expected to be wise or brilliant. There are two aspects to brilliance. Being far-sighted when others are near-sighted is brilliance; observing subtleties when others observe only a rough sketch is astuteness. Brilliant people can see for miles because they perch themselves atop a tall building or even a mountain, whereas others stay inside and thus see only the few meters in front of them. Astute people are like those who use a microscope to observe the smallest

加大一倍、十倍、百倍矣。又如粗糙之米，再舂则粗糠全去，三舂、四舂则精白绝伦矣。高明由于天分，精明由于学问。吾兄弟忝居大家，天分均不甚高明，专赖学问以求精明。好问若买显微之镜，好学若舂上熟之米。总须心中极明，而后口中可断。能明而断谓之英断，不明而断谓之武断。武断自己之事，为害犹浅；武断他人之事，招怨实深。惟谦退而不肯轻断，最足养福。

慎

古人曰钦、曰敬、曰谦、曰谨、曰虔恭、曰祗惧，皆慎字之义也。慎者，有所畏惮之谓也。居心不循天理，则畏天怒；作事不顺人情，则畏人言。少贱则畏父师，畏官长。老年则畏后生之窃议。高位则畏僚属之指摘。凡人方寸有所畏惮，则过必不大，鬼神必从而原之。若嬉游、斗牌等事而毫无忌惮，坏邻党之风气，作子孙之榜样，其所损者大矣。

thing, allowing them to enlarge it as much as a hundredfold, or just like unpolished rice that becomes fine after several rounds of polishing. Brilliance is a natural gift, whereas astuteness must be learned. We brothers were born into a large family. We are not naturally gifted, therefore we must rely on learning to become astute. Asking questions is just like buying a microscope; being studious is just like polishing rice. We need to be clear-minded so as to make good judgments. A judgment made with a clear mind is wise; a judgment made without a clear mind is arbitrary. Arbitrary judgments about oneself are less harmful than those about others, as the latter may incur rancor. The best way to ensure good fortune is by being reserved and refraining from making hasty judgments.

On Discretion

When discussing admiration, respect, modesty, discretion, piety, and awe, the ancient sages were really focusing on the meaning of discretion. Discretion implies awe and dread. Failing to conform to the natural order, one should fear the wrath of Nature; failing to conform to human feelings, one should fear the criticism of others. Being young and from humble origins, one fears parents, teachers, and superiors; being older, one fears the opinions of younger generations; serving in a high position, one fears the criticism of colleagues and subordinates. Everyone harbors fears that prevent them from making major mistakes; consequently, the gods are willing to forgive them. However, great suffering shall be handed down if people engage in merry-making and card games without any scruples and corrupt their hometowns, thus setting bad examples for their descendants.

恕

圣门好言仁，仁即恕也。曰富，曰贵，曰成，曰荣，曰誉，曰顺，此数者，我之所喜，人亦皆喜之。曰贫，曰贱，曰败，曰辱，曰毁，曰逆，此数者，我之所恶，人亦皆恶之。吾辈有声势之家，一言可以荣人，一言可以辱人。荣人，则得名、得利、得光耀。人尚未必感我，何也？谓我有势，帮人不难也。辱人，则受刑，受罚，受苦恼，人必恨我次骨。何也？谓我倚势，欺人太甚也。吾兄弟须从恕字痛下工夫，随在皆设身以处地。我要步步站得稳，须知他人也要站得稳，所谓立也。我要处处行得通，须知他人也要行得通，所谓达也。今日我处顺境，预想他日也有处逆境之时；今日我以盛气凌人，预想他日人亦以盛气凌我之身，或凌我之子孙。常以恕字自惕，常留余地处人，则荆棘少矣。

静

静则生明，动则多咎，自然之理也。家长好动，子弟必纷纷扰扰。朝生一策，暮设一计，虽严禁之而不能止。欲求一家之安静，先求一身之清静。静有二道：一曰不入是非之场，二曰不入

On Forgiveness

Confucianism focuses heavily on benevolence, which implies forgiveness. We all appreciate wealth, status, success, honor, praise, and good fortune; we all detest poverty, lowliness, defeat, humiliation, defamation, and adversity. As part of an influential family, we have the power to honor or humiliate with a single word. Those who are honored gain access to fame, profit, and glory, for which they may be ungrateful. Why? Because they believe that our influence makes it easy to extend help to others. Those who are humiliated are subject to punishment, penalties, and distress, for which they hate us bitterly. Why? Because they believe that we use our influence to take advantage of others. Therefore, we brothers should put time and energy into forgiveness and try to stand in other people's shoes. If we want to stride firmly ahead, we should realize that others also want to strive firmly ahead. This is called "establishment." If we want to achieve things, we should understand that others also want to achieve things. This is called "attainment." Today, we enjoy favorable circumstances, but we should prepare for future adversity. Today, we can be overbearing, but we should prepare for others to treat us and our descendants the same way in the future. Therefore, we should monitor ourselves to ensure that we are forgiving towards others and give them space so that our own life may be less troubled.

On Quiet

Quiet produces clarity, and action incurs faults; this is natural reasoning. Restless parents produce disorderly children who cause disturbances. They dream up ideas and plans all day long despite being forbidden from doing so. In order to cultivate a quiet family, the parents must first quiet themselves internally. This may be achieved in two ways. First, avoid areas fraught with disputes; sec-

势利之场。乡里之词讼曲直，于我何干？我若强为剖断，始则赔酒饭，后则惹怨恨。官场之得失升沉，于我何涉？我若稍为干预，小则招物议，大则挂弹章。不若一概不管，可以敛后辈之躁气，即可保此身之清福。

ond, avoid areas fraught with greed. What do local lawsuits have to do with us? If we attempt to pronounce judgments, we may start out having to compensate for food and drink, but may eventually provoke hatred from the parties involved. What do success and failure in officialdom have to do with us? If we venture to intervene, we may invite criticism or even be impeached in a memorial to the emperor. It would be better to pay no heed to any of them so that the younger generation may tamp down their restless energy and enjoy a quiet and easy life.

劝学篇示直隶士子

此文作于同治八年（1869），当时曾氏的身份是直隶总督。

作为读书人出身的高级官员，曾氏深知文化的重要性，又很清楚士人在四民之中的表率性，以及对社会稳定的独特作用。以劝学为题来勉励士人，的确是一省之主的要务。直隶属慷慨悲歌的燕赵之地。于是，曾氏从比较豪侠之质与圣人之道入手，将豪侠之质引入圣人之道，希望直隶士子致力于义理、考据、辞章、经济之学，并以义理为先，以立志为本，以乡贤为榜样，营造良好的学风，进而以此学风来培植良好的社会风气。

人才随士风为转移，信乎？曰：是不尽然，然大较莫能外也。前史称燕赵慷慨悲歌，敢于急人之难，盖有豪侠之风。余观直隶先正，若杨忠愍、赵忠毅、鹿忠节、孙征君诸贤，其后所诣各殊，

A Note to Encourage Learning Among Hebei Scholars

This essay was written in the eighth year of Emperor Tongzhi's reign (1869), when Zeng Guofan was governor of Zhili (present-day Hebei Province).

As a scholar-turned senior official, Zeng Guofan was well aware of the importance of culture, the example that educated people played among the four social classes, [1] and the unique role of scholars in social stability. It is indeed an important task for the governor of a province to encourage learning among scholars. Zhili (Hebei Province) was home to the ancient states of Yan and Zhao and was famed for its heroic yet mournful poetry. Zeng began by introducing the concept of gallantry to the way of sages. He hoped that scholars in Zhili would dedicate themselves to the Confucian way, textual research, literary composition, and social administration. He thought that prioritizing the Confucian way would build their resolve and foster local scholars upon whom others could model themselves. He wanted to nurture a positive academic atmosphere to use as the basis for cultivating a good social environment.

Is it true that talented people are swayed by changes in their academic environment? Yes, for the most part. According to historical records, the states of Zhao and Yan were famous for their heroic yet mournful poetry, and their people were gallantly willing to help those in need. From my perspective, prominent past residents of Zhili, such as Yang Jisheng ,[2] Zhao Nanxing ,[3] Lu Shanji ,[4]

1 The four social classes include scholars, farmers, artisans, and merchants.

2 Yang Jisheng (1516-1555, posthumous name Zhongmin) was a famous official of admonition in the Ming Dynasty.

3 Zhao Nanxing (1550-1628, posthumous name Zhongyi) was a famous statesman and literary writer in the Ming Dynasty.

4 Lu Shanji (1575-1636, posthumous name Zhongjie) was a famous official of admonition in the Ming Dynasty.

其初皆于豪侠为近。即今日士林，亦多刚而不摇，质而好义，犹有豪侠之遗。才质本于士风，殆不诬与？

豪侠之质，可与入圣人之道者，约有数端。侠者薄视财利，弃万金而不眄；而圣贤则富贵不处，贫贱不去，痛恶夫墦间之食、龙断之登。虽精粗不同，而轻财好义之迹则略近矣。侠者忘己济物，不惜苦志脱人于厄；而圣贤以博济为怀。邹鲁之汲汲皇皇，与夫禹之犹己溺，稷之犹己饥，伊尹之犹己推之沟中，曾无少异。彼其能力救穷交者，即其可以进援天下者也。侠者轻死重气，圣贤罕言及此。然孔曰成仁，孟曰取义，坚确不移之操，亦未尝不

and Sun Qifeng [1], each followed their own path yet shared similar gallant temperaments. Even today, most scholars from Zhili are upright, outspoken, honest, and loyal, with an air of traditional gallantry. These qualities probably originated from their academic environment.

Several aspects of a gallant temperament may be introduced to the way of the sages. The gallant look down on property and profits; they would discard a pile of gold without hesitation. Sages would neither linger on account of wealth or status, nor turn away on account of poverty or humble rank. They hate to eat sacrificial food or monopolize benefits. Although the gallant and the sages have differences, they share a generous and philanthropic nature. The gallant are selfless about helping others and willingly suffer hardships to rescue people from danger. Sages feel compelled to extend their blessings to others. For example, Zou Yan and Lu Zhonglian of the Warring States period roamed the land to solve social problems. Similarly, Yu the Great, an ancient king who founded the Xia Dynasty, was so moved by those who drowned that he developed flood control; Houji, an ancestor of the ancient Zhou family, was so moved by those who starved that he introduced millet to the country; Yiyin, a statesman and thinker of the Shang Dynasty, felt as though he himself had been pushed into a ditch when he learned that others had been treated poorly. Helping individuals in need, they proceeded to the next step: attempting to save humanity. The gallant sneer at death and embrace a code of brotherhood, yet the sages seldom mention it. However, Confucius and Mencius argued for benevolence and righteousness, respectively. Their unswerving integrity may be compared to gallantry. And Sima Qian, the grand historian, was ridiculed for lauding gal-

1 Sun Qifeng (1584-1675, courtesy name Qitai, also known as Sun Zhengjun and Master Xiafeng) was a famous Neo-Confucianist in the late Ming and early Qing dynasties.

与之相类。昔人讥太史公好称任侠，以余观此数者，乃不悖于圣贤之道。然则豪侠之徒，未可深贬，而直隶之士，其为学当较易于他省，乌可以不致力乎哉？

致力如何？为学之术有四：曰义理，曰考据，曰辞章，曰经济。义理者，在孔门为德行之科，今世目为宋学者也。考据者，在孔门为文学之科，今世目为汉学者也。辞章者，在孔门为言语之科，从古艺文及今世制义诗赋皆是也。经济者，在孔门为政事之科，前代典礼、政书及当世掌故皆是也。

人之才智，上哲少而中下多；有生又不过数十寒暑，势不能求此四术遍观而尽取之。是以君子贵慎其所择，而先其所急。择其切于吾身心不可造次离者，则莫急于义理之学。凡人身所自具者，有耳、目、口、体、心思；日接于吾前者，有父子、兄弟、夫妇；稍远者，有君臣，有朋友。为义理之学者，盖将使耳、目、口、体、心思，各敬其职，而五伦各尽其分，又将推以及物，使凡民皆有以善其身，而无憾于伦纪。夫使举世皆无憾于伦纪，虽

lantry. In my opinion, embracing gallantry is consistent with the way of the sages. Therefore, the gallant should not be reproached. Since scholars in Zhili maintain an advantage over scholars from other provinces, how could they not dedicate themselves to learning?

How should one commit oneself to learning? There are four disciplines of learning in Confucianism: the Confucian way, textual research, literary composition, and social administration. The Confucian way is classified under virtuous conduct and is considered the philosophical theory of Song scholars nowadays. Textual research is classified under literature and is currently known as Sinology. Literary composition is classified under language, encompassing everything from ancient art and literature to contemporary eight-legged essays. And social administration is classified under political affairs, including everything from ceremonial rules of past dynasties to contemporary anecdotes.

Truly brilliant people are rare in the world, with people of average and below-average intelligence constituting most of the population. Limited lifespans prevent most of us from mastering the four disciplines of learning outlined above, thus a scholar should choose wisely and prioritize that which is urgent. Nothing is more vital to our body and mind than the Confucian way. Humans have ears, eyes, a mouth, a body, and a mind. Our days involve relationships such as those between father and son, older and younger brothers, and husband and wife, and they may even involve more distant relationships, such as those between ruler and subject and between friends. Those who study the Confucian way should let their ears, eyes, mouth, body, and mind manage their respective duties, let the five relationships outlined above fulfill their respective roles, and then apply this concept to the rest of the world. In this way, every person will treat his body well and have no regrets

唐虞之盛有不能逮。苟通义理之学，而经济该乎其中矣。程朱诸子遗书具在，曷尝舍末而言本、遗新民而专事明德？观其雅言，推阐反复而不厌者，大抵不外立志以植基，居敬以养德，穷理以致知，克己以力行，成物以致用。义理与经济初无两术之可分，特其施功之序，详于体而略于用耳。

今与直隶多士约：以义理之学为先，以立志为本，取乡先达杨、赵、鹿、孙数君子者为之表。彼能艰苦困饿，坚忍以成业，而吾何为不能？彼能置穷通、荣辱、祸福、死生于度外，而吾何为不能？彼能以功绩称当时，教泽牖后世，而吾何为不能？

洗除旧日晻昧卑污之见，矫然直趋广大光明之域；视人世之浮荣微利，若蝇蚋之触于目而不留；不忧所如不耦，而忧节概之少贬；不耻冻馁在室，而耻德不被于生民。志之所向，金石为开，

about ethics and discipline, thereby achieving even more than the flourishing age of Emperors Yao and Shun. A proficiency in the study of the Confucian way provides a foundation for the study of social administration. We still have access to the books written by the Cheng brothers (Cheng Hao and Cheng Yi) and Zhu Xi. Do they seek the incidentals while abandoning the fundamentals? Do they focus on explaining morality while disregarding the education of the people? To read their elegant speeches and untiringly infer and elaborate on them falls under the scope of nurturing ideals to lay our foundation, conducting ourselves respectfully for self-cultivation, pursuing the truth to acquire knowledge, restraining ourselves to apply what we have learned, and contributing to the world through our achievements. The separation of the Confucian way and social administration into two disciplines is unnecessary as they share the same nature. In terms of efficacy, however, the former leans heavier on fundamental research while the latter focuses more on practical research.

Now, we have come to an agreement with scholars in Zhili to prioritize the Confucian way, use the establishment of ideals as our foundation, and model ourselves on ancient sages from Zhili, including Yang Jisheng, Zhao Nanxing, Lu Shanji, and Sun Qifeng. They could endure hardships and hunger to achieve great things, so why can't we? They could ignore considerations such as distress, dishonor, misfortune, and death, so why can't we? Their achievements won them praise and enlightened later generations, so why can't ours?

We should wash away ignorant and foul thoughts from the past, hold our heads high and shoulders squared as we strive toward brilliance, and dismiss vanity and petty profits as no more than flies and midges before our eyes. Rather than worrying about failing to achieve what we pursue, we should worry about our integ-

谁能御之？志既定矣，然后取程朱所谓居敬穷理、力行成物云者，精研而实体之。然后求先儒所谓考据者，使吾之所见，证诸古制而不谬；然后求所谓辞章者，使吾之所获，达诸笔札而不差，择一术以坚持，而他术固未敢竟废也。其或多士之中，质性所近，师友所渐，有偏于考据之学，有偏于辞章之学，亦不必遽易前辙，即二途皆可入圣人之道。其文经史百家，其业学问思辨，其事始于修身，终于济世，百川异派，何必同哉？同达于海而已矣。

若夫风气无常，随人事而变迁。有一二人好学，则数辈皆思力追先哲；有一二人好仁，则数辈皆思康济斯民。倡者启其绪，

rity falling short of that of others. Rather than feeling ashamed of suffering from cold and hunger, we should feel ashamed that our virtuous conduct does not benefit the common people. A determination to work hard can split even metal and stone, so who can stop us? Once we are determined, we should work to understand and then apply what the Cheng brothers and Zhu Xi referred to as being respectful, getting to the root of things, practicing diligence, and cultivating all things. Next, we ought to study what ancient scholars called textual research to ensure that what we have learned does not contradict the various ancient systems. Then, we should study what ancient scholars called rhetoric so that the bounty we have harvested can be shared through good writing free from errors. If we choose to focus on one subject of learning, we should not completely abandon the other subjects. Some scholars are drawn together by common academic interests or by the influence of teachers and friends. When switching between textual research and literary composition, scholars need not discard their previous course of study as both approaches can lead to becoming a sage. In terms of literature, there are an untold number of Confucian classics and histories available; in terms of learning, there are various schools of thought; in terms of undertakings, begin with self-cultivation to ultimately benefit society. Why should a hundred rivers be the same? Each may be unique as long as they all flow into the sea.

A social environment is not static; it changes in accordance with human affairs. If one or two people enjoy studying, then many more fall in line to learn from the ancient sages; if one or two people are interested in benevolence and righteousness, then many more follow suit and strive to improve the well-being of the common people. Those who introduce a concept are like a fountainhead, and their followers are like billowing waves; they

和者衍其波；倡者可传诸同志，和者又可禮诸无穷；倡者如有本之泉放乎川渎，和者如支河沟浍交汇旁流。先觉后觉，互相劝诱，譬之大水小水，互相灌注。以直隶之士风，诚得有志者导夫先路，不过数年，必有体用兼备之才，彬蔚而四出，泉涌而云兴。

余忝官斯土，自愧学无本原，不足仪型多士。嘉此邦有刚方质实之资，乡贤多坚苦卓绝之行，粗述旧闻，以勖群士；亦冀通才硕彦，告我昌言，上下交相劝勉，仰希古昔与人为善、取人为善之轨，于化民成俗之道，或不无小补云。

communicate a concept to like-minded people, and their followers spread it to countless more; they are like a spring with its own source to a river, and their followers are the streams and creeks that branch off it. Just as rivers and streams pour into one another, visionaries and their followers advise and guide one another. Take Zhili, for example. If scholars who harbor ideals really take the lead, their ideals would flourish across the land in both theory and practice within a few years, just like gushing springs and billowing clouds.

When I first assumed my official post here, I felt ashamed that I was unequipped with the proper learning and unable to set a good example for more scholars. I am envious of the scholars in Zhili who can take advantage of the academic environment and of the local sages who have shown great fortitude. I have shared some of the past with you in order to encourage you to press ahead. I have also taken this as an opportunity to solicit recommendations from learned scholars. I hope that blending the ancient sages' path of helping others into the academic environment of local Zhili scholars proves beneficial.

湘乡昭忠祠记

同治八年（1869）九月上旬，曾氏以三日之功写下这篇文章。此文章大笔勾勒了湘勇诞生、成长、壮大乃至建功立业的过程，可视为湘勇的一份简历。这篇文章的最大价值，在于揭示了湘勇在乱世中做成大事业的最重要的内在原因——拙诚。

曾氏一贯倡导拙诚：人以伪来，我以诚应；人以巧来，我以拙应。拙诚是一个内涵异常丰富而深刻的理念，因曾国藩、罗泽南等人的提倡，以及湘勇的成功实践，而成为近世湖湘文化的厚重底色。

咸丰二年十月，粤贼围攻湖南省城。既解严，巡抚张公亮基檄调湘乡团丁千人至长沙备防守。罗忠节公泽南、王壮武公錱等，以诸生率千人者以往。维时国藩方以母忧归里，奉命治团练于长沙。因奏言团练保卫乡里，法当由本团醵金养之，不食于官，缓

A Note on Zhaozhong Ancestral Temple in Xiangxiang County

Early in the ninth month of the eighth year of Emperor Tongzhi's reign (1869), Zeng Guofan spent three days writing this essay, which outlines the growth and contributions of the army that originated from Xiangxiang County and may be regarded as its curriculum vitae. The great value of this essay lies in his attributing the army's success during chaotic times to simplicity and sincerity.

Zeng Guofan always advocated simplicity and sincerity. He revealed, "When a man approaches me with hypocrisy, I respond with sincerity; when a man approaches me with cleverness, I respond with simplicity." The concepts of simplicity and sincerity have rich connotations. Advocated by people such as Zeng Guofan and Luo Zenan, they were successfully ingrained into the army from Xiangxiang County and eventually expanded to underpin modern Hunan culture.

In the tenth month of the second year of Emperor Xianfeng's reign (1852), the Yue rebels [1] besieged Changsha, the capital of Hunan. In response, Zhang Liangji, the governor of Hunan, mobilized a thousand militiamen to help defend the city, and Luo Zenan, Wang Zhen, and others led the militia to Changsha's rescue. I was in my hometown attending to my mother's funeral when I received an imperial order to recruit and train the militias in Changsha. Militias were expected to pool local funds to sustain themselves as they were organized to protect local communities. Since militias were not maintained by the government, they were unreli-

1 The "Yue rebels," "Yue rebel army," and "Taiping rebel army" were derogatory terms that the Qing government used for the army of the Taiping Heavenly Kingdom.

急终不可恃，不若募团丁为官勇，粮饷取诸公家。请就现调之千人，略仿戚元敬氏成法，束伍练技，以备不时之卫。由是吾邑团卒，号曰“湘勇”。

三年春，平土寇于衡山，破逆党于桂东。其夏，粤贼围江西省城。国藩募湘勇二千、楚勇千人，罗忠节公辈率之东援。初战失利，营官谢邦翰、易良幹等殉难。湘勇之越境剿贼，将领之力战捐躯，实始于此。余闻而悼之，议立忠义祠于县城，祀湘人与于南昌之难者。

其冬，余奉命筹备舟师，乃募湘勇水陆万人。明年，率之东讨。岳州之役，陆兵败挫，虽旋有湘潭之捷，而湘士中熸。既而整军再出，罗公暨李忠武公续宾率湘勇以从。于是大隽于岳州，

able in emergencies. Therefore, I proposed to the imperial government that the militiamen be recruited as government-backed official soldiers and that I mobilize and train a thousand militiamen in accordance with Qi Jiguang's [1] military strategies. Consequently, militiamen from my hometown of Xiangxiang County became known as the Xiang Army (Hunan Army).

In the spring of the third year of Emperor Xianfeng's reign (1853), the Xiang Army suppressed local bandits in Hengshan County and defeated the rebel faction in Guidong County. In the summer of that same year, the Yue rebels laid siege to Nanchang, the capital of Jiangxi Province. In response, I recruited two thousand men from Xiangxiang County and a thousand from the Chu militia. [2] Then, Luo Zenan led them eastward toward Jiangxi to shore up resistance against the Yue rebels. The initial battle was lost, and two battalion officials, Xie Banghan and Yi Lianggan, were killed. So began the Xiang Army's cross-border crackdown on rebel factions and the supreme sacrifices of Xiang Army leaders. Upon receiving the news, I mourned for the dead and discussed the establishment of the Zhongyi Ancestral Temple in Xiangxiang to memorialize the officers and soldiers of the Xiang Army who died defending Nanchang.

In the winter of that same year, I received an imperial order to assemble a navy. I responded by recruiting ten thousand militiamen from Xiangxiang for both the navy and the army and led them eastward the following year. The battle of Yuezhou (present-day Yueyang City) ended in defeat for the army despite a victory in Xiangtan. The army soon rallied under the leadership of Luo Zenan and Li Xubin. This time, they secured a major victory in Yuezhou and captured Wuhan, the capital of Hubei. Later, the

1 Qi Jiguang, a Ming Dynasty general, was famous for his exploits fighting against the invading Japanese navy.

2 Chu militiamen were initially natives of Xinning County, Hunan Province.

克武汉，下蕲、黄，破田家镇，复江西弋阳、信州、宁州。又以其间由江还鄂，扫荡枝县，再克武昌省会。

咸丰五六年间，罗、李湘勇之名震天下，而王壮武公与刘武烈公腾鸿、萧壮果公启江暨巡抚蒋公益澧，皆提湘勇征战湖北、江西、广西、广东等省，所在有声。然罗公、王公、刘公遂以六七年间先后徂谢，而将士伤亡者滋益多。前所议建之忠义祠，规制隘庳，不足以严典祀。咸丰八年秋，国藩乃与李公具疏会奏，请立昭忠祠于湘乡，令有司春秋致祭。天子许之。吾邑军士，没有余荣已。

未几而舒城、三河之难作，李公殉节，部下死者殆六千人。国藩私忧，以谓湘中士气恐不复振。其后李公之弟勇毅公续宜重辑部曲，转战皖北，张忠毅公运兰及唐总戎义训辈之师转战皖南，而吾弟国荃遂以湘士克复安庆、金陵两省，蒋公暨杨公昌濬亦用

Xiang Army marched south to Qizhou and Huangzhou to capture Tianjiazhen Town and then recaptured Yiyang, Xinzhou, and Ningzhou in Jiangxi Province. Afterward, the Xiang Army returned to Hubei via the Yangtze River, raided Zhijiang County, and once again recaptured Wuhan.

During the fifth and the sixth years of Emperor Xianfeng's reign (1855-1856), word of the Xiang Army led by Luo Zenan and Li Xubin reverberated across the country. Wang Zhen, Liu Tenghong, Xiao Qijiang, and Jiang Yili all referenced the Xiang Army's military campaigns in Hubei, Jiangxi, Guangxi, Guangdong, and other provinces. However, Luo Zenan, Wang Zhen, and Liu Tenghong died one after another in the sixth and the seventh years of Emperor Xianfeng's reign (1856-1857), and the number of generals and soldiers who became casualties soared. Consequently, the Zhongyi Ancestral Temple that had been proposed became insufficient to accommodate sacrificial ceremonies. In the autumn of the eighth year of Emperor Xianfeng's reign (1858), Li Xubin and I submitted a memorial to the throne for the establishment of Zhaozhong Ancestral Temple in Xiangxiang to conduct sacrificial ceremonies in spring and autumn. Emperor Xianfeng approved, and now Xiang Army officers and soldiers can enjoy posthumous glory.

Soon after, Li Xubin was killed in the Shucheng-Sanhe battle together with nearly six thousand soldiers. I worried that the Xiang Army's morale may have been irrevocably broken; however, Li Xuyi, the younger brother of Li Xubin, continued to rally the militia and took the fight to the rebels in northern Anhui. Zhang Yunlan and Tang Yixun led their troops to southern Anhui, and my younger brother, Zeng Guoquan, led his troops to seize Anqing and Jinling. Jiang Yili and Yang Changjun led their forces to capture Zhejiang and Fujian, where Zhang Yunlan met his death. Consequently, the colors of the Xiang Army flew over the southeast to

湘人平浙江，伐福建，张忠毅公亦战没于闽。东南数省，莫不有湘军之旌旗，中外皆叹异焉。

其西北诸道，则提督刘君松山追逐捻匪于河南、山东、直隶，征叛回于陕西、甘肃，而按察使陈君湜防守山西。其西南诸道，则萧壮果公率师入蜀，而巡抚刘公蓉屡平蜀寇，总督刘公岳昭暨诸湘军，又自蜀而南入黔，西入滇。一县之人，征伐遍于十八行省，近古未尝有也。

当其负羽远征，乖离骨肉，或苦战而授命，或邂逅而戕生，残骸暴于荒原，凶问迟而不审，老母寡妇，望祭宵哭，可谓极人世之至悲。然而前者覆亡，后者继往，蹈百死而不辞，困厄无所遇而不悔者，何哉？岂皆迫于生事，逐风尘而不返与？亦由前此死义数君子者为之倡，忠诚所感，气机鼓动，而不能自已也。

君子之道，莫大乎以忠诚为天下倡。世之乱也，上下纵于亡等之欲，奸伪相吞，变诈相角，自图其安而予人以至危，畏难避害，曾不肯捐丝粟之力以拯天下。得忠诚者起而矫之，克己而爱人，去伪而崇拙，躬履诸艰而不责人以同患；浩然捐生，如远游

the amazement of people at home and abroad.

Liu Songshan, commander-in-chief of the northwestern provinces, pursued the Nian rebel army [1] across Henan, Shandong, and Zhili (Hebei) and conducted a punitive campaign against the Hui ethnic rebels in Shaanxi and Gansu. Meanwhile, Chen Shi, the chief inspector of the northwestern provinces, defended Shanxi. In the southwest, Xiao Qijiang led his troops to Sichuan; the governor of Sichuan, Liu Rong, repeatedly suppressed local bandits; and the governor of Yunnan and Guizhou, Liu Yuezhao, led the Xiang Army to Guizhou and Yunnan from Sichuan. As the above documents, soldiers from just one county fought in punitive campaigns across an unprecedented eighteen provinces!

Punitive expeditions forced them to leave family members behind while either offering their own lives in battle or killing their enemies in combat. Their corpses were exposed to the wilderness, and news of their deaths only reached their families after long delays. Elderly mothers and widows were torn by the deepest sorrow and wept over their deaths. However, new faces followed in the footsteps of the fallen without fear or regret. Are they all forced to make a living and chase after worldly gains, unable to return home? They are encouraged and moved by those who have proven their loyalty by dying for a righteous cause and thus could not help themselves.

The way of the superior man is to advocate loyalty everywhere. In a chaotic world, people indulge in desires that defy etiquette and law. Wicked and disingenuous, they seek out safety while abandoning others to danger. Flinching at difficulties and abstaining from anything harmful, they are unwilling to lift a finger to save the rest of the world. Those who are loyal rise to correct wrongs; they practice self-restraint and love others; they eliminate

1 The Nian rebel army was influential in northern China despite being composed mainly of peasants.

之还乡而无所顾悸。由是众人效其所为，亦皆以苟活为羞，以避事为耻。呜呼！吾乡数君子所以鼓舞群伦，历九州而戡大乱，非拙且诚者之效与？亦岂始事时所及料哉！

今海宇粗安，昭忠祠落成有年，而邑中壮士效命疆场者，尚不乏人。能常葆此拙且诚者，出而济世，入而表里，群材之兴也，不可量矣！又岂仅以武节彪炳寰区也乎？

hypocrisy and value humbleness; they bear burdens but never blame or invite others to share their suffering; they sacrifice their lives as easily as though they were returning home from a long journey. As a result, people view these behaviors as examples to be imitated, and they feel ashamed of their unworthy and irresponsible lives. Alas, several noble gentlemen from my hometown have encouraged many of their peers and suppressed upheaval across the country. Is this not the result of humbleness and sincerity? And how can this be expected from the outset?

Nowadays, the world is generally a safe place. It has been years since Zhaozhong Ancestral Temple was built, and many warriors from my hometown still fight on the battlefields. Those who can remain humble and sincere benefit society when away and set good examples for their communities when at home, thus the success of talented people cannot be measured! Their renown the world over cannot be attributed solely to military feats!

罗忠节公神道碑铭

罗泽南是早期湘军的重要领导人之一。

罗泽南出身于湘乡县的清贫之家，刻苦力学，直到三十三岁才中秀才。太平天国运动爆发前，他一直以教师为业，勤奋研习理学，著述等身，是湖南学界的一位著名学者。咸丰二年（1852），已经四十六岁的罗泽南奉县令之命招募乡勇，以后一直在曾国藩麾下带兵打仗。咸丰六年三月，阵亡于武昌，年仅五十。

罗泽南是曾国藩的挚友兼儿女亲家。同治八年（1869）十月，应罗氏后人之请，曾国藩写下了这篇铭文。

公讳泽南，字仲岳，号罗山，湘乡罗氏。咸丰四五年间，公以诸生提兵破贼，屡建大勋。朝野叹仰，以为名将，而不知其平生志事学，盖素定者久矣。

公之学，其大者以为天地万物本吾一体，量不周于六合，泽不被于匹夫，亏辱莫大焉。凛降衷之大原，思主静以协中，于是

Inscription on Luo Zenan's Tombstone

Luo Zenan was an important leader of the early Xiang Army.

Luo Zenan was born into a poor family in Xiangxiang County. Through hard work, he passed the county-level imperial exam to become a *xiucai* at the age of 33. Until the start of fighting to defeat the Taiping rebels, Luo was a teacher and prolific writer who studied Neo-Confucianism; thus, he was a familiar sight in Hunan's academic circles. In the second year of Emperor Xianfeng's reign (1852), 46-year-old Luo Zenan received an order from the county magistrate to recruit a militia and, thereafter, served as a military officer under Zeng Guofan. He died at the age of 50 during a battle in Wuchang in the third month of the sixth year of Emperor Xianfeng's reign (1856).

Luo Zenan was Zeng's close friend and the father-in-law of his third eldest daughter. In the tenth month of the eighth year of Emperor Tongzhi's reign (1869), Zeng wrote the following inscription at the request of Luo Zenan's family.

Luo Zenan, who had the courtesy name Zhongyue and the pen name Luoshan, was a native of Xiangxiang County. During the fourth and fifth years of Emperor Xianfeng's reign (1854-1855), Luo Zenan was celebrated for helping to lead the Xiang Army to defeat the Taiping rebels, winning the admiration of the imperial government and the public. However, people tend to be unfamiliar with other aspects of his life that were overshadowed by his military career.

Regarding learning, Luo Zenan argued that all things in heaven and on earth belong to one body, and that the quantity of all things is insufficient for the universe; grace does not permeate

乎宗张子而著《西铭讲义》一卷，宗周子而著《人极衍义》一卷。幼仪不慎，则居敬无基；异说不辨，则谬以千里，于是乎宗朱子而著《小学韵语》一卷、《姚江学辨》二卷。严取与出处之义，参阴阳消息之幾，旁及州域之形势，百家之述作，靡不研讨，于是乎有《读孟子札记》二卷、《周易本义衍言》若干卷、《皇舆要览》若干卷、诗文集八卷。其为说虽多，而其本躬修以安四海，未尝不同归也。

始，公家世贫甚。曾祖王父日阮、王父拱诗皆以公贵，赠通奉大夫。父嘉旦，公没后赏加头品顶戴。曾祖王母萧氏、王母贺氏、母萧氏皆赠夫人。公少就学，王父屡典衣市米，节缩于家，专饷于塾。年十九，即藉课徒取资自给。丧其母，又丧其兄，旋

down to the common man, and this is unfortunate. Taking inspiration from great sources and promoting harmony through contemplation, Luo Zenan responded to Zhang Zai, a famous Confucianist in the Northern Song Dynasty, by writing *Lecture Notes on Zhang Zai's "Western Inscription"* (*Xi Ming Jiang Yi*); he was also influenced by Zhou Dunyi, a famous neo-Confucianist in the Northern Song Dynasty, to write *Derivations of Ultimate Ethics* (*Ren Ji Yan Yi*). A child who is careless with etiquette has no foundation for his conduct; a failure to differentiate dissenting views could lead one a thousand miles astray. Therefore, Luo Zenan was inspired by Zhu Xi, a famous neo-Confucianist in the Southern Song Dynasty, to write *A Rhymed Text for Primary School Education* (*Xiao Xue Yun Yu*) and *Yaojiang Academic Thoughts* (*Yao Jiang Xue Bian*). He selected meanings of the classics and discerned messages in ancient Chinese philosophy. He touched upon the situations in different regions and analyzed the spoken and written traditions of different schools of thinking. Consequently, Luo Zenan wrote *Reading Notes on Mencius* in two volumes, *Derivations of Original Meanings in the Zhou Book of Change* (*Zhou Yi Ben Yi Yan Yan*) in multiple volumes, *An Anthology of Imperial Readings* (*Huang Yu Yao Lan*) in multiple volumes, and a collection of poems and essays in eight volumes. Although Luo proposed various theories, he never strayed from his original principle of preserving peace and order in the world.

Luo Zenan came from a humble background, yet his family was awarded many honors due to his service. His great-grandfather, Luo Riruan, and grandfather, Luo Gongshi, were awarded the title of Tongfeng Dafu (an official of the third rank in the Qing Dynasty). His father, Luo Jiadan, was awarded an official title of the first rank. And his great-grandmother (surnamed Xiao), grandmother (surnamed He), and mother (surnamed Xiao) were awarded the

丧王父。十年之中，连遭期功之戚十一。尝以试罢，徒步夜归，家人以岁饥不能具食，妻以连哭三子丧明。公益自刻厉，不忧门庭多故，而忧所学不能拔俗而入圣；不耻生事之艰，而耻无术以济天下。

其后年逾三十，乃补学官附生。逾四十，乃以廪生举孝廉方正。假馆四方，穷年汲汲与其徒讲论濂洛关闽之绪，无日不熟于口，悦诸心，因以措诸事为，显诸笔札。未几，兵事起，湘中书生多拯大难、立勋名，大率公弟子也。

咸丰二年，粤贼度岭北犯，攻围长沙，县令召公练乡勇以备不虞，会城解围。明年春，巡抚张公亮基檄公带勇至长沙。维时国藩奉命督治团练，因与公讲求束伍技击之法，晨夕训练，击土

title of Furen (Madame). Luo Zenan was able to attend a private boarding school thanks to the efforts of his grandfather, who pawned clothes to buy rice and eliminated all possible household expenditures to save money. At the age of 19, Luo Zenan began teaching and became self-sufficient. He lost his mother, his elder brother, and then his grandfather in quick succession. Within ten years, he had lost one tenth of his family members. Upon returning home one night after an exam, he found his family starving and his wife blind from mourning the loss of three children. The experience only increased his diligence. He worried more about improving his education than about family emergencies. He was shamed by his inability to serve the world rather than his dire financial circumstances.

After turning 30, Luo Zenan attended the county-level government school as an associate scholar. After turning 40, he was recommended to serve as a government-sponsored scholar after becoming a successful second-degree candidate. He traveled widely and taught students the works of Zhou Dunyi, the Cheng brothers, Zhang Zai, and Zhu Xi. He accommodated his students' interests and welcomed them to observe what he did and the records he kept. However, it was not long before war broke out. Scholars from Hunan who would go on to provide assistance in dire times and establish their reputations tended to be students of Luo Zenan.

In the second year of Emperor Xianfeng's reign (1852), the Yue rebels crossed the mountains and attacked Changsha, the capital of Hunan. The county magistrate ordered Luo Zenan to train and ready a local militia, which then rescued Changsha from the siege. The next spring, the provincial governor, Zhang Liangji, ordered Luo Zenan to lead the militia once again to Changsha. At that time, I received orders to supervise military training. Naturally, Luo Zenan and I discussed how best to discipline the militia and

寇于桂东，擒逆党于衡山。其夏，贼围江西省城，乃益募湘勇二千，附以新宁之勇、镇筸之兵，檄公赴援南昌。湘军越境讨贼，自此始矣。

既解南昌之围，复破贼于安福。归及衡州，歼土匪于永兴。无何，湖北之贼大举南侵，官军失利于岳阳，克捷于湘潭。提督塔齐布公追贼至岳州，余檄公与李公续宾佐之。公扼大桥以遏其冲，凡七战而群贼溃，岳州平，乘胜逐北，连复三县。将攻武昌，公手一图，就余决策。师出两路，以塔公进洪山一路，而自请攻花园一路，当其坚者。如其策，果克武昌、汉阳两城。贼既东奔，追及于兴国，大膊于田家镇。公提卒二千，御数百倍之寇，蹙之江滨，挂石坠崖死者万计。而水师亦断横江铁锁，燔贼舟数千。

hone their fighting skills. The militia trained from morning to night, eventually defeating local bandits in Guidong and capturing rebel factions in Hengshan. When the Yue rebels surrounded the capital of Jiangxi Province over the summer, another two thousand troops were recruited to shore up the Xinning and Zhengan militias, and Luo Zenan was ordered to lead them to recover Nanchang. This signified the Xiang Army's first foray into other provinces to fight the rebels.

The Xiang Army broke the siege of Nanchang and then defeated the rebels in Anfu. After returning to Hengzhou in Hunan, they annihilated the rebels in Yongxing. Soon after, the rebels in Hubei conducted a large-scale invasion moving south, where official government troops suffered a defeat in Yueyang but emerged victorious in Xiangtan. Tacibu, the commander-in-chief of the province, led government troops to chase the Taiping rebels to Yuezhou, and I ordered Luo Zenan and Li Xubin to offer him their assistance. Luo Zenan's troops controlled the bridge, preventing the rebels from advancing, and then fought the rebels seven times before finally routing them. After recapturing Yuezhou, Luo Zenan's troops pursued the rebels northward, recovering three counties. At my direction, he drew up plans to attack the rebels in Wuchang. The Xiang Army took a two-pronged approach: Tacibu led one group to attack Hongshan, and Luo Zenan led another to bear the brunt of the rebel forces in Huayuan. This strategy enabled the Xiang Army to capture Wuchang and Hanyang. The rebels fled eastward into Xingguo, and a battle erupted in Tianjiazhen. Luo Zenan led two thousand soldiers to fight the rebel forces, which were more than a hundred times stronger. Nevertheless, the rebels became trapped near the Yangtze River, and thousands died after being forced to jump from the cliffs into the water below. The navy broke the iron lock that the rebels had on the river and set thousands of enemy boats aflame.

当是时，公名震天下。前此累功保至道员、花翎，至是有宁绍台道之命，加按察使衔。既而引兵北渡，克广济、黄梅，赏叶普铿额巴图鲁名号。又引兵南渡，攻围九江，进规湖口。贼坚守不可遽下。适会水师分兵入宫亭湖，江上之军不利，而湖北诸军屡败，贼自黄梅长驱西上，武昌再陷。公太息深忧，叹利钝之无常，世变之未已，或解说《周易》以自遣。

时别贼陷饶州、弋阳。檄公入江西援剿，大战弋阳，克之。贼陷广信，又战信州，克之。又以其间收复德兴、景德镇。东路甫定，而义宁复陷。公军渡湖汉而西，至则示形杭口，而暗进鳌岭，屯高峰以瞰敌，设三伏以要之，四战而贼大熸。义宁既克，有诏加布政使衔。

During this time, Luo Zenan was celebrated throughout the land. Having previously been promoted to *daoyuan* [1] with honors, he was then promoted to commander-in-chief and chief inspector of the Ningbo-Shaoxing-Taizhou region. Next, he led troops northward to capture Guangji and Huangmei and was awarded the title of Yebkengge Baturu (outstanding warrior). Then, he led troops southward to lay siege to Jiujiang and attempt to take Hukou. However, the Taiping rebels stood firm and refused to be defeated easily. The Qing navy set sail on Gongting Lake (Poyang Lake) but was crushed on the Yangtze River. As Qing troops were defeated again and again, the Taiping rebels charged west through Huangmei to recapture Wuchang. Troubled by the unstable military situation and the changing world, Luo Zenan sometimes turned to the *Zhou Book of Change* for solace.

Meanwhile, other rebel forces captured Raozhou and Yiyang in Jiangxi Province. Luo Zenan and his troops received orders to quash the rebels in Jiangxi, and they succeeded in routing the rebel forces in Yiyang after a major battle. The rebels then captured the Guangxin District of Shangrao, leading to a battle in the nearby Xinzhou District, where the rebels were quashed once again. Meanwhile, Luo Zenan's troops also recovered Dexing and Jingdezhen. The Taiping rebels responded by capturing Yining Town, and Luo Zenan's troops crossed Poyang Lake and the Han River as they moved westward in hot pursuit. His troops made a maneuver in Hangkou Town but marched covertly to Aoling Village, where they positioned themselves atop a mountain overlooking the rebel forces. They eventually defeated the rebels after conducting three ambushes and engaging in four skirmishes. Consequently, Yining was recaptured, and Luo Zenan was awarded the title of commissioner by an imperial edict.

1 Daoyuan, also known as Daotai, is the title of an intermediate-level official in the Qing Dynasty.

公以书抵国藩，具论吴楚形势：欲取九江、湖口，法当先图武昌；欲取武昌，法当先清岳、鄂之交。于是草奏，以公回援武汉，遂略通城，克崇阳，挫衄于濠头堡，大捷于蒲圻。将达武昌，巡抚胡文忠公欢迎劳问，凡事咨而后行。城外贼垒铲除略尽，殄灭有绪矣。公以雾中搏战，中枪子伤，创甚，咸丰六年三月初八日卒于军，春秋五十。病中索笔作书，皆军国要事、艰危支拄之语，左右藏去宝之。事闻，天子震悼，照巡抚例赐恤，二子皆赏给举人，三省建立专祠，予谥忠节。

公在军四载，论数省安危，皆视为一家骨肉之事，与其所注《西铭》之指相符。其临阵审固乃发，亦本主静察幾之说。而行军

Luo Zenan wrote me a letter elaborating on the situation in the Wu-Chu region (the middle and lower reaches of the Yangtze River). He recommended that the Qing army recapture Wuchang before attempting to target Jiujiang and Hukou and clear the border region between Yueyang and Hubei Province. Thus, I drafted a memorial to the throne, and Luo Zenan's troops headed toward Wuchang. Enroute, they seized back Tongcheng and Chongyang before suffering a defeat in Haotoubao and then winning a major victory in Puqi. Hu Linyi, the governor of Hubei, welcomed Luo's troops to Wuchang and consulted him before taking any action. Rebel fortresses on the outskirts of the city were largely destroyed, and most of the rebel forces were wiped out. Then, during a savage battle in dense fog, Luo Zenan was mortally wounded by gunshots and passed away at the age of 50 on the eighth day of the third month in the sixth year of Emperor Xianfeng's reign (1856). As he lay dying, Luo Zenan asked for a pen to record his thoughts on important military and national matters and on the best way to serve the country in difficult times. His attendants treasured his writings. News of his death was greeted with mourning by the emperor, who awarded him a posthumous title commensurate with provincial governor and granted his sons the title of *juren* (a scholar who has passed the provincial-level imperial examination). Three provinces also established temples in his honor for his contributions to society.

Having served in the army for four years, Luo Zenan considered the stability of several provinces to be his personal mission, which is consistent with his writing in *Lecture Notes on Zhang Zai's "Western Inscription"* (*Xi Ming Jiang Yi*). He contemplated his options before striding onto the battlefield, a practice that was rooted in the concept of quietly observing subtleties. He also believed that maneuvering troops should analyze terrain and make good

好相度山川脉络，又其讲求舆图之效。君子是以知公之功，所蓄积者夙也，非天幸也。

配张氏，诰封夫人，妾周氏。子兆作，配胡氏；兆升，配曾氏，国藩第三女也。余与公以学行相勖，又相从于金革，申之以婚姻，乃摭其大节，铭诸墓道。铭曰：

渐车之涧，
积潦纵横；
崇朝即涸，
卷势收声。

大江西来，
其源万里；
泽溥寰区，
不矜厥美。

无本者竭，
有本者昌。
罗公渊默，
所蓄孔长。

洞澈天人，
潜睎往圣；
一物未康，
终亏吾性。

use of maps. Thus, Luo Zenan's military exploits were obviously the result of accumulated achievements rather than simply good luck.

Luo Zenan had a wife surnamed Zhang, who was awarded the title of Furen (Madame), and a concubine surnamed Zhou. He was a father to two sons: Zhaozuo, whose wife was surnamed Hu, and Zhaosheng, whose wife was surnamed Zeng (my third eldest daughter). Luo Zenan and I encouraged each other with regard to scholarship and moral conduct. We were comrades-in-arms who became linked when our children married. Therefore, I have highlighted major events in his life and written this inscription on his gravestone. It reads,

A brook grows gradually,
Water flowing freely.
It dries up in an instant,
Going in its own time.

The Great River runs east,
Its source thousands of miles away.
It nourishes folk across the land,
Yet never flaunts its beauty.

That which has no root is depleted,
And that which has roots blooms.
Luo is silent,
Yet has left much behind.

He walks with men of great talent,
And admires ancient sages.
If one aspect is weak,
Within, he feels flawed.

提师苦战，
荆扬二州；
斧彼凶竖，
为民复仇。

矫矫学徒，
相从征讨；
朝如鏖兵，
暮归讲道。

洛闽之术，
近世所捐；
姚江事业，
或迈前贤。

公慎其趋，
既辨其诡；
仍立丰功，
一雪斯耻。

大本内植，
伟绩外充。
兹谓豪杰，
百世可宗。

He leads troops into battle,
At Jingzhou and Yangzhou.
He slays the rebels,
Avenging the common folk.

Courageous apprentices,
Joined military campaigns.
Warriors at dawn,
Return as students at dusk.

The Cheng Brothers and Zhu Xi,
Bestowed much to the modern world.
Luo's cause at the Yao River,
Places him in their midst.

Ever cautious,
He is adept at maneuvers.
With feats aplenty,
He avenges past shames.

The essence within,
Fuels conquests without.
He is a hero,
For all generations.

大界墓表

祖父去世二十三年后，同治十年（1871）七月，曾氏满怀深情，写下这篇垂暮之年的大文章，作为祖父祖母坟茔墓表。

此文的特色是以大段祖父自述的文字，勾画出一位平凡又不平凡的乡民的人生经历与性格特点，为我们研究曾氏家族以及曾国藩本人，留下一份难得的史料。

曾氏兄弟事功巨大，声名显赫，但在这篇文章中，晚年的曾氏却说“高年及见吾祖者，咸谓吾兄弟威重智略，不逮府君远甚也”。这句话，看似行文的技巧，其实不然。终其一生，祖父都是曾氏的精神偶像。从这点上说，此文为我们提供了一把打开曾氏家族密码的钥匙。

王考府君以道光二十九年十月四日弃养，倏历二十三年。当初葬时，吾父以书抵京师，命国藩为文，纪述先德，揭诸墓道。国藩窃观王考府君威仪言论，实有雄伟非常之概，而终老山林，曾无奇遇重事一发其意。其型于家，式于乡邑者，又率依乎中道，无峻绝可惊之行。独其生平雅言，有足垂训来叶者，敢敬述一二，以示后昆。

府君之言曰：“吾少耽游惰，往还湘潭市肆，与裘马少年相

Inscription on the Dajie Gravestone

In the seventh month of the tenth year of Emperor Tongzhi's reign (1871), Zeng Guofan marked 23 years since his grandfather's death by composing this essay that was inscribed on his paternal grandparents' gravestone.

This essay is unusual in that Zeng Guofan quotes his grandfather extensively when sketching the experiences and character of a seemingly ordinary local villager, providing a rare glimpse into the lives of the Zeng family and Zeng Guofan himself.

The Zeng brothers were celebrated for their great achievements. In this essay written in his later years, however, Zeng explains, "The elders who knew my grandfather declare that my brothers and I cannot match the dignity and wisdom he displayed."These words were far from a mere writing exercise. Zeng had idolized his grandfather his entire life. This knowledge offers us a unique perspective for understanding the Zeng family.

On the fourth day of the tenth month in the 29th year of Emperor Daoguang's reign (1849), my grandfather passed away. That was 23 years ago. On the day of his funeral, my father wrote me in Beijing asking if I would compose a few lines about my grandfather's character to be etched onto his gravestone. I felt a majestic presence in my grandfather's speech. However, he passed away quietly in the countryside with no opportunity to voice his ideas. My grandfather provided an example for both our family and our hometown; he followed the doctrine of the golden mean, never achieving astonishing feats. I can only recount his earnest advice, which is worthy enough to be passed down to later generations.

My grandfather said, "In my youth, I was prone to laziness and

逐，或日高酣寝。长老有讥以浮薄，将覆其家者。余闻而立起自责，货马徒行，自是终身未明而起。余年三十五，始讲求农事。居枕高嵋山下，垅峻如梯，田小如瓦。吾凿石决壤，开十数畛而通为一，然后耕夫易于从事。吾昕宵行水，听虫鸟鸣声以知节候，观露上禾颠以为乐。种蔬半畦，晨而耘，吾任之；夕而粪，庸保任之。入而饲豕，出而养鱼，彼此杂职之。凡菜茹手植而手撷者，其味弥甘；凡物亲历艰苦而得者，食之弥安也。吾宗自元明居衡阳之庙山，久无祠宇。吾谋之宗族诸老，建立祠堂，岁以十月致祭。自国初迁居湘乡，至吾曾祖元吉公，基业始宏。吾又谋之宗族，别立祀典，岁以三月致祭。世人礼神徼福，求诸幽遐。吾以为神之陟降，莫亲于祖考，故独隆于生我一本之祀，而他祀姑阙焉。后世虽贫，礼不可隳；子孙虽愚，家祭不可简也。吾早岁失

had no purpose. I frequented the shops in Xiangtan, fraternized with the well-off, and rose late. The elders in my hometown ridiculed my frivolity and predicted that I would ruin my family. Their words inspired self-reproach, prompting me to sell my horse and go on foot. Since then, I have always been an early riser. At the age of 35, I turned to farming. Near the foot of Mount Gaomei, the ridges are steep as ladders, and the fields are small as tiles. I broke the stones, cultivated the soil, and combined more than ten paddies into one for easier tending. I irrigated the paddies from dawn until dusk, recognized the seasons by the sound of insects and birds, and took pleasure in watching dew form on the rice plants. I reserved one section for growing vegetables, which I weeded in the morning and fertilized in the evening. I raised pigs on the farm and bred fish further away, which took me out of my routine. Vegetables planted and picked with one's own two hands taste sweet; food that comes from one's hard work can be eaten with peace of mind. Despite living on Hengyang's Mount Miao since the Yuan and Ming dynasties, my family never built any ancestral shrines there. So, I approached our elders about building one so that we could offer sacrifices to our ancestors in every tenth month. After moving to Xiangxiang in the early Qing Dynasty, our family became deeply rooted in the land during the time of my great-grandfather, Zeng Yuanji. So, I also asked our elders about performing annual religious rites for our ancestors in the third month. People worship faraway gods in search of blessings. Communication with the gods is best realized through our own ancestors. Thus, ancestral sacrifices should take precedence over other types of sacrifices, which may be paused temporarily. Poverty is no excuse for abandoning rites, and foolishness is no reason for descendants to simplify rites. As an adult, I have felt deep shame for leaving school at an early age. I have not only ordered my chil-

学，壮而引为深耻，既令子孙出就名师，又好宾接文士，候望音尘，常愿通材宿儒接迹吾门，此心乃快。其次老成端士，敬礼不怠，其下泛应群伦。至于巫医、僧徒、堪舆、星命之流，吾屏斥之惟恐不远。旧姻穷乏，遇之惟恐不隆。识者观一门宾客之雅正疏数，而卜家之兴败，理无爽者。乡党戚好，吉则贺，丧则吊，有疾则问，人道之常也，吾必践焉，必躬焉。财不足以及物，吾以力助焉。邻里讼争，吾尝居间以解两家之纷。其尤无状者，厉辞诘责，势若霆摧而理如的破，悍夫往往神沮。或具樽酒通殷勤，一笑散去。君子居下则排一方之难，在上则息万物之嚣，其道一耳。津梁道途废坏不治者，孤嫠衰疾无告者，量吾力之所能，随时图之，不无小补。若必待富而后谋，则天下终无可成之事。”

盖府君平昔所恒言者如此。国藩既稔闻之，吾父暨叔父又传述而告诫数数矣。

府君讳玉屏，号星冈。声如洪钟，见者惮慑；而温良博爱，物无不尽之情。其卒也，远近感唏，或涕泣不能自休。配我祖妣

dren and grandchildren to learn from famous teachers but also welcomed scholars and intellectuals to my home. I look forward to hearing their news. Moreover, individuals with experience and integrity are also welcome. As for shamans, monks, geomancers, astrologists, and the like, I keep them as far away as possible. My elderly in-laws are destitute, and I worry about their livelihood when I meet them. A discerning mind can predict the rise and fall of a family by examining the integrity and number of the guests who visit; this is well accepted. As far as townspeople and relatives are concerned, I congratulate them on their good fortune, mourn them at their funerals, and ask after their health when they are ill. I follow the norms of mankind. I offer to work when others are in need. I offer to mediate when disputes arise between local families. As for those who are ill-mannered, I berate them with reason as though hurling a thunderbolt, thus subduing those who are fierce. Sometimes, I prepare a few cups of alcohol to entertain them. After imbibing, they laugh and depart. In a lowly position, the superior man solves problems where he lives; in a lofty position, he quiets the clamor of the world. The way of the superior man remains unchanged. If a bridge or road is in disrepair, I do my best to fix it; if the widowed or the sickly are in need, I do my best to help them. Waiting until I become rich to help others will achieve nothing."

These are the familiar words that I often heard my grandfather speak. Not only did I hear them from him, I also heard them repeated by my father and uncles, who would admonish me to keep these words in mind.

My grandfather had the given name Yuping and the pen name Xinggang. His voice rang out like a great bell, intimidating those around him. However, he was a gentle and kindhearted man who was willing to help others with all he had. News of his death sad-

王太夫人，孝恭雍穆，娣姒钦其所为，自酒浆缝纫以至礼宾承祭，经纪百端，曲有仪法。虔事夫子，卑诎已甚，时逢愠怒，则竦息减食，甘受折辱以回眷睐。年逾七十，犹检校内政，丝粟不遗。其于子妇孙曾，群从外姻，童幼仆妪，皆思有惠逮之。权量多寡，物薄而意长，阅时而再施。太夫人道光二十六年九月十八日卒，春秋八十，葬于木兜冲。其后三年而府君卒，春秋七十有六，葬于八斗冲，迁太夫人之柩祔焉。其后十年为咸丰九年己未十二月，均改葬于大界。

府君之先，六世祖曰孟学，初迁湘乡者也。曾祖曰元吉，别立祀典者也。祖曰辅臣，考曰竟希。曾祖妣氏曰刘，祖妣氏曰蒋，曰刘，妣氏曰彭。以国藩忝窃禄位，府君初贻封中宪大夫，后累

dened those near and far, with some unable to stop weeping. My grandmother was obedient, respectful, and friendly. She was well admired by her sisters-in-law for how she conducted herself. From brewing wine and sewing clothes to following official etiquette and performing ceremonial sacrifices, her many responsibilities were always conducted in line with moral standards. She was a devout yet humble wife and mother. When my grandfather was inwardly angry, she would curtail her diet respectfully in order to win back my grandfather's favor. Even after turning 70, she still examined the family's household affairs with attention to the smallest detail. She was considerate and kind to her children and grandchildren, people who married into the family, and servants young and old. She gave great thought to how her actions affected people in the household and was consistent in giving attention. On the 18th day of the ninth month in the 26th year of Emperor Daoguang's reign (1846), my grandmother passed away at the age of 80. She was later buried in Mudouchong. Three years later, my grandfather passed away at the age of 76. He was buried in Badouchong, where the coffin of my grandmother was relocated to be entombed with his. A decade later, in the 12th month of the ninth year of Emperor Xianfeng's reign (1859), their joint tomb was relocated to Dajie.

My sixth-generation ancestor, by the name of Mengxue, was the first to settle in Xiangxiang. My great-grandfather, who was named Yuanji, was given a separate sacrificial rite. My grandfather had the given name Fuchen but was called Jingxi by his father. My great-grandmother was surnamed Liu, my two grandmothers (my grandfather's two wives) were surnamed Jiang and Liu, respectively, and my mother was surnamed Peng. As I was fortunate enough to obtain a position at the imperial court, my grandfather was first awarded the title of *Zhongxian Dafu* (a fourth-rank senior official)

赠为光禄大夫、大学士、两江总督。祖妣初封恭人，后累赠为一品夫人。圣朝推恩，追而上之，竟希公累赠光禄大夫，妣彭氏亦赠一品夫人。府君生吾父兄弟三人，仲父上台早卒，季父骥云无子，以吾弟国华为嗣。孙五人。军兴以来，惟国潢治团练于乡，四人者皆托身兵间。国华、贞幹没于军，国藩与国荃遂以微功列封疆而膺高爵，而高年及见吾祖者，咸谓吾兄弟威重智略，不逮府君远甚也。其风采亦可想已。曾孙七人，元孙七人，凡兹安居足食，列于显荣者，繄维祖德是赖。于是叙其大致，表于斯阡，令后嗣无忘彝训，亦使过者考求事实，知有众征，无虚美云。

长孙太子太保武英殿大学士两江总督一等毅勇侯国藩谨撰

第四孙太子少保兵部侍郎前任湖北巡抚一等威毅伯国荃谨书

and was later awarded the titles of *Guanglu Dafu* (a first-rank senior official), *Daxueshi* (Grand Secretary), and Viceroy of Liangjiang. My grandmother was first awarded the title of *Gongren* (wife of a fourth-rank senior official) and was later awarded the title of *Yipin Furen* (wife of the first-rank official). The imperial court later bestowed further honor on our family by awarding my grandfather the title of *Guanglu Dafu* and my mother, surnamed Peng, the title of Yipin Furen. My grandfather had three sons and five grandsons. The eldest son was my father. The second son, who was named Shangtai, passed away when he was young. The youngest son, who was named Jiyun, had no children, and thus, my younger brother Guohua was chosen to be his heir. Since the rise of the Xiang Army, Guohuang has been the only grandson to direct a militia in our hometown; the other four joined the army. Guohua and Guobao died while serving in the military, and Guoquan and I rose to become generals and were awarded titles of nobility. However, the elders who knew my grandfather declare that my brothers and I cannot match the dignity and wisdom he displayed. His brilliance was beyond words. My grandfather has seven great-grandsons and seven great-great-grandsons. Those who live a peaceful life or achieve a high rank enjoy the fruits of the deeds performed by their forefathers. This is a summary of my grandfather's life inscribed on his gravestone. This inscription serves to ensure that we, as his descendants, never forget his earnest advice, and that passers-by may examine the facts, for what I have written is evidence-based and not empty praise.

Authored by Zeng Guofan, eldest grandson, Grand Guardian, Grand Secretary of the Hall of Martial Valor, Viceroy of Liangjiang, and First-class Marquis of Yiyong

Handwritten by Zeng Guoquan, fourth eldest grandson, Deputy Grand Secretary, Vice Minister of War, Governor of Hubei Province, First-class Count of Weiyi

《湖南文征》序

这篇序作于同治十年（1871），是曾氏晚年的一篇重要文章。

湘潭学者罗汝怀编了一部湖湘文章汇集，文集多达一百九十余卷。应罗之请，曾氏作了这篇序言。此文虽为友人所托而写，却不是应景，而是厚积薄发之作。

曾氏一生对古文用功最勤，研究心得最多。他以六百来字的精炼文笔，勾勒出古文发展演变的粗略轮廓，向世人呈现了他一生对古文苦苦思索的成果。尤为精彩的是最后一段，更能代表湘乡文派的特色：气势宏大，声光炯然。“湖南之为邦，北枕大江，南薄五岭，西接黔蜀，群苗所萃，盖亦山国荒僻之亚。”这二十九个字，一百多年来广为后人引用，成为对湖湘人文地理的经典概括。

吾友湘潭罗君研生以所编撰《湖南文征》百九十卷示余，而属为序其端。国藩陋甚，齿又益衰，奚足以语文事？窃闻古之文，初无所谓法也。《易》《书》《诗》《仪礼》《春秋》诸经，其体势声

Foreword to *Hunan Anthology*

This foreword, written in the tenth year of Emperor Tongzhi's reign (1871), stands out as an important essay from Zeng Guofan's later years.

Luo Ruhuai (courtesy names Yansheng and Niansun), a scholar from Xiangtan, compiled a collection of essays by Hunan scholars comprising more than 190 volumes. Zeng Guofan wrote this foreword for the collection at Luo's request. Nevertheless, rather than introducing a collection of essays, Zeng seized this opportunity to condense all that he had learned into one piece of writing.

Zeng Guofan dedicated much of his life to researching and perfecting classical Chinese prose. In an elegant essay of about 600 characters, he outlined the development and evolution of the essay and shared what a lifetime of contemplation had taught him about classical Chinese prose. The brilliant last paragraph, in particular, is representative of the vigor and resonance that distinguish the Xiangxiang school. "Hunan approaches the Yangtze River in the north and the Five Ridges in the south and borders Guizhou and Sichuan in the west. As an often remote and mountainous area, Hunan has been a gathering place for different ethnic groups." These succinct words have been quoted for more than a century to encapsulate the culture and geography of Hunan Province.

Luo Yansheng, my friend from Xiangtan in Hunan Province, presented me with the 190 volumes that form his compilation, *Hunan Anthology*, and asked me to write the foreword. Unskilled and aged, how am I qualified to write about literary matters? It is said that the art of composition did not exist in ancient times. The stylistic rules, layout, and language of Confucian classics such as *The Zhou Book of Change*, *The Book of Documents*, *The Book of Poetry*, *The Book of Rites*, and *The Spring and Autumn Annals* did

色，曾无一字相袭。即周秦诸子，亦各自成体。持此衡彼，画然若金玉与卉木之不同类，是乌有所谓法者。后人本不能文，强取古人所造而摹拟之，于是有合有离，而法不法名焉。

若其不俟摹拟，人心各具自然之文，约有二端：曰理，曰情。二者人人之所固有。就吾所知之理而笔诸书，而传诸世，称吾爱恶悲愉之情而缀辞以达之，若剖肺肝而陈诸简策，使吾缱绻之怀的然呈露，斯皆自然之文。性情敦厚者，类能为之。而浅深工拙，则相去十百千万而未始有极。自群经而外，百家著述，率有偏胜。以理胜者，多阐幽造极之语，而其弊或激宕失中；以情胜者，多悱恻感人之言，而其弊常丰缛而寡实。自东汉至隋，文人秀士大抵义不孤行，辞多俪语。即议大政，考大礼，亦每缀以排比之句，间以婀娜之声。历唐代而不改。

虽韩、李锐志复古，而不能革举世骈体之风。此皆习于情韵

not follow an accepted universal practice. Prose from the Zhou and Qin dynasties was also composed without any established principles. Just as flowers and plants cannot be judged by the same standard as gold and jade, one essay cannot be measured against another. Not knowing how to compose an essay, later generations reluctantly turned to ancient prose for examples to model their writing on. Consequently, their essays conformed to each other to create a standard in some areas and deviated from each other, going against any standard, in others.

If they refrained from imitation, people wrote in a natural style that may be divided into argumentation and emotional expression. Everyone is inherently capable of these natural essays, which involve recording what one knows in book form and then widely disseminating it. Natural essays use the written word to express likes and dislikes, sorrows and joys, just as though one had opened one's chest to expose the words within. Those who are honest and sincere are capable of composing such essays. Whether an essay has depth or is written well are just a few of the infinite ways that essays may differ. Apart from the Chinese classics, schools of thought tend to dominate different areas of writing. Those who excel in argumentation clarify hidden truths but weaken their essays by using passionate and biased language; those who excel in expressing emotion compose essays that are brimming with pathos but lacking in any real substance. From the Eastern Han Dynasty to the Sui Dynasty, scholars expressed more complicated ideas through magnificent rhetoric and employed parallel sentences and, occasionally, beautiful language in their essays, even when debating government affairs or conducting textual research on rites. This practice continued through the Tang Dynasty.

Although Han Yu and Li Ao [1] were determined to return to an

1 Li Ao (772-841) was a famous literary writer and philosopher of the Tang Dynasty.

者类也。宋兴既久，欧、苏、曾、王之徒崇奉韩公，以为不迁之宗。适会其时，大儒迭起，相与上探邹鲁，研讨微言。群士慕效，类皆法韩氏之气体，以阐明性道。自元、明至圣朝康、雍之间，风会略同，非是不足与于斯文之末。此皆习于义理者类也。

乾隆以来，鸿生硕彦稍厌旧闻，别启途轨，远搜汉儒之学，因有所谓考据之文。一字之音训，一物之制度，辨论动至数千言。曩所称义理之文，淡远简朴者，或屏弃之，以为空疏不足道。此又习俗趋向之一变已。

湖南之为邦，北枕大江，南薄五岭，西接黔蜀，群苗所萃，盖亦山国荒僻之亚。然周之末，屈原出于其间，《离骚》诸篇为后

ancient writing style, they could not disentangle themselves from the parallelism and ornateness that marked the style of rhythmical prose, which derived from a preference toward emotion-oriented essays. After the establishment of the Song Dynasty, scholars such as Ouyang Xiu, Su Shi, Zeng Gong, and Wang Anshi admired Han Yu and considered him the grand master. This period was celebrated for the plethora of neo-Confucian scholars who traced their learning to Confucius and Mencius, studying and deliberating on their profound yet simple words. Other scholars emerged who studied and followed Han Yu's writing style in order to expound on the nature and way of writing. From the Yuan and Ming dynasties to the reigns of Emperors Kangxi and Yongzheng in the current Qing Dynasty, the writing style remained roughly the same, as otherwise it would have lost its place among the literati. All this stemmed from the Confucian way.

Since Emperor Qianlong's reign, great scholars have tired of the old style and embarked on new trails. Their exploration of Han Dynasty scholars developed into textual research. They would produce arguments composed of thousands of words on the exegesis of one character or the system for one thing. Essays that used to be categorized under the Confucian way were abandoned if they seemed lofty and simplistic, as their critics believed them to be empty and superficial. This stood out as another change in the writing style.

Hunan approaches the Yangtze River in the north and the Five Ridges in the south and borders Guizhou and Sichuan in the west. As an often remote and mountainous area, Hunan has been a gathering place for different ethnic groups. During the last years of the Eastern Zhou Dynasty, Qu Yuan emerged in Hunan, and his poem, *The Lament* (*Li Sao*), was esteemed by later generations who preferred an emotional tone in their writing. During the Northern

世言情韵者所祖。逮乎宋世，周子复生于斯，作《太极图说》《通书》，为后世言义理者所祖。两贤者，皆前无师承，创立高文，上与《诗经》《周易》同风，下而百代逸才举莫能越其范围，而况湖湘后进沾被流风者乎？兹编所录，精于理者盖十之六，善言情者约十之四，而骈体亦颇有甄采，不言法而法未始或紊。惟考据之文搜集极少，前哲之倡导不宏，后世之欣慕亦寡。研生之学，稽《说文》以究达诂，笺《禹贡》以晰地志，固亦深明考据家之说。而论文但崇体要，不尚繁称博引，取其长而不溺其偏，其犹君子慎于择术之道欤！

Song Dynasty, Zhou Dunyi was born in Hunan. His *Diagram Explaining the Supreme Polarity* (*Tai Ji Tu Shuo*) and *Penetrating the Zhou Book of Change* (*Tong Shu*) were also esteemed by later generations. These two great scholars did not imitate previous writing styles. Instead, they made their own unique contributions that put their writing on par with the *Book of Poetry and the Zhou Book of Change*. Talented people who came after them failed to surpass their achievements, not to mention Hunan's younger generation, who has been heavily influenced by their predecessors. About 60 percent of the writings complied in this anthology have a strong basis in the Confucian way, with the remaining 40 percent exhibiting an emotional tone. Elegant writing in the style of rhythmical prose is also included selectively. The lack of a standard writing style does not equate to chaos. However, the proportion of essays dedicated to textual research is lacking, as such essays were not advocated by past sages and are unpopular with later generations. Luo Yansheng has studied the *Origin of Chinese Characters* (*Shuo Wen Jie Zi*) for exegesis, annotated *Yu Gong*, China's oldest known book of geography, for a thorough understanding of topography, and familiarized himself with theories on textual research. He advocates for concise and practical writing instead of excessive quotations. He believes in making the most of people's strengths without accommodating their biases. This is the same reasoning that the superior man uses when cautiously choosing an approach to learning!

奏折

Memorials to the Throne

应诏陈言疏

这篇奏折作于道光三十年（1850）三月初二日。

道光三十年正月十四日，道光皇帝去世，二十岁的奕訢继位，改年号为咸丰。但这一年，仍用道光年号。所以，这篇写于道光三十年三月的奏折，实际上是写给新主咸丰皇帝的。

刚登位的年轻皇帝想有所作为，于是号召大臣们积极上疏言事。身为礼部侍郎的曾国藩响应皇上的号召，一连上了五道有关国计民生，甚至给皇帝本人提意见的奏折。《应诏陈言疏》就是著名的曾氏“五疏”中的一道。

这道奏疏讲的是关于人才的事。曾氏认为，治理国家的第一要务是用人，而现在朝廷内外最缺的是人才。曾氏针对这一严重问题提出三条建议，即转移之道、培养之方、考察之法。

奏为应诏陈言事。

二月初八日奉皇上谕令：“九卿科道有言事之责者，于用人、行政一切事宜，皆得据实直陈，封章密奏。”仰见圣德谦冲，孜孜

Memorial in Response to an Imperial Edict

This memorial to the throne was written on the second day of the third month in the 30th year of Emperor Daoguang's reign (1850).

Emperor Daoguang passed away on the 14th day of the first month in the 30th year of his reign (1850). He was succeeded to the throne by twenty-year-old Yizhu, who adopted the reign title "Xianfeng." Written more than one month after the death of Emperor Daoguang, this memorial was actually intended for Emperor Xianfeng.

Having just ascended the throne, the young emperor was determined to make a difference and thus called on his ministers to submit memorials on various matters. As the Vice Minister of Rites, Zeng Guofan responded to the emperor by writing five memorials concerning the national economy and the people's livelihood, even going so far as to advise the emperor in person. This was the first of Zeng Guofan's five famous memorials.

The following memorial to the throne discusses talented people. Zeng Guofan believed that the first priority for governing a country should be making the best use of its officials, yet talented people were exactly what the imperial court and the government at large were lacking. Consequently, he proposed three areas of focus: modeling behavior, development, and examinations.

This memorial is submitted in response to an imperial edict.

In accordance with the emperor's decree of the eighth day of the second month, the nine Great Ministers of State, the six officials at the Department of Supervision, and the 15 provincial-level supervisory officials across the country are expected to speak frankly by means of confidential memorials about all matters

求治。臣窃维用人、行政，二者自古皆相提并论。独至我朝，则凡百庶政，皆已著有成宪，既备既详，未可轻议。今日所当讲求者，惟在用人一端耳。方今人才不乏，欲作育而激扬之，端赖我皇上之妙用。大抵有转移之道，有培养之方，有考察之法，三者不可废一，请为我皇上陈之。

所谓转移之道，何也？我朝列圣为政，大抵因时俗之过而矫之，使就于中。顺治之时，疮痍初复，民志未定，故圣祖继之以宽；康熙之末，久安而吏弛，刑措而民偷，故世宗救之以严。乾隆、嘉庆之际，人尚才华，士骛高远，故大行皇帝敛之以镇静，以变其浮夸之习。一时人才循循规矩准绳之中，无有敢才智自雄、锋芒自逞者。然有守者多，而有猷有为者渐觉其少。大率以畏葸为慎，以柔靡为恭。

concerning the use of talented people and the administration. The imperial edict informs us that Your Majesty is of modest character and committed to good governance. Since ancient times, the use of talented people and the administration have always been discussed together. In the present dynasty, government affairs must be written into established laws that are detailed and hence cannot be discussed carelessly. The focus today should be solely on the use of talented people. There is no shortage of them, but whether they can be developed and allowed to distinguish themselves depends upon the ingenuity of Your Majesty. The three general areas of focus are modeling behavior, development, and examinations, none of which can be neglected. Please allow me to interpret this for Your Majesty.

What is the meaning of modeling behavior? In the present dynasty, the monarch governing the country addressed mistakes that arose from prevailing customs in order to attain the golden mean. During the reign of Emperor Shunzhi, the people had recently recovered from the wounds of war, and popular sentiment was uncertain; thus the emperor governed the people with tolerance and leniency. During the final years of the reign of Emperor Kangxi, the long period of peace and stability encouraged officials to be lax in their duties. Punishments were not issued, causing the people to become lazy. Thus, Emperor Yongzheng attempted to remedy the situation through strict measures. During the reigns of Emperor Qianlong and Emperor Jiaqing, literary talents were admired, causing scholars to be overambitious. Therefore, Emperor Daoguang restrained them with calmness in order to correct the harmful atmosphere of exaggeration. Talented people strictly abided by conventions, and no one dared to boast of their brilliance. As a result, talented people became conservative and few were proactive. They grew to equate timidity with caution and gentleness with respect.

以臣观之，京官之办事通病有二，曰退缩，曰琐屑。外官之办事通病有二，曰敷衍，曰颟顸。退缩者，同官互推，不肯任怨，动辄请旨，不肯任咎是也。琐屑者，利析锱铢，不顾大体，察及秋毫，不见舆薪是也。敷衍者，装头盖面，但计目前剜肉补疮，不问明日是也。颟顸者，外面完全，而中已溃烂，章奏粉饰，而语无归宿是也。有此四者，习俗相沿，但求苟安无过，不求振作有为。将来一有艰巨，国家必有乏才之患。我大行皇帝深知此中之消息，故亟思得一有用之才，以力挽颓风。去年京察人员，数月之内，擢臬司者三人，擢藩司者一人。盖亦欲破格超迁，整顿积弱之习也。无如风会所趋，势难骤变。今若遽求振作之才，又恐躁竞者因而幸进，转不足以收实效。

臣愚以为，欲使有用之才不出范围之中，莫若使之从事于学

In my humble opinion, officials who work in the capital are prone to two common failings: recoiling from work and focusing on the trivial. Local government officials also suffer from two common failings: being indifferent and being careless. Those who recoil from work shift their responsibilities onto colleagues, refuse to do more than the minimum, frequently request imperial edicts, and do not assume blame. Those who focus on the trivial are calculating and fail to see the bigger picture because they are mired in the details. Those who are indifferent handle busy work instead of dealing with important matters, regardless of long-term interests. Those who are careless pretend that everything is fine when they know that their work is a complete shambles. Their memorials to the throne simulate peace and posterity but lack any substance. Officials who suffer from these four common failings may pass them down to others as these failings become accepted; they seek only ease and comfort without assuming any responsibility or stirring themselves to action. When difficult times arise, the country will lack enough talented people to address them. With this realization, Emperor Daoguang urgently sought outstanding people to reverse these negative practices. Within a few months last year, three officials were promoted to provincial prosecutors upon examination by the imperial government, and one official was promoted to provincial treasurer in order to make exceptions that allowed talented people to distinguish themselves and address deep-rooted negative practices. Unfortunately, ingrained habits are difficult to break and thus cannot be reversed quickly. Today, if people are quickly appointed to important positions, there is a chance that some of them may be opportunistic, which would not have the desired effect.

In my humble opinion, if an emperor wants to make the best use of talented people who will not go beyond the laws and regu-

术。汉臣诸葛亮曰："才须学，学须识。"盖至论也。然欲人才皆知好学，又必自我皇上以身作则，乃能操转移风化之本。臣考圣祖仁皇帝登极之后，勤学好问，儒臣逐日进讲，寒暑不辍；万寿圣节，不许间断；三藩用兵，亦不停止；召见廷臣，辄与之往复讨论。故当时人才济济，好学者多。至康熙末年，博学伟才，大半皆圣祖教谕而成就之。今皇上春秋鼎盛，正与圣祖讲学之年相似。臣之愚见，欲请俟二十七月后，举行逐日进讲之例。四海传播，人人响风。召见臣工，与之从容论难。见无才者，则勖之以学，以痛惩模棱罢软之习；见有才者，则愈勖之以学，以化其刚愎刻薄之偏。十年以后，人才必大有起色。一人典学于宫中，群英鼓舞于天下，其幾在此，其效在彼。康熙年间之往事，昭昭可

lations, it would be best to encourage them to engage in learning. Zhuge Liang, a minister in the Han Dynasty, remarked, "Competence requires learning, and learning requires knowledge." This is very apt. However, if an emperor would like talented people to be studious, he himself must set an example that lays the foundation for a positive change in the culture. After Emperor Kangxi ascended the throne, I observed his diligence and curiosity. Confucian scholars gave daily lectures in the imperial court regardless of the weather. This practice never stopped, not even for the emperor's birthday celebrations or in wartime. He would also summon ministers for repeated discussions on areas of learning. As a result, a wealth of talent emerged and the number of diligent scholars grew. In the final years of Emperor Kangxi's reign, the majority of learned officials serving at their posts had been cultivated by him. Your Majesty is in the prime of life and about the same age as Emperor Kangxi when he listened to lectures by Confucian scholars. In my humble opinion, Your Majesty should resume Kangxi's old practices for daily improvement after 27 months. [1] People will quickly follow Your Majesty's example when they hear the news. Your Majesty can summon officials to the court for leisurely consultations on difficult issues. Your Majesty can encourage people without talent to embrace learning and take stern measures to address indifference and carelessness; Your Majesty can encourage people with talent to further embrace learning to correct any obstinacy and harshness. Within ten years, the issue of talented people will have improved greatly. One person advocating learning from the imperial palace will inspire multitudes of outstanding people across the country. It begins here and then ripples throughout the land. The influence of Emperor Kangxi is still clearly evi-

1 In the Qing Dynasty, officials who suffered the loss of their parents were expected to observe a mourning period of 27 months. Emperor Xianfeng also observed a period of mourning for his late father, Emperor Daoguang.

观也。以今日之委靡因循，而期之以振作；又虑他日更张偾事，而泽之以《诗》《书》。但期默运而潜移，不肯矫枉而过正。盖转移之道，其略如此。

所谓培养之方，何也？凡人才未登仕版者，姑不具论。其已登仕版者，如内阁、六部、翰林院最为荟萃之地，将来内而卿相，外而督抚，大约不出此八衙门。此八衙门者，人才数千，我皇上不能一一周知也。培养之权，不得不责成于堂官。所谓培养者，约有数端：曰教诲，曰甄别，曰保举，曰超擢。堂官之于司员，一言嘉奖，则感而图功；片语责惩，则畏而改过。此教诲之不可缓也。榛棘不除，则兰蕙减色；害马不去，则骐骥短气。此甄别之不可缓也。嘉庆四年、十八年，两次令部院各保司员，此保举之成案也。雍正年间，甘汝来以主事而赏人参，放知府；嘉庆年间，黄钺以主事而充翰林，入南斋。此超擢之成案也。盖尝

dent. Despite the despondency and stagnancy that prevail today, we can look forward to a future created by talented people. In order to prevent the negative effects of arrogance, we can enlighten talented people with the *Book of Poetry* and the *Book of Documents*. However, we should exert subtle influence on their character rather than being heavy-handed. This is modeling behavior.

How should talented people be developed? Let us put aside any discussion about talented people who have yet to enter officialdom. Those who have already become officials tend to be concentrated in the cabinet, the Six ministries, and Hanlin Academy. In the future, ministers and governors will mostly come from the aforementioned eight government offices. Thousands of talented people fill their ranks, making it impossible for Your Majesty to know them all. The responsibility for their development must be entrusted to superior officials in government offices. [1] Development is focused on the following areas: education, screenings, recommendations, and promotions. A word of praise from a senior official may encourage a subordinate to strive for success; a word of criticism may inspire fear and compel him to correct his faults. This type of education cannot be underestimated. The brambles will overrun the orchid if not pulled out; the black sheep will bring down the whole flock if not removed. This type of screening cannot be undervalued. In the fourth and the 18th years of Emperor Jiaqing's reign (1799 and 1813, respectively), the ministries and branches of government were ordered to recommend subordinate officials, thus setting a precedent for future recommendations. During the reign of Emperor Yongzheng, Gan Rulai was rewarded with ginseng for his work and given the position of prefectural magistrate. During the reign of Emperor Jiaqing, Huang Yue was appointed to Hanlin Academy as a reward for his work and served

1 Here, "superior officials" refer to those who are in charge of the ministries of the imperial government.

论之，人才譬之禾稼，堂官之教诲犹种植耘耔也。甄别则去其稂莠也，保举则犹灌溉也。皇上超擢，譬之甘雨时降，苗勃然兴也；堂官常到署，譬之农夫日日田间，乃能熟悉穑事也。今各衙门堂官，多内廷行走之员，或累月不克到署，与司员恒不相习，自掌印、主稿数人而外，大半不能识面，譬之嘉禾、稂莠，听其同生同落于畎亩之中，而农夫不问。教诲之法无闻，甄别之例亦废。近奉明诏保举，又但及外官，而不及京秩，培养之道，不尚有未尽者哉！自顷岁以来，六部人数日多，或二十年不得补缺，或终身不得主稿；内阁、翰林院员数亦三倍于前，往往十年不得一差，不迁一秩，固已英才摧挫矣。而堂官又多在内廷，终岁不获一见，如吏部六堂，内廷四人；礼部六堂，内廷四人；户部六堂，皆直内廷；翰林两掌院，皆直内廷。在诸臣随侍御园，本难分身入署，而又或兼摄两部，或管理数处。为司员者，画稿则匆匆一面，白事则寥寥数语，纵使才德俱优，曾不能邀堂官之一顾，又焉能达天子之知哉！以若干之人才，近在眼前，不能加意培养，甚可惜也。臣之愚见，欲请皇上稍为酌量，每部须有三四堂不入直内廷者，令其日日到署，以与司员相砥砺。翰林掌院亦须有不直内廷者，令其与编、检相濡染，务使属官之性情、心术，长官一一周

the emperor at the Southern Study.[1] These are precedents for promotions. In my humble opinion, talented people may be compared to crops. Educating them is similar to cultivating plants; screening them is similar to weeding; recommending them is similar to irrigation; and the emperor promoting them is similar to the rainfall that allows crops to flourish. Superior officials often visit government departments, just as farmers tend daily to their fields to become familiar with their crops. Nowadays, most superior officials serve in positions at the imperial court and may spend months without setting foot in government offices. They are unfamiliar with their subordinates and only recognize the faces of the few who hold power or are chief writers. This is just like the farmer who cares not whether wheat or weeds grow in his fields. Education is no longer mentioned, and examples of screening have disappeared. Recently, an imperial edict was issued regarding the recommendation of officials; however, it only pertained to officials serving outside the capital. Development has yet to be applied to all talented people! In recent years, the ranks of officials working in the Six ministries have been growing. Some may wait decades for a post with any real power or spend a lifetime waiting for the position of chief drafter. The number of officials serving in the cabinet and at Hanlin Academy has grown threefold. Some officials may wait over a decade for an assignment or a promotion. Consequently, talented people have become frustrated. Most superior officials work at the imperial court without ever showing their faces at their department offices. For example, four of the six superior officials in the Ministry of Personnel are posted at the imperial court, and the same is true of the Ministry of Rites. The six superior officials in the Ministry of Revenue all serve at the im-

1 The Southern Study was where emperors (from Emperor Kangxi onwards) of the Qing Dynasty consulted with courtiers on major decisions.

知。皇上不时询问，某也才，某也直，某也小知，某也大受，不特属官之优劣粲然毕呈，即长官之深浅亦可互见。旁考参稽，而八衙门之人才，同往来于圣主之胸中。彼司员者，但令姓名达于九重，不必升官迁秩，而已感激无地矣。然后保举之法，甄别之例，次第举行乎旧章。皇上偶有超擢，则楩楠一升，而草木之精神皆振。盖培养之方，其略如此。

所谓考察之法，何也？古者询事、考言，二者并重。近来各

perial court. And the two chancellors of Hanlin Academy are both posted at the imperial court. Superior officials have little time to spare for working in their own departments, and some are even responsible for two or more departments. Lower-level officials may only see their superiors long enough to ask for a signature to endorse a document or to make a simple report. How can a talented and virtuous lower-level official become known to the emperor if he has no opportunity to even speak with his superiors! It is a pity that there is not an abundance of talented people close at hand that we can develop. I would humbly ask that Your Majesty consider requiring every department to retain three or four superior officials who work together with their subordinates daily at their government offices rather than work at the imperial court. Only one of the chancellors of Hanlin Academy should work at the imperial court; the other should be immersed in the work of editors and reviewers so as to learn the temperament and intentions of their subordinates. From time to time, I humbly suggest that Your Majesty question superior officials to determine if any of their subordinates show talent, exhibit a strong moral character, appear knowledgeable, or are prepared to assume larger responsibilities. In this way, Your Majesty can measure not only the quality of lower-level officials but also the capabilities of their superiors. These indirect assessments and cross-checks provide Your Majesty with a clear understanding of the talented people in the eight government offices. Even without a promotion, lower-level officials will be utterly grateful that Your Majesty is familiar with their names. Thus, recommendations and screenings will conform to traditional regulations. If Your Majesty occasionally promotes a man of tremendous promise so that he skips a few ranks, ordinary officials will be motivated by his promotion. This is development.

How should examinations be administered? In ancient times,

衙门办事，小者循例，大者请旨。本无才猷之可见，则莫若于言考之。而召对陈言，天威咫尺，又不宜喋喋便佞，则莫若于奏折考之矣。国家定例，内而九卿科道，外而督抚藩臬，皆有言事之责。各省道员，不许专折谢恩，而许专折言事。乃十余年间，九卿无一人陈时政之得失，司道无一折言地方之利病，相率缄默，一时之风气，有不解其所以然者。科道间有奏疏，而从无一言及主德之隆替，无一折弹大臣之过失，岂君为尧、舜之君，臣皆稷、契之臣乎？一时之风气，亦有不解其所以然者。臣考本朝以来，匡言主德者，孙嘉淦以自是规高宗，袁铣以寡欲规大行皇帝，皆

an official's work and speech were equally important areas of examination. In recent years, government offices have handled routine matters by following established rules and requested imperial instructions when dealing with important business. As talent cannot be demonstrated through routine matters, it would be better to examine an official based on his speech. When called to make a statement before the emperor, however, officials are too intimidated to speak freely, thus examining their memorials to the throne would be more effective. According to national regulations, the officials who have a responsibility to submit memorials to the throne include the nine Great Ministers of State, the six Investigating Censors of the Censorate, the 15 provincial-level supervisory officials who work at the imperial court, as well as governors, provincial treasurers, and provincial judges who work outside the imperial court. Provincial-level intendants are not allowed to submit memorials of gratitude, but they are allowed to submit memorials about business. However, it has been more than a decade since any of the nine Great Ministers of State has explained the successes and failures of the current political situation or since any official from the provincial government has submitted a memorial to discuss the advantages and disadvantages of local government affairs. Everyone has remained silent. Nobody knows how this type of atmosphere developed. Officials have submitted memorials, but none has addressed the state of the emperor's moral conduct or impeached high-ranking officials. Could it be that the emperor is as flawless as Emperors Yao and Shun and the ministers are as virtuous as Houji and Xie? [1] Nobody understands how this type of atmosphere developed. In the present dynasty, the officials who have addressed the moral character of the emperor include Sun Jiagan, who advised Emperor Qianlong against believing he was

1 Houji and Xie were virtuous and sagacious ministers during the reigns of Emperors Yao and Shun, respectively.

蒙优旨嘉纳，至今传为美谈。纠弹大臣者，如李之芳参劾魏裔介，彭鹏参劾李光地，厥后四人，皆为名臣，亦至今传为美谈。自古直言不讳，未有盛于我朝者也。今皇上御极之初，又特诏求言，而褒答倭仁之谕，臣读之至于抃舞感泣。此诚太平之象。然臣犹有过虑者，诚见我皇上求言甚切，恐诸臣纷纷入奏，或者条陈庶政，颇多雷同之语，不免久而生厌；弹劾大臣，惧长攻讦之风，又不免久而生厌。臣之愚见，愿皇上坚持圣意，借奏折为考核人才之具，永不生厌斁之心。涉于雷同者，不必交议而已；过于攻讦者，不必发钞而已。此外则但见其有益，初不见其有损。人情狃于故常，大抵多所顾忌。如主德之隆替，大臣之过失，非皇上再三诱之使言，谁肯轻冒不韪？如藩臬之奏事，道员之具折，虽

infallible, and Yuan Xian, who advised Emperor Daoguang against being self-indulgent. Their advice was met with the emperors' approval, and their stories have been passed down with admiration. As for the impeachment of high-ranking officials, Li Zhifang impeached Wei Yijie, and Peng Peng impeached Li Guangdi. All four eventually became well-known, and their stories have been passed down for generations. This tradition of candor has not flourished as much among officials in the present dynasty. Just after ascending the throne, Your Majesty issued a special imperial edict soliciting advice and responded with praise to Woren, the Grand Secretary of Hanlin Academy. Reading Your Majesty's response excited and moved me to tears. This is truly a prospect for peace. However, I am still anxious. Your Majesty is sincere about soliciting advice, but I worry that the number of memorials being submitted and the proportion of similar views on government and politics being expressed might become tedious for Your Majesty. I also worry that the impeachment of high-ranking officials may encourage a negative atmosphere that might discourage Your Majesty. I hope that Your Majesty will persist in your original intentions and use the memorials as a gauge for appraising talented people without becoming disgusted or irritated. Memorials that echo each other need not be passed on to the departments concerned for discussion; memorials written to disparage specific officials need not be copied and sent to government departments. Apart from this, look at the benefits of the memorials and ignore those aspects which might be harmful. Human feelings are bound by conventions so that most people have scruples. Officials will avoid offering opinions on the moral conduct of Your Majesty and the faults of high-ranking officials unless repeatedly encouraged to do so by Your Majesty. Although rules and regulations exist for provincial treasurers and provincial judges to submit memorials to

有定例，久不遵行，非皇上再三迫之使言，又谁肯立异以犯督抚之怒哉？臣亦知内外大小，群言并进，即浮伪之人，不能不杂出其中。然无本之言，其术可以一售，而不可以再试，明鉴高悬，岂能终遁！方今考九卿之贤否，但凭召见之应对；考科道之贤否，但凭三年之京察；考司道之贤否，但凭督抚之考语。若使人人建言，参互质证，岂不更为核实乎？臣所谓考察之法，其略如此。三者相需为用，并行不悖。

臣本愚陋，顷以议礼一疏，荷蒙皇上天语褒嘉，感激思所以报。但憾识见浅薄，无补万一。伏求皇上怜其愚诚，俯赐训示，幸甚。谨奏。

the throne and for provincial-level intendants to make proposals, they have not been followed for a long time. Without the repeated encouragement of Your Majesty, who would be willing to offer their opinion and draw the ire of the governors by attracting too much attention! As officials of various ranks working in different areas within the government submit proposals to Your Majesty, some impulsive and hypocritical officials will inevitably be among them. Groundless advice may be offered once but never twice. Your Majesty is like an impartial and wise judge. How could those who have promoted falsehoods be allowed to escape? Currently the nine Great Ministers of State are appraised during interviews based only on their responses; provincial-level Imperial Censors who work in Beijing are appraised by an examination once every three years; provincial treasurers, provincial judges, and provincial-level intendants are appraised based on the comments of their governors. Wouldn't this process be more accurate if everyone offered advice and consulted with one another? This is what is meant by examination. Modeling behavior, development, and examinations should be combined to work in coordination. They are not mutually exclusive.

I am ignorant and backward. Having been commended by Your Majesty for a recent memorial to the throne, I felt such gratitude that I have been thinking of ways to repay Your Majesty's grace. It is regretful that I lack enough experience to be helpful. I entreat Your Majesty to show mercy on my foolishness, and I await Your Majesty's instructions. I hereby respectfully submit this memorial to the throne.

备陈民间疾苦疏

这道奏折写于咸丰元年（1851）十二月十八日。

这是曾氏“五疏”中的另一疏，奏疏将当时民间的三大疾苦告诉初执国政的皇帝。

第一大疾苦是银价太昂，钱粮难纳。百姓向官府纳税，不能纳实物，要折算成银子，而银价日涨，百姓负担也便加重。第二大疾苦是盗贼太众，良民难以生存。第三大疾苦是冤狱太多，民气难伸。

曾氏借此提醒皇帝，须存爱民之心，应革除弊政，以抒民间困难，以图社会安宁。

奏为备陈民间疾苦，仰副圣主爱民之怀事。

臣窃闻国贫不足患，惟民心涣散，则为患甚大。自古莫富于隋文之季，而忽致乱亡，民心去也；莫贫于汉昭之初，而渐致乂安，能抚民也。我朝康熙元年至十六年，中间惟一年无河患，其

Memorial on the People's Hardships

This memorial to the throne was written on the 18th day of the 12th month in the first year of Emperor Xianfeng's reign (1851).

One of Zeng Guofan's five famous memorials, it provided the emperor, who had newly taken charge of state affairs, with a detailed explanation of the three major hardships that people faced.

The first major hardship was the excessive land tax caused by the high price of silver. Since land taxes could not be paid with goods, people had to exchange goods for silver. As the price of silver increased, the burden on the people grew heavier. The second major hardship was the proliferation of thieves, which made it difficult for law-abiding people to make a living. The third major hardship was the escalation in unjust verdicts, which stifled people's morale.

Zeng Guofan viewed this memorial as an opportunity to remind the emperor of his responsibility to take care of the people and reform bad policies in order to improve their circumstances and promote a peaceful society.

This memorial was prepared to provide details about the people's hardships in response to Your Majesty's desire to improve their lives.

I have heard that rather than worrying about poverty in our country, we should be concerned about calamities brought about by declining public morale. The latter years of Emperor Wen of the Sui Dynasty's reign are considered the greatest period of prosperity, but a sudden upheaval brought about by the people's declining morale caused the dynasty to fall; the early years of Han Emperor Zhao's reign are considered the greatest period of poverty, but the government was able to gradually bring about social stability by

余岁岁河决，而新庄、高堰各案，为患极巨。其时又有三藩之变，骚动九省，用兵七载，天下财赋去其大半，府藏之空虚，殆有甚于今日。卒能金瓯无缺，寰宇清谧，盖圣祖爱民如伤，民心固结而不可解也。我皇上爱民之诚，足以远绍前徽。特外间守令，或玩视民瘼，致圣主之德意不能达于民，而民间之疾苦不能诉于上。臣敢一一缕陈之：

一曰银价太昂，钱粮难纳也。苏、松、常、镇、太钱粮之重，甲于天下。每田一亩，产米自一石五六斗至二石不等。除去佃户平分之数与抗欠之数，计业主所收，牵算不过八斗。而额征之粮已在二斗内外，兑之以漕斛，加之以帮费，又须各去米二斗。计

pacifying the common people. From the first through the sixteenth year of Emperor Kangxi's reign (1661-1677), the Yellow River flooded every year but one, with the worst flooding occurring in the Gaoyan and Xinzhuang areas of Huai'an. During the same period, there was the revolt of the three feudatories,[1] which affected nine provinces and launched seven years of armed conflict. The majority of the country's wealth was consumed, and the central treasury was even emptier than it is today. Fortunately, territorial integrity was restored, and peace washed over the land. This was due in large part to Emperor Kangxi's deep concern for the people, which strengthened their morale. Your Majesty's concern for the people follows a glorious precedent set by previous emperors. However, prefects and county heads may underestimate the importance of addressing people's hardships. Consequently, Your Majesty's grace fails to reach the people, and the people's hardships cannot be communicated to Your Majesty.

Allow me to explain the people's hardships one by one. The first is the exorbitant land tax caused by the high price of silver. The land tax in Suzhou, Songjiang, Changzhou, Zhenjiang, and Taicang is the highest in the country. One *mu* of paddy field produces about 1.5-2.0 *dan*[2] of rice. After deducting the tenant's share and the amount that some tenants refuse to pay, the average production rate of rice is only eight *dou*[3] per *mu*[4]. According to quotas, the grain to be collected by the government is about two *dou*, and the water transport cost for the rice plus the subsidy paid to the transporters amount to about four *dou*. As such, the landowners are required to pay the government six *dou* of rice per *mu* of pad-

1 The revolt was led by Wu Sangui in Yunnan Province, Shang Kexi in Guangdong Province, and Geng Jingzhong in Fujian Province.

2 *Dan* is a unit of dry measure. One *dan* equals ten *dou* and one *dou* equals ten *sheng* (liter). .

3 *Dou* is a unit of dry measure. One dou equals ten *sheng* (liter).

4 *Mu* is a unit of area. One *mu* equals 1/15 of a hectare.

每亩所收八斗，正供已输其六，业主只获其二耳。然使所输之六斗，皆以米相交纳，则小民犹为取之甚便。无如收本色者少，收折色者多。即使漕粮或收本色，而帮费必须折银，地丁必须纳银。

小民力田之所得者米也。持米以售钱，则米价苦贱而民怨；持钱以易银，则银价苦昂而民怨。东南产米之区，大率石米买钱三千，自古迄今，不甚悬远。昔日两银换钱一千，则石米得银三两。今日两银换钱两千，则石米仅得银两五钱。昔日卖米三斗，输一亩之课而有余。今日卖米六斗，输一亩之课而不足。朝廷自守岁取之常，小民暗加一倍之赋。此外如房基，如坟地，均须另纳税课。准以银价，皆倍昔年。无力监追者，不可胜计。州县竭全力以催科，犹恐不给，往往委员佐之，吏役四出，昼夜追比，鞭朴满堂，血肉狼籍，岂皆酷吏之为哉！不如是，则考成不及七

dy field, leaving only two *dou* of rice per *mu* left over for themselves. It would be convenient for the landowners to pay the land tax with six *dou* of rice. However, only a small part of the land tax can be paid with goods, as most of it must be paid in silver. Even if landlords were allowed to fulfill the rice quota with rice, the subsidy to the transporters, the land tax and corvee must all be paid in silver.

People labor in the paddy fields to harvest rice. When exchanging rice for money, they feel resentful if they must sell the rice at too low a price. When exchanging money for silver, they feel resentful if the price of silver is too high. In the southeast where rice is grown, one *dan* of rice can be sold for 3,000 coppers (copper coins), which has generally been the price since ancient times. In the past, one tael of silver was worth 1,000 coppers, so one *dan* of rice could be sold for three taels of sliver. Today, one tael of silver is worth 2,000 coppers, thus one *dan* of rice can only be sold for 1.5 taels of sliver. In the past, the price for three *dou* of rice was more than enough to cover the land tax of one *mu* of paddy field. Today, the price of six *dou* of rice is not enough to cover the land tax of one *mu* of paddy field. Although the imperial court has kept the annual land tax unchanged, the tax burden on ordinary people has doubled. In addition, a homestead, including the site of a grave, also comes with a tax that must be paid in silver, which is now worth twice the amount of rice as before. Countless people are no longer capable of paying the land tax. Local governments at the prefecture and county levels spare no effort to collect taxes and often entrust a group of people to help. Government clerks are everywhere, collecting taxes day and night. Those who fail to pay are whipped in government halls. This is what oppressive officials do! If government officials fail to collect at least 70 percent of taxes, they might be impeached and have to make compensations of

分，有参劾之惧，赔累动以巨万，有子孙之忧。故自道光十五年以前，江苏尚办全漕，自十六年至今，岁岁报歉，年年蠲缓，岂昔皆良而今皆刁！盖银价太昂，不独官民交困，国家亦受其害也。

浙江正赋与江苏大略相似，而民愈抗延，官愈穷窘，于是有"截串"之法。"截串"者，上忙而预征下忙之税，今年而预截明年之串。小民不应，则稍减其价，招之使来。预截太多，缺分太亏，后任无可复征，使循吏亦无自全之法，则贪吏愈得借口鱼肉百姓，巧诛横索，悍然不顾。江西、湖广课额稍轻，然自银价昂贵以来，民之完纳愈苦，官之追呼亦愈酷。或本家不能完，则锁拿同族之殷实者而责之代纳，甚者或锁其亲戚，押其邻里。百姓怨愤，则抗拒而激成巨案。如湖广之耒阳、崇阳，江西之贵溪、

up to tens of thousands of taels of silver. Even their descendants may be implicated. Fifteen years ago, Jiangsu Province handled all water transportation. Prior to the 15th year of Emperor Daoguang's reign (1835), Jiangsu Province was still able to successfully handle the rice transport business. Since then, however, Jiangsu has reported a failure to collect taxes every year. It has applied to reduce taxation and postpone the deadline for tax collection every year. Is this because the people of Jiangsu are less upright than they once were? It is because the price of silver is too high, making times difficult not only for the government and the people but also for the country at large.

The situation in Zhejiang Province is much like that in Jiangsu. As more people resist and delay tax payments, the circumstances of local governments become direr, thus giving rise to the concept of *jie chuan* (literally, cutting a tax receipt). Under this concept, local governments seek to collect taxes anywhere from six to 12 months in advance. If taxpayers refuse to comply, local governments reduce tax rates to encourage swift compliance. An excess of advanced tax payments exacerbate shortages, leaving no opportunity for future officials to collect taxes and no way for upright officials to cope. As a result, corrupt officials feel justified in bleeding the people dry through ruthless taxation. Tax quotas are slightly lower in Jiangxi, Hunan, and Hubei; however, the rising price of silver makes it increasingly difficult for people to pay their taxes, leading local governments to institute harsher measures for collecting taxes. If a family is unable to pay in full, the local government may seize well-off members of the extended family and force them to pay instead. Sometimes, local governments even detain relatives and neighbors of those unable to pay. Increased resentment has spawned resistance in the form of major crimes. For example, there are the Leiyang and Chongyang cases in Hunan and Hubei and the Guixi and Fuzhou cases in Jiangxi. Although

抚州，此四案者，虽闾阎不无刁悍之风，亦由银价之倍增，官吏之浮收，差役之滥刑，真有日不聊生之势。臣所谓民间之疾苦，此其一也。

二曰盗贼太众，良民难安也。庐、凤、颍、亳一带，自古为群盗之薮。北达丰、沛、萧、砀，西接南、汝、光、固，此皆天下腹地。一有啸聚，患且不测。近闻盗风益炽，白日劫淫，捉人勒赎，民不得已而控官。官将往捕，先期出示，比至其地，牌保辄诡言盗遁。官吏则焚烧附近之民房，示威而后去；差役则讹索事主之财物，满载而后归，而盗实未遁也。或诡言盗死，毙他囚以抵此案，而盗实未死也。案不能雪，赃不能起，而事主之家已破矣。吞声饮泣，无力再控。即使再控，幸得发兵会捕，而兵役平日皆与盗通，临时卖放，泯然无迹；或反借盗名以恐吓村愚，

the people involved may be considered cunning and fierce, one must also remember that the doubling of the price of silver, the over-collection of taxes, and the imposition of excessive penalties have made it impossible for people to make a living. This is one of the people's major hardships.

The second is the proliferation of thieves and robbers, which threatens the peace that law-abiding people seek. Since ancient times, Luzhou, Fengyang, Yingzhou, and Bozhou [1] have served as breeding grounds for bandits. The region that includes Feng, Pei, Xiao, and Dangshan counties [2] in the north, and Nanyang, Ruyang, Guangzhou, and Gushi counties [3] in the west form the heart of our country. The gathering of bandits in this region would invite disaster. Robberies and thefts have grown rampant, and locals have reported that these and other crimes, such as rape and kidnapping, have occurred in broad daylight. Local governments dispatch officers to make arrests and post-arrest announcements; however, local chiefs cover for criminals and allow them to evade capture. Officers respond by setting nearby homes alight to put on a show of force, and then they leave. Officers seize stolen property and return home with their hands full, never informing victims that the perpetrators were caught. Officers execute prisoners on death row, deceiving victims into believing that they were the criminals convicted in their cases. Crimes remain unsolved, stolen goods cannot be recovered, and victims lose everything. They must stomach the injustice as they are powerless to submit another appeal. In those cases that do elicit a proper response that ends in an arrest, the criminals are released in return for a bribe because criminals often

1 Luzhou Prefecture (present-day Hefei City), Fengyang County, Yingzhou Prefecture (present-day Fuyang City), and Bozhou County (present-day Bozhou City) are located in Anhui Province.

2 Feng County and Pei County are in present-day Xuzhou City, Jiangsu Province; Xiao County and Dangshan County are in present-day Suzhou City, Anhui Province.

3 Nanyang County (present-day Nanyang City), Ruyang County (present-day Runan County), Guangzhou County, and Gushi County are located in Henan Province.

要索重贿，否则，指为盗伙，火其居而械系之；又或责成族邻，勒令缚盗来献，直至缚解到县，又复索收押之费，索转解之资。故凡盗贼所在，不独事主焦头烂额，即最疏之戚，最远之邻，大者荡产，小者株系，比比然也。

往者嘉庆川陕之变，盗魁刘之协者，业就擒矣，太和县卖而纵之，遂成大乱。今日之劣兵蠹役，豢盗纵盗，所在皆是，每一念及，可为寒心。臣在刑部见疏防盗犯之稿，日或数十件，而行旅来京言被劫不报，报而不准者，尤不可胜计。南中会匪名目繁多，或十家之中，三家从贼，良民逼处其中，心知其非，亦姑且输金钱、备酒食以供盗贼之求，而买旦夕之安。臣尝细询州县所以讳盗之故，彼亦有难焉者。

move in the same circles as the military personnel who hold them. Indeed, they may even work together to help the criminals disappear. The military intimidates ordinary people and extorts heavy bribes under the guise of catching thieves and robbers. Those who refuse to comply are framed as gangsters, their homes are burned down, and they themselves are imprisoned. The military may even order the relatives and neighbors of those who have been framed to bind and deliver them to the county government and pay the cost of their imprisonment and transportation. Therefore, everyone from the victim of the crime to their most distant relatives and neighbors is made to suffer. At the very worst, the victims lose everything; at the very least, they are implicated in a crime. This phenomenon is commonplace.

Liu Zhixie, the leader of a group of outlaws, was captured in the Sichuan-Shaanxi region during a tumultuous period of Emperor Jiaqing's reign. The Taihe County government accepted a bribe to release him from custody, thus sparking great upheaval. Today, corrupt soldiers are everywhere, willing to overlook or even abet robbers and thieves. How bitterly disappointing. While at the Ministry of Punishment, I saw dozens of documents every day that detailed how lapses in security enabled robbers and thieves to escape. An untold number of visitors from outside Beijing are robbed yet never report the crime or never have their case pursued by the local government. Bandits are so commonplace in the south that as many as three out of every ten families engage in robberies and thefts in some areas. Law-abiding people must find a way to survive amongst them. Good people have no choice but to defy their conscience and provide bandits with money or food and drink in exchange for a short respite. I once delicately questioned county officials about their reticence to investigate robberies and discovered that they had their reasons. When responding

盖初往踩缉，有拒捕之患；解犯晋省，有抢夺之患；层层勘转，道路数百里，有繁重之患；处处需索，解费数百金，有赔累之患；或报盗而不获，则按限而参之，或上司好粉饰，则目为多事而斥之。不如因循讳饰，反得晏然无事。以是愈酿愈多，盗贼横行，而良民更无安枕之日。臣所谓民间之疾苦，此又其一也。

三曰冤狱太多，民气难伸也。臣自署理刑部以来，见京控、上控之件，奏结者数十案，咨结者数百案。惟河南知府黄庆安一案，密云防御阿祥一案，皆审系原告得失，水落石出。此外各件，大率皆坐原告以虚诬之罪，而被告者反得脱然无事。其科原告之罪，援引例文，约有数条：或曰申诉不实，杖一百；或曰蓦越进京告重事不实，发边远军；或曰假以建言为由，挟制官府，发附近军；或曰挟嫌诬告本管官，发烟瘴军。又不敢竟从重办也，则

to a robbery and investigating a crime, they risk being injured by criminals who resist arrest. When escorting criminals to provincial cities, they risk being robbed enroute. They travel hundreds of miles to conduct investigations at multiple levels, which places a heavy burden on their shoulders. They confront extortion at every turn and spend hundreds of taels of silver on escorting prisoners, thus making robbery investigations a losing venture. Some county officials are impeached for reporting a case but failing to make an arrest within a certain timeframe. This contradicts the false image of peace and prosperity that their superiors may like to present. County officials may choose to remain quiet because reporting too many robberies may incur the disapproval of their superiors. Consequently, the number of bandits soars unchecked, creating an increasingly worrisome environment for those who abide by the law. This represents another of the people's major hardships.

The third is the surge in unjust verdicts that inhibit people from venting their grievances. As acting Minister of Punishment, I have found that, among the cases submitted to the provincial and central governments, a few dozen were settled by imperial edicts and several hundred were settled through negotiation. Only the cases of Huang Qing'an, who was the prefectural magistrate of Henan Province, and A Xiang, who was a military guard in Miyun County, were settled through trials that exposed the whole truth, proving the plaintiffs were guilty. In most cases, the plaintiffs were convicted of making false accusations, and the defendants were released. The judgments outlined punishments for those who made false accusations: caning the accuser 100 times if the complaint is proven false; exiling the accuser to a remote area if the complaint is filed in Beijing, bypassing the first level of the judicial process, and is inconsistent with the facts; exiling the accuser to an area near Beijing if he submits advice for the purpose of pressuring

曰怀疑误控，或曰诉出有因。于是有收赎之法，有减等之方，使原告不曲不直，难进难退，庶可免于翻案；而被告则巧为解脱，断不加罪。夫以部民而告官长，诚不可长其刁风矣。若夫告奸吏舞弊，告蠹役作赃，而谓案案皆诬，其谁信之乎？即平民相告，而谓原告皆曲，被告皆直，又谁信之乎？圣明在上，必难逃洞鉴矣。臣考定例所载，民人京控，有提取该省案卷来京核对质讯者，有交督抚审办者，有钦派大臣前往者。近来概交督抚审办，督抚发委首府，从无亲提之事；首府为同寅弥缝，不问事之轻重，一概磨折恫喝，必使原告认诬而后已。风气所趋，各省皆然。一家

local authorities; exiling the accuser to an epidemic-stricken area if he makes false accusations against officials in charge and the local government to satisfy a grudge. Reticent to re-examine cases, some court officials claim to suspect false accusations or admit that there are grounds for an appeal; however, they handle the cases by bailing out people from exile or mitigating their punishment, which puts the accuser in a tough position, being judged neither right nor wrong. Meanwhile, court officials try every means to extricate the defendant and downplay his crime. Suing the officials in charge and the local government cannot be encouraged. However, who will believe that every accusation of fraud, embezzlement, and perversion of the law leveled against officials is judged false? Even in cases that do not involve officials, who would believe that all of the plaintiffs are wrong and all of the defendants are right? Your Majesty sees all and knows all; this surely will not go beyond your insight. After examining cases recorded in laws and regulations, I found that appeals to the imperial government were processed in the following three ways. They were examined in Beijing after provincial courts were ordered to bring their files to the capital. They were entrusted to provincial governors for settlement. And they were settled with the assistance of imperial envoys who had been sent to the provincial capital. Recently, all such cases have been entrusted to provincial governors for examination and settlement; the governors, in turn, entrust the cases to officials in the provincial capital for examination and settlement. Officials in the provincial capital cover up the mistakes of their colleagues by threatening and torturing the plaintiffs, regardless of the seriousness of the case, until they admit that the accusations are false. This atmosphere sits like a cloud over all of the provinces. If one family is bogged down in a long-running lawsuit, then ten will be driven to bankruptcy; if one person is the victim of gross injustice,

久讼，十家破产，一人沉冤，百人含痛。往往有纤小之案，累年不结，颠倒黑白，老死囹圄。令人闻之发指者。臣所谓民间之疾苦，此又其一也。

此三者皆目前之急务。其盗贼太众，冤狱太多二条，求皇上申谕外省，严饬督抚，务思所以更张之。其银价太昂一条，必须变通平价之法。臣谨胪管见，另拟银钱并用章程一折，续行入奏。国以民为本，百姓之颠连困苦，苟有纤毫不得上达，皆臣等之咎也。区区微诚，伏乞圣鉴。谨奏。

then one hundred will end up suffering. There are often very minor cases that remain open for years because the truth has been deliberately distorted, closing only when the accuser passes away in prison. This represents still another of the people's hardships.

All three hardships cry out for solutions. The proliferation of thieves and robbers and the surge in unjust verdicts may be addressed by Your Majesty issuing an imperial edict to local authorities that orders governors to initiate reforms. The exorbitant land tax may be resolved by stabilizing the price of silver. I respectfully voice my humble opinions and offer to draft and submit a memorial on regulations for the acceptance of both silver and cash. The people constitute the foundation of the country. Officials are to blame if Your Majesty is unfamiliar with the hardships of the people. These are my humble opinions. I hereby respectfully submit this memorial to the throne.

遵旨复奏借俄兵助剿发逆并代运南漕折

咸丰十年（1860）八月，英法联军打进北京，咸丰皇帝仓皇逃奔热河避暑山庄。留在北京的恭亲王奕䜣，代表朝廷与英法联军谈判。九月，英法联军退出北京。这就是近代史上的“第二次鸦片战争”。这份奏折便写在如此背景下。

在这道写于咸丰十年十一月初八日的奏折中，身为两江总督的曾国藩，建议朝廷拒绝俄国派兵助剿，而接受代运漕粮的要求，并提出师夷智以造炮制船让国家获永远之利的主张。对于曾氏的建议与主张，朝廷予以接受。朝廷随即下达建立总理各国通商事务衙门之令，并命曾国藩购买洋枪洋炮。从那以后，洋务运动兴起。史学界将此折视为揭开洋务运动序幕的第一份重要文献。

奏为遵旨复陈，仰祈圣鉴事。

Memorial on Russia's Offer to Suppress the Taiping Rebel Army and Transport Northbound Grain in Response to an Imperial Edict

In the eighth month of the tenth year of Emperor Xianfeng's reign (1860), the British and French allied forces entered Beijing, forcing Emperor Xianfeng to flee to the Rehe Mountain Resort. Prince Gong (Yixin) remained in Beijing and represented the imperial court in negotiations with the British and French allied forces, which withdrew from Beijing in the ninth month of that year. This was the Second Opium War in modern Chinese history and the background for this memorial to the throne.

In this memorial dated the eighth day of the 11th month of the tenth year of Emperor Xianfeng's reign (1860), Zeng Guofan exerted his position as Viceroy of Liangjiang to suggest that the imperial court refuse Russia's offer to help suppress the Taiping Rebel Army but accept its offer to help transport grain from the south. He also proposed that the government study Western science and technology, manufacture armaments, and build ships to benefit future generations. The imperial court accepted Zeng's proposals, issued an edict establishing the Office for the General Management of Business Affairs Concerning Various Countries,[1] and ordered Zeng to purchase Western guns and cannons. Historians regard this memorial as the first major document to set the stage for the Westernization Movement.[2]

This memorial was prepared for Your Majesty in response to the following imperial edict.

1 The official name of the Office for the General Management of Business Affairs Concerning Various Countries later became "The Office for the General Management of Affairs Concerning Various Countries", "The Ministry of Foreign Affairs" for short.

2 The Westernization or Western Affairs Movement (c. 1861-1895), also known as the Self-Strengthening Movement, was a period of radical institutional reforms initiated in China during the late Qing dynasty following the military disasters of the Opium Wars.

窃臣于十月二十五日承准军机大臣密寄十月十一日上谕：

本年秋间，嘆、咈两国带兵扑犯都城，业经换约退兵。俄罗斯使臣伊格那替业幅，亦即随后换约。该酋见恭亲王奕䜣等面称，发逆在江南等处横行，请令中国官军于陆路统重兵进剿，该国拨兵三四百名在水路会击，必可得手。又称，明年南漕运京，恐沿途或有阻碍。伊在上海时，有咪国商人及中国粤商，情愿领价采办台米、洋米运津。如令伊寄信上海领事官，将来洋船、沙船均可装载，用俄、咪旗帜，即保无虞等语。中国剿贼、运漕，断无专借资外国之理。惟思江浙地方糜烂，兵力不敷剿办，如借俄兵之力帮同办理，逆贼若能早平，我之元气亦可渐复。但恐该国所贪在利，借口协同剿贼，或格外再有要求，不可不思患预防。咈郎西在京时，亦有此请。着曾国藩等公同悉心体察，如利多害少，

On the 25th day of the tenth month, I received a confidential imperial edict from the Grand Minister of State dated the 11th day of the tenth month.

This past autumn, Great Britain and France led an invasion of Beijing. Eventually, they each signed a treaty agreeing to withdraw their troops, and Ambassador Ignatyev signed a treaty on behalf of Russia soon after. During a meeting with Prince Gong (Yixin) and others, the ambassador warned that the Taiping rebels were dominating southern China and other regions. Therefore, he advised the imperial court to order official government troops to attack the rebel army by land. His country would order 300-400 troops to attack the rebels by sea, assisting the official Chinese army to secure a victory. He further stated that he believed rice would be blocked from being transported to the capital next year. While in Shanghai, some merchants from Guangdong and the United States confided they were willing to approach Taiwan and foreign countries to purchase rice which would be transported to Tianjin. A letter from him to officials at the Shanghai consulate would allow foreign ships and large junks to be loaded to transport the rice. The ships and junks would sail under the Russian and American flags to safeguard their cargo. China has no reason to depend on foreign countries for help suppressing rebels or transporting grain. Jiangsu and Zhejiang provinces have been devastated, and the local military lacks the strength to suppress the rebels; accepting Russian military assistance would accelerate the rebels' defeat and provide our country with time to build up our strength. However, we must understand that Russia is greedy for profit and may have hidden motives for helping us defeat the rebel army. We must take precautions against future troubles. When the French were in Beijing, they extended a similar offer. Zeng Guofan and other officials will weigh the Russian offer. If the benefits outweigh the harm,

尚可为救急之方，即行迅速奏明，候旨定夺。至代运南漕一节，江、浙地方沦陷，明岁能否办理新漕，尚无定议。然漕粮为天庾正供，自不可缺。该酋所称采办运津之说，是否可行？应如何妥议章程办理之处，并着曾国藩、薛焕、王有龄酌量情形，迅速具奏。将此由六百里各密谕知之。钦此。

具仰皇上圣虑周详，驭夷之方，达变之略，无微弗至，钦服莫名。臣就俄酋所陈二事思之。其请拨夷兵三四百名助剿金陵发逆一节。查大西洋暎、咈、咪各国，恃其船坚炮大，横行海上。俄罗斯国都紧接大西洋，所用船炮及所习技艺均足相抗，近始由重洋以通中国。该夷与我向无嫌怨，其请用兵船助剿发逆，自非别有诡谋。康熙年间进攻台湾，曾调荷兰夹板船助剿，亦中国借

the offer may be accepted to meet urgent needs. Their conclusion should be reported promptly to the throne, pending another imperial edict. As for the transportation of grain from the south, Jiangsu and Zhejiang provinces are occupied by the rebel army. The possibility of transporting next year's rice from the south is still unknown. However, it is the primary source of the imperial court's grain storage, which makes it indispensable. The Russian ambassador has proposed purchasing foreign rice and transporting it to Tianjin – is this feasible, and how should we proceed? Zeng Guofan, Xue Huan, [1] and Wang Youling [2] will give due consideration and promptly report their findings to the throne. We shall hereby inform you by express mail delivered at a speed of 600 *li* [3] per day. That is all. [4]

Your Majesty is thoughtful, adept at foreign interactions and flexible tactics, and attentive to detail. I have such great admiration for Your Majesty. I have considered the two issues raised by the Russian ambassador. He proposed dispatching 300-400 Russian troops to help attack and suppress the Taiping rebel army in Jinling [present-day Nanjing]. Our investigation found that strong seagoing warships and large cannons enable Great Britain, France, and the United States to sail the seas without fear. The Russian capital is not far from the Atlantic Ocean, and Russia can compete with other countries in terms of ships, guns, and technical skills. Despite vast distances, Russia has recently begun to communicate with China. No grudges exist between our two countries. Their offer to assist in suppressing the Taiping rebel army appears to be genuine, and a precedent exists for using foreign ships: we attacked Taiwan using Dutch sailing ships during the reign of

1 Xue Huan (1815-1880) was the Minister of Foreign Trade.

2 Wang Youling (1810-1861) was the Governor of Zhejiang.

3 A *li* is a unit of distance. One *li* is roughly equivalent to half a kilometer.

4 The literal translation of "钦此" is "This is the end of the edict."

资夷船之一证。惟长江二千余里，上游安庆、芜湖等处有杨载福、彭玉麟等水师，下游扬州、镇江等处有吴全美、李德麟之水师。臣现又在长沙、吴城等处添造师船，为明年驶赴淮扬之用。是皖、吴官军之单薄在陆而不在水，金陵发逆之横行亦在陆而不在水。此时我之陆军，势不能遽进金陵。若俄夷兵船即由海口上驶，亦未能遂收夹击之效。应请饬下王大臣等，传谕该夷酋，奖其效顺之忱，缓其会师之期。俟陆军克复皖、浙、苏、常各郡后，再由统兵大臣约会该酋，派船助剿。庶在我足以自立，在彼亦乐与有成。咈郎西亦有此请，亦可奖而允之，许其来助，示以和好而无猜，缓其师期，明非有急而来救。自古外夷之助中国，成功之后，每多意外要求。彼时操纵失宜，或致别开嫌隙。似不如先与约定兵船若干只，雇价若干，每船夷兵若干，需月饷若干，军火一切

Emperor Kangxi. However, the Yangtze River is more than 2,000 *li* long. Yang Zaifu and Peng Yulin command navy ships stationed in its upper reaches, specifically, Anqing and Wuhu. Wu Quanmei and Li Delin lead navy ships stationed in its lower reaches, specifically, Yangzhou and Zhenjiang. I am currently building more warships in Changsha, Wucheng, and other places, with an eye on the battlefields in Huaiyang[1] next year. This indicates that official government troops in Anhui and southern Jiangsu are stretched thin across land, not water; conversely, the rebel army in Jinling has a substantial presence on land but not water. At this time, our ground army is unable to recapture Jinling. As such, even if Russian warships enter the Yangtze River from the sea and sail upriver, a pincer attack cannot be executed. Therefore, we should ask the princes and ministers to inform the Russian ambassador that while his enthusiasm for serving our country will be rewarded, the time for joining forces has not yet arrived. Once our official army recaptures Suzhou, Changzhou, and major cities in Anhui and Zhejiang, our commanders-in-chief will meet the ambassador and request that Russian warships assist in suppressing the rebel army. This strategy allows us to remain independent. Russia will be eager to participate in a promising campaign, and France, which has extended a similar offer, will likewise be rewarded if we accept it. Accepting their offer expresses friendship and trust, and delaying the date for joining our forces indicates that we are not simply accepting their assistance because we are cornered. Since ancient times, foreign countries that have successfully helped China in a crisis have issued unexpected requests afterward. In order to avoid unnecessary resentment, it would be better to agree with foreign countries in advance on the number of warships, the cost for using each ship, the number of foreign soldiers on board, the

1 Huaiyang is the name of the region that covers the lower reaches of the Huai and Yangtze Rivers.

经费若干，一一说明。将来助剿时，均由上海粮台支应，庶可免争竞而杜衅端。

至所称咪商领价采米运津一节。江、浙各郡县地方沦陷既多，明年新漕势难赴办。咪商、粤商情愿领价采办台米、洋米，由海道运至津、沽，实亦济变之要着。俄酋既以此为请，似即可因而许之。除粤商采办之米，应由该商自行经理，毋庸插用俄、咪旗帜外，所有咪商采办运津之米，亦请饬薛焕在上海就近与该商订明。粤商领价，须取保户。咪商则听咪酋经理，当可无误要需。为时局计，似亦舍此别无良策。伏乞圣明察酌行之。

抑臣窃有请者，驭夷之道，贵识夷情。以大西洋诸夷论之，暎咭唎狡黠最甚，咈郎西次之，俄罗斯势力大于暎、咈，尝与暎夷争斗，为暎所惮。咪唎坚人性质醇厚，其于中国素称恭顺。道

salaries of foreign soldiers, the cost of munitions, and other issues. The Shanghai commissariat will be responsible for the above-mentioned costs once foreign troops and ships are mobilized to suppress the Taiping rebels. This will prevent unnecessary disputes that may arise in the future.

Next is the matter of the American merchants who have offered to purchase and transport rice north to Tianjin. Since many areas in southern Jiangsu and Zhejiang have fallen into enemy hands, purchasing rice from those areas next year will be difficult. Merchants from the United States and Guangdong are willing to purchase rice from Taiwan and foreign countries and then ship it to the Port of Tianjin.[1] This is an urgent measure of coping with the situation. Since the Russian ambassador has extended his hand, we may accept his offer. Rice purchased by merchants from Guangdong should be transported by those merchants and not loaded on boats sailing under the Russian or American flags. Xue Huan should be directed to meet the American merchants near Shanghai to sign a contract for all the rice they purchase and transport to Tianjin. The contract with the merchants from Guangdong must have a guarantor. The American merchants will be handled by the American ambassador to ensure that the rice is delivered smoothly. This is the best plan in light of the current situation. Your Majesty, please examine and implement it with discretion.

I must respectfully ask for instructions regarding another matter. The key to handling foreigners is to understand their national characteristics. Among the Atlantic countries, Great Britain is the most cunning, followed by France. Russia is more powerful than either France or Great Britain, which it once fought and instilled with dread. The Americans are simple and kind by nature, and they are always respectful and submissive to China. In the 19th

1 The Port of Tianjin was also known as the Port of Tanggu.

光十九年，暎夷因鸦片肇衅之始，兵船闯入广州省河。咪酋曾于参赞大臣杨芳处递禀，愿为居间调处。暎酋义律旋出亲笔，有只求通商、不讨别情等语。是并烟价亦不敢索也。杨芳曾据以入奏，而不敢专主其议。会官军烧抢洋行，误伤咪夷数人，其事遂寝，而夷患遂炽。咸丰三年，贼踞金陵，闻咪酋亦曾于向荣处托人关说，请以兵船助剿。未知向荣曾据以入奏否？暎、咈两夷犯广东省城时，咪酋未尝助逆。上年天津击败夷船时，咪酋即首先赴京换约，并无异词。是咪夷于中国时有效顺之诚，而于暎、咈诸夷，并非固结之党，已可概见。此次俄夷既称咪商情愿领价采米，似可即饬薛焕与咪酋面订章程，妥为筹办。庶几暗杜俄夷见好中国、

year of Emperor Daoguang's reign (1839), at the beginning of the First Opium War, British warships broke the Chinese blockade of the Pearl River in Guangzhou City. The American ambassador sent the ministerial attaché, Yang Fang,[1] an official document expressing his willingness to mediate between Great Britain and China. Charles Elliot, the British representative for trade in China, soon issued a personal letter with the words "only requesting trade relations, not any other business" written in his own handwriting. Elliot did not press for the cost of opium. Yang Fang reported this to the imperial government as he did not dare to make the decision himself. Around this time, official government troops robbed and burned foreign firms, unintentionally injuring a number of Americans. Although things settled down, anxieties about foreign countries continued to build. In the third year of Emperor Xianfeng's reign (1853), the Taiping rebel army occupied Jinling. It was believed that the American ambassador had entrusted an envoy to meet with Xiang Rong[2] and offer to help suppress the rebel army. I do not know whether Xiang Rong reported this to the imperial court. The United States did not participate when Great Britain and France invaded the capital of Guangdong Province, and the American ambassador hurried to Beijing to quickly sign a treaty last year when foreign warships were defeated in Tianjin. These examples prove that the United States is sincere about complying with China and is not an ally of Great Britain, France, and other countries. Since American merchants are willing to purchase rice on our behalf, we can direct Xue Huan to meet with the American ambassador to draw up regulations and make necessary arrangements. This may also prevent Russia from fawning over China in

1 Yang Fang (1770-1846), a native of Songtao County, Guizhou Province, was a famous general in the late Qing Dynasty.

2 Xiang Rong (1792-1856), a native of Daning County, Sichuan Province (present-day Wuxi County of Chongqing Municipality), was a famous general in the late Qing Dynasty.

市德咪夷之心，而咪夷知中国于彼毫无疑忌，或且输诚而昵就于我，未可知也。此次款议虽成，中国岂可一日而忘备？河道既改海运，岂可一岁而不行？如能将此两事妥为经画，无论目前资夷力以助剿、济运，得纾一时之忧；将来师夷智以造炮制船，尤可期永远之利。区区愚虑所及，合并陈明，伏乞皇上圣鉴训示。谨奏。

secret while seeking favor with the United States. This ensures that the United States understands that China harbors no suspicions or hatred toward the United States, thus it may freely engage in a close friendship with China. Although the peace talks have concluded, how can we afford to let down our guard for even a single day? How can sea transportation replace river transportation over the course of just one year? Regardless of how we employ foreign troops to suppress the Taiping rebel army and help with the sea transportation of rice, properly handling these two matters will help alleviate present woes. Moreover, studying the military technology that foreign countries utilize to manufacture armaments and build warships will lead to permanent benefits. I entreat Your Majesty to forgive my ignorance as I await Your Majesty's instructions. I hereby respectfully submit this memorial to the throne.

参翁同书片

这是中国近代官场上的一道著名参折，写于同治元年(1862)正月初十日。它的著名源于两点：

一是参的人非同一般。翁同书官居巡抚，职位已很高了，而且，他的家族名望显赫。他的父亲翁心存，翰林出身，历任工部、户部尚书及体仁阁大学士，在上书房做过二十多年的老师，咸丰帝与恭亲王都是他的学生。翁同书有两个弟弟：大弟同爵官至督抚，小弟同龢状元出身，做过同治、光绪两朝帝师，官至协办大学士。翁同书的儿子后来也成了状元。这就是有名的“两朝帝师、叔侄状元”的江苏常熟翁氏家族。

二是文章水平高。此折深得参折“辣”的要诀，文章虽短，却字字峻厉，掷地作金石声，不容辩驳，亦无力回护。一句“臣职分所在，例应纠参，不敢因翁同书之门第鼎盛瞻顾迁就”，就连有心保护的慈禧也不敢徇私。

Memorial Attachment to Impeach Weng Tongshu

This is a famous memorial that addresses the impeachment of an official in modern China. Written on the 10th day of the first month in the first year of Emperor Tongzhi's reign (1862), the memorial is famous for two reasons.

The first is that the impeached official was no ordinary man. Weng Tongshu served as a provincial governor. He was not only a high-ranking official but also a member of a celebrated family. His father, Weng Xincun, built his reputation at Hanlin Academy and taught for more than two decades at the imperial school, where his students included Emperor Xianfeng and Prince Gong. He also served as the Minister of Works, the Minister of Revenue, and the Grand Secretary of the Tiren Library. Weng Tongshu's two younger brothers were quite accomplished. Weng Tongjue served as a provincial governor, and the youngest brother, Weng Tonghe, gained his reputation by becoming a *zhuangyuan*[1] on the highest imperial examination. He then served as the Imperial Tutor for Emperors Tongzhi and Guangxu, eventually being promoted to Assistant Grand Secretary. Years later, Weng Tongshu's son also became a *zhuangyuan*. Thus, the Wengs of Changshu, Jiangsu Province, were an extraordinarily accomplished family that, in two generations, boasted two imperial tutors and two *zhuangyuan*.

The second is that the quality of the writing is excellent. Sharply written, this brief memorial is merciless in its condemnation of Weng. The writing rings with a force and clarity that makes its claims irrefutable. Zeng states, "It is my duty to impeach and correct Weng Tongshu regardless of the status and splendor of the Weng family." This line was so powerful that even Empress Dowager Cixi, who wanted to intercede on Weng Tongshu's behalf, abandoned her personal stake in the matter.

1 *Zhuangyuan* is the title for the top scorer on the highest imperial examination.

再，前任安徽巡抚翁同书，咸丰八年七月间，梁园之挫，退守定远。维时接任未久，尚可推诿。乃驻定一载，至九年六月，定远城陷，文武官绅殉难甚众。该抚独弃城远遁，逃往寿州，势穷力绌，复倚苗沛霖为声援，屡疏保荐，养痈贻患，绅民愤恨，遂有孙家泰与苗练仇杀之事。逮苗逆围寿，则杀徐立壮、孙家泰、蒙时中以媚苗，而并未解围。

寿城既破，则合博崇武、庆瑞、尹善廷以通苗，而借此脱身。苗沛霖攻陷城池，杀戮甚惨，蚕食日广，翁同书不能殉节，反具疏力保苗逆之非叛，团练之有罪。始则奏称苗练入城并未杀害平民，继则奏称寿州被害及妇女殉节者不可胜计，请饬彭玉麟查明旌恤，已属自相矛盾。至其上年正月奏称苗沛霖之必应诛剿一折

Furthermore, Weng Tongshu, the former provincial governor of Anhui, led his men to be defeated at Liangyuan Town and retreated to Dingyuan County in the seventh month of the eighth year of Emperor Xianfeng's reign (1858). He blamed the failure to perform his duties on the short time he had been at his post. He had been stationed at Dingyuan County for one year before it fell to enemy hands in the sixth month of the ninth year of Emperor Xianfeng's reign (1859). Despite the number of government officials, military officers, and civilians who died fighting for Dingyuan County, Weng Tongshu, the Provincial Governor of Anhui, abandoned them and fled alone to Shouzhou City. When the official government army had almost reached the point of exhaustion, Weng attached himself to Miao Peilin's [1] militia for support. He repeatedly recommended Miao Peilin for promotions, which sowed the seeds of disaster and stirred up the resentment of the gentry and the common people. As a result, Sun Jiatai [2] and Miao Peilin became mortal enemies. When Miao Peilin besieged Shouzhou, Weng killed Xu Lizhuang, Sun Jiatai, and Meng Shizhong to appease him, [3] but it was all for naught.

After Shouzhou was captured, Weng joined Bo Chongwu, Qing Rui, and Yin Shanting to plead with Miao Peilin for their own release. After seizing Shouzhou, Miao Peilin's militia slaughtered residents and gradually expanded its territory. Weng Tongshu chose not to die for his country and took special pains to exonerate Miao Peilin while shifting blame on his militia. Initially, Weng reported that Miao Peilin's militia never killed civilians in Shouzhou. He then contradicted himself by stating that countless civilians had been killed, including women who had killed them-

1 Miao Peilin (?-1863), a native of Fengtai County, Anhui Province, was a militia head in the late Qing Dynasty.

2 Sun Jiatai (1817-1861), a native of Shouzhou County, Anhui Province, was ordered by the imperial government to recruit and train militias in Shouzhou.

3 Xu Lizhuang and Meng Shizhong were both famous squires in Shouzhou County, Anhui Province.

三片，脍炙人口。有“身为封疆大吏，当为朝廷存体制，兼为万古留纲常。今日不为忠言，毕生所学何事”等语，又云“誓为国家守此疆域，保此残黎”，俨然刚正不屈，字挟风霜。

逮九月寿州城破，翁同书具奏一折二片，则力表苗沛霖之忠义。视正月一疏，不特大相矛盾，亦且判若天渊。颠倒是非，荧惑圣听，败坏纲纪，莫此为甚。若翁同书自谓已卸抚篆，不应守城，则当早自引去，不当处嫌疑之地；为一城之主，又不当多杀团练，以张叛苗之威。若翁同书既奉谕旨，责令守城，则当与民效死，不当濡忍不决，又不当受挟制而草奏，独宛转而偷生。事定之后，翁同书寄臣三函，全无引咎之辞，廉耻丧尽，恬不为怪。

selves to protect their chastity, and thus he made a request to the emperor for Peng Yulin to make a full account of the war dead for commendation and compensation. Last January, Weng submitted a sensational memorial with three attachments that called for the annihilation of Miao Peilin. The memorial included language such as the following line, "As the commander of a border province, I strive to preserve the system of the imperial court and instill the Three Cardinal Guides and Five Constant Virtues in future generations. If we cannot offer earnest advice to the imperial court today, then to what purpose have we been studying all our life?" He also stated, "On behalf of our country, I swear to defend this territory and protect the remaining inhabitants." In his memorial, he presents himself as upright and unyielding and describes the various hardships he has experienced.

After Shouzhou fell into enemy hands in September, Weng submitted another memorial to the throne, this time with two attachments praising Miao Peilin for his loyalty. This memorial contradicts the one he submitted in January, as even the sky and the sea could not be further apart than these two memorials. Nothing is more abominable than his inversion of right and wrong, misleading Your Majesty and undermining social order and law. If Weng Tongshu declared that he had been dismissed from office and was not responsible for guarding the city, then he should have retired as soon as possible and not remained in a suspicious place. As the head of a city, he should not have killed members of the militia to incite the wrath of the traitor Miao Peilin. If Weng Tongshu had received imperial orders to defend the city, he should have sacrificed his life for the cause instead of testing the people's forbearance; they should neither be coerced into drafting memorials nor forced into a prolonged ignoble existence. After the rebel army was suppressed, Weng Tongshu wrote me three letters, none of which ex-

军兴以来，督抚失守逃遁者皆获重谴，翁同书于定远、寿州两次失守，又酿成苗逆之祸，岂宜逍遥法外？应请旨即将翁同书革职拿问，敕下王大臣九卿会同刑部议罪，以肃军纪，而昭炯戒。臣职分所在，例应纠参，不敢因翁同书之门第鼎盛瞻顾迁就。是否有当，伏乞皇上圣鉴训示。谨附片具奏。

pressed any shouldering of blame or sense of honor. Since fighting against the Taiping rebel army began, governors who chose to flee after failing to guard their territory have been punished severely. Weng Tongshu allowed Dingyuan and Shouzhou to fall into enemy hands and fomented Miao Peilin's rebellion. How can he walk away unpunished? I respectfully ask for an imperial edict to discharge Weng Tongshu from office and detain him for questioning. Princes and the nine Great Ministers of State should work with the Ministry of Punishment to determine his guilt and then set a clear example for strict military discipline. It is my duty to impeach and correct Weng Tongshu regardless of the status and splendor of the Weng family. I eagerly await Your Majesty's instructions and hereby respectfully submit this memorial attachment.

拟选聪颖子弟赴泰西各国肄业折

这是曾国藩去世前一年，即同治十年（1871）七月初三日，与直隶总督李鸿章联名上的一道奏折。

洋务运动在中国轰轰烈烈开启之后，洋务人才的奇缺，便成了当时的最大问题。第一位在美国高等院校拿到学位的中国人容闳，向江苏巡抚丁日昌建议：朝廷出钱，选拔一批十几岁的聪颖少年，去西方各国学习科学技术，学成归国报效，以使中国徐图自强。处理“天津教案”期间，丁日昌将这个建议向曾国藩与李鸿章汇报，获得他们的赞许，于是便有了这道奏折。

曾国藩去世后不久，这个建议付诸实践。同治十一年七月，第一批三十名幼童赴美，接下来又派出第二批、第三批、第四批，共一百二十名幼童赴美。光绪七年（1881），所有留美幼童全部回国，成为中国第一批“海归”。

奏为拟选聪颖子弟前赴泰西各国肄习技艺，以培人才，恭折

Memorial on the Selection of Bright Young Scholars to Study in the West

This memorial was written by Zeng Guofan and Li Hongzhang, the Viceroy of Zhili (present-day Hebei Province), on the third day of the seventh month in the tenth year of Emperor Tongzhi's reign (1871), one year before Zeng's death.

After the dynamic start of the Westernization Movement in China, the dire shortage of experts in foreign affairs emerged as its most pressing problem. Rong Hong, the first person from China to obtain an academic degree in the United States, made the following suggestion to Ding Richang, the Provincial Governor of Jiangsu Province: the imperial court should select a group of bright young scholars and fund them to study science and technology in Western countries so that they can return home after graduation to promote the Self-strengthening Movement. [1] While handling the case of the Tianjin Massacre, [2] Ding Richang reported this proposal to Zeng and Li. They commended it and prepared this memorial to the throne.

This proposal was implemented soon after Zeng's passing. In the seventh month of the 11th year of Emperor Tongzhi's reign (1872), the first group of 30 young scholars was sent to the United States. Another three groups were also sent to the United States, eventually bringing the total to 120 youths. By the seventh year of Emperor Guangxu's reign (1881), almost all of the young scholars who had been sent to the United States had returned home, thus becoming the first group of students to return to China after gaining experience overseas.

To prepare for the selection of bright young scholars who will be sent to the West to learn new skills, and with a view to training

1 The Self-Strengthening Movement, also known as the Westernization Movement (c.1861-1895), featured radical institutional reforms in China during the late Qing Dynasty following the military disasters of the Opium Wars.

2 The Tianjin Massacre occurred in 1870 when Tianjin civilians attacked Catholic churches in protest against forceful evangelization.

仰祈圣鉴事。

窃臣国藩上年在天津办理洋务，前任江苏巡抚丁日昌奉旨来津会办，屡与臣商榷，拟选聪颖幼童送赴泰西各国书院学习军政、船政、步算、制造诸书，约计十余年，业成而归，使西人擅长之技中国皆能谙悉，然后可以渐图自强。且谓携带幼童前赴外国者，如四品衔刑部主事陈兰彬、江苏候补同知容闳皆可胜任等语。臣国藩深韪其言，曾于上年九月、本年正月两次附奏在案。臣鸿章复往返函商。窃谓自斌椿及志刚、孙家谷两次奉命游历各国，于海外情形亦已窥其要领。如舆图、算法、步天、测海、造船、制器等事，无一不与用兵相表里。凡游学他国得有长技者，归即延入书院，分科传授，精益求精。其余军政、船政，直视为身心性命之学。今中国欲仿效其意而精通其法，当此风气既开，似宜亟

talented people, I sincerely request Your Majesty's judgment.

While I was handling foreign affairs in Tianjin last year, Ding Richang, the former provincial governor of Jiangsu, came to Tianjin to assist me at the request of Your Majesty. He and I often discussed the prospect of sending bright young scholars to academies in the West, where they could study subjects such as military and political affairs, shipping, mathematics, and manufacturing. The students would require at least ten years to complete their studies and return home, thus enabling China to learn from the West and apply those skills for self-strengthening at home. Ding also suggested that the young scholars could be taken to the West by competent officials such as Chen Lanbin, a fourth-rank manager at the Ministry of Punishment, and Rong Hong, an alternate associate prefect of Jiangsu Province. I fully agree with Ding's plan. Last ninth month and this past first month, I wrote two memorial attachments on this matter. Li Hongzhang has also corresponded with me many times on this subject. I think that Yao Binchun, Zhi Gang,[1] and Sun Jiagu[2] have completed two tours around the world under imperial orders, and thus they have some understanding of the situation overseas. Skills such as mapping, arithmetic, astronomy, navigation, shipbuilding, and manufacturing are all connected to military affairs. Those young scholars who learn special skills will be invited to pass them on by teaching at academies upon their return to China. Other areas, such as military and political affairs and shipbuilding, may be regarded as studies of the greatest significance. Now that China hopes to emulate the intentions of Western countries and become proficient in their methods, the environment is right for selecting bright young scholars to study

1 Yao Binchun and Zhi Gang were low-ranking officials of the late Qing Dynasty who were designated to lead a delegation to the Western countries in 1866.

2 Sun Jiagu (1823-1888), a native of Shouzhou County, Anhui Province, was the director of the Foreign Affairs Department under the imperial government.

选聪颖子弟携往外国肄业，实力讲求，以仰副我皇上徐图自强之至意。

查美国新立和约第七条内载，嗣后中国人欲入美国大小官学学习各等文艺，须照相待最优国人民一体优待。又，美国可以在中国指准外国人居住地方设立学堂，中国人亦可在美国一体照办等语。本年春间，美国公使过天津时，臣鸿章面与商及，允俟知照到日，即转致本国妥为照料。三月间，英国公使来津接见，亦以此事有无相询。臣鸿章当以实告，意颇欣许，亦谓先赴美国学习，英国大书院极多，将来亦可随便派往。此固外国人所深愿，似于和好大局有益无损。

臣等伏思外国所长，既肯听人共习，志刚、孙家谷又已导之先路，计由太平洋乘轮船径达美国，月余可至，当非甚难之事。或谓天津、上海、福州等处，已设局仿造轮船、枪炮、军火，京师设同文馆选满汉子弟延西人教授。又，上海开广方言馆选文童

abroad in order to realize Your Majesty's sincere intention for self-strengthening.

According to the seventh article of the new peace treaty signed with the United States, people from China who want to study at official schools in the United States must be given the same treatment as people from its most favored countries. In addition, the United States may build schools in areas that China has designated for foreign residences, and China may do the same in the United States in accordance with this provision. When an American envoy passed through Tianjin in the spring of this year, Li Hongzhang discussed the matter with him in person. The American envoy promised that great care would be given to this message to ensure its secure delivery to his home country. In March, a British envoy visiting Tianjin inquired about the existence of such an arrangement. Li Hongzhang explained it to him, and the British envoy also agreed to this arrangement. He suggested that China first send young scholars to the United States and then eventually send them to Britain, which he claimed was home to many great academies. Foreign countries appear to be very pleased with this arrangement as it benefits all parties and has no downside.

We have contemplated the advantages of foreign countries. A willingness to study with others combined with previous experience makes Zhi Gang and Sun Jiagu ideal candidates as the journey across the Pacific Ocean to the United States takes just over one month. Some people will say that Tianjin, Shanghai, Fuzhou, and other cities have established manufacturing bureaus for building ships and manufacturing guns, cannons, and munitions. Beijing has established a School of Combined Learning (Tong Wen Guan), where selected students of Manchu and Han backgrounds learn from Western teachers. Shanghai has also established a School of Foreign Languages (Guang Fang Yan Guan), where se-

肄业，似中国已有基绪，无须远涉重洋。不知设局制造，开馆教习，所以图振奋之基也。远适肄业，集思广益，所以收远大之效也。西人学求实济，无论为士、为工、为兵，无不入塾读书，共明其理，习见其器，躬亲其事，各致其心，思巧力递相师授，期于月异而岁不同。中国欲取其长，一旦遽图尽购其器，不惟力有不逮，且此中奥密，苟非遍览久习，则本源无由洞彻，而曲折无以自明。古人谓学齐语者，须引而置之庄岳之间，又曰百闻不如一见，比物此志也。况诚得其法，归而触类引伸，视今日所为，孜孜以求者，不更扩充于无穷耶？

惟是试办之难有二：一曰选材，一曰筹费。盖聪颖子弟不可多得，必其志趣远大，品质朴实，不牵于家累，不役于纷华者，方能远游异国，安心学习，则选材难。国家帑项，岁有常额，增

lected students study translation. It would appear that China has laid the foundation for Western studies, thus eliminating the need for students to study abroad. People may not realize that the establishment of manufacturing bureaus and schools of combined learning is to encourage self-strengthening, whereas studying abroad to draw on collective wisdom and absorb useful ideas is for reaping long-term benefits. Western learning emphasizes practical results. Anyone can attend school regardless of whether they are scholars, laborers, or soldiers. Together, they study theories, become familiar with instruments, and participate in learning activities. They challenge their minds, learn from one another, and are expected to achieve goals. China would like to adopt the advantages of Western countries and purchase their machinery within a small amount of time. However, that is beyond our current capabilities. Moreover, we cannot understand the mysteries and origins of Western advantages without reading widely and studying at length. The ancients said that those who wish to learn the Qi language must live in a neighborhood where the Qi language is spoken. They also declared that seeing something once was better than hearing about it one hundred times. Surely, it would be easier to understand the way of things if we could make comparative studies of actual objects. We should probe into the mysteries so that we might extend their meanings by analogy. Considering the current situation, shouldn't we put more effort into expanding our fields of learning?

This plan presents two obstacles: selecting bright people and raising funds. Bright youths are hard to find. Only those sincere few who embrace lofty aspirations yet are unburdened by family woes or the need for luxurious surroundings have the right temperament for travelling and studying abroad. Since the national revenue is a fixed sum, implementing a study-abroad program

此派人出洋肄习之款，更须措办，则筹费又难。凡此二者，臣等亦深知其难，第以成山始于一篑，蓄艾期以三年，及今以图，庶他日继长增高稍易为力。爰饬陈兰彬、容闳等悉心酌议，加以复核，拟派员在沪设局访选沿海各省聪颖幼童，每年以三十名为率，四年计一百二十名，分年搭船赴洋在外国肄习，十五年后按年分起挨次回华。计回华之日，各幼童不过三十岁上下，年力方强，正可及时报效。闻前此闽、粤、宁波子弟亦时有赴洋学习者，但只图识粗浅洋文洋话，以便与洋人交易，为衣食计。此则入选之初，慎之又慎。至带赴外国，悉归委员管束，分门别类，务求学术精到。又有翻译教习，随时课以中国文义，俾识立身大节，可冀成有用之材。虽未必皆为伟器，而人才既众，当有瑰异者出乎其中。此拔十得五之说也。

至于通计费用，首尾二十年需银百二十万两，诚属巨款。然

would increase expenditures, thus requiring that additional funds be raised. We are well aware of the difficulty of overcoming these obstacles. Just as a mountain grows from a clump of dirt, and moxa sticks take three years to prepare, our choices today are made easier, knowing that they will pay off in the long run. Therefore, Chen Lanbin, Rong Hong, and others were ordered to carefully deliberate and review the plan. They are preparing to send staff members to set up a bureau in Shanghai for the examination and selection of bright youths from coastal provinces. Each year, no more than 30 youths will be sent to study abroad, thus totaling 120 youths over four years. Their staggered departure across several years means that they will return to China in waves 15 years after first leaving their home country. According to this calculation, the youths who were sent abroad will be no more than 30 years old, still young, energetic, and with ample opportunity to serve their country, by the time they return. It has been said that some youths from Fujian, Guangdong, and Ningbo went abroad to acquire just enough foreign language skills to do business with foreigners. Their motives were purely to satisfy basic needs such as food and clothing. This is just the beginning of the selection process, so we cannot be too cautious. After being sent abroad, the youths will be under the supervision of committee members, who will divide them into groups to ensure that proficiency in a broad range of science and technology is nurtured. In addition to translation, they will be taught Chinese literature so that they learn how to conduct themselves and develop integrity, with the expectation that they will become contributing members of society when they return to China. Although not all will become great talents, some of them surely will. As the saying goes, "Only five out of ten live up to their potential."

This plan will cost a total of 1.2 million taels of silver over 20

此款不必一时凑拨，分析计之，每年接济六万，尚不觉其过难。除初年盘川发给委员携带外，其余指有定款按年预拨交与银号陆续汇寄，事亦易办。

总之，图事之始，固不能予之甚吝，而遽望之甚奢，况远适异国，储才备用，更不可以经费偶乏浅尝中辍。近年来设局制造，开馆教习，凡西人擅长之技，中国颇知究心，所需经费，均蒙谕旨准拨，亦以志在必成，虽难不惮，虽费不惜，日积月累，成效渐有可观。兹拟选带聪颖子弟赴外国肄业，事虽稍异，意实相同。谨将章程十二条恭呈御览，合无仰恳天恩，饬下江海关于洋税项下按年指拨，勿使缺乏。恭候命下，臣等即饬设局挑选聪颖子弟，妥慎办理，如有章程中未尽事宜，并请敕下总理衙门酌核更改，臣等亦可随时奏请更正。所有拟选聪颖子弟前赴泰西各国肄习技艺缘由，谨合词恭折具奏，伏乞皇太后、皇上圣鉴训示。谨奏。

years—a huge sum of money indeed. However, there is no need to allocate the whole sum at once. Instead, we can allocate 60,000 taels of silver annually. This should not prove to be too difficult. Except for the initial travel expenses, moreover, the rest of the money may be remitted in advance to a designated bank on an annual basis.

In short, we cannot start by underfunding our plan, and we cannot expect too much at once. These youths will travel abroad to develop into a wealth of talents for our country's future; we cannot undermine them by failing to fully provide for their expenses. In recent years, China has established manufacturing bureaus and schools of combined learning. We have been diligently learning skills that Westerners have dominated. All the necessary funds have been approved by imperial edicts because we are determined to succeed. We should be neither daunted by the difficulties nor reticent about funding. Over time, our efforts will reap considerable results. Although the approach is somewhat different, the plan to send bright youths to study overseas shares the same goals as the establishment of manufacturing bureaus and schools of combined learning. The 12th article of the agreement is presented to Your Majesty. We humbly ask for Your Majesty's favor to order Customs to annually allocate the funds collected as import tariffs for the study-abroad plan, thus ensuring it never lacks funding. After the imperial edict is issued, we will immediately set up a bureau in Shanghai to select bright youths and handle matters with care. If any matters are not covered in the articles of the agreement, we will invite the Ministry of Foreign Affairs to review and revise them. We may also request corrections at any time. For all the reasons outlined above for selecting bright youths to study in the West to learn skills, I hereby respectfully submit a detailed memorial to Empress Dowager and Your Majesty for review and instructions.

家书

Family Letters

致诸弟 (1842)

这封信写于道光二十二年（1842）九月十八日。此时，曾国藩进京已两年多了，在翰林院做一个小京官。进京两年多来，他最大的收获，一是读圣贤书要落实到自己的人生中去，也就是说要修身自律；二是在学习上，他已从应试之学中走出来，进入大本大源之学。这封信里，曾氏与诸弟谈及的，也是这两方面的事。

在谈到为学时，此信有两点特别值得我们重视：一是“猛火煮，慢火温”。这是子思、朱熹等人从熬肉中得到的启发。读书好比熬肉，先在短期内大量阅读，掌握所读之书的概貌；然后再对其中的章节字句细细咀嚼，以求探取精义。二是乾坤礼乐之道。这种将对立融为一体的思维方式，不但可用于读书，而且可用于我们面对的一切事物。

四位老弟足下：

九弟行程，计此时可以到家。自任邱发信之后，至今未接到第二封信，不胜悬悬。不知道上不甚艰险否？四弟、六弟院试，

To My Brothers (1842)

This letter was written on September 18 of the 22nd year of Emperor Daoguang's reign (1842). At that time, Zeng Guofan had been in Beijing for more than two years and was serving as a lower-level official at Hanlin Academy. Over those two years, he reaped two great rewards: first, he realized that books written by the ancient sages should be read and then applied to his own life, namely by cultivating his moral character and practicing self-discipline; second, he recognized that the purpose of studying was no longer to pass an exam but to understand the essential principles of life. In this letter, Zeng discusses these two breakthroughs with his brothers.

In this discussion about studying, two points deserve special attention. The first point is, "We must boil it over a fierce fire, and then simmer it over a gentle heat." This concept of likening studying to boiling meat was developed by Zisi, Zhu Xi, and others. Initially, one reads a great deal in a small amount of time to grasp the general idea of a book; then, one carefully reads a sentence, chapter, or section at a time to explore the essence of the book. The second point is the way of heaven and earth and rites and music. This mode of thinking may be applied not only to studying but also to everything we encounter in life.

My four brothers,

By my estimates, Guoquan [1] has completed his journey home by now. As I have yet to receive any word since the letter he sent from Renqiu County, I have been very anxious. I wonder if the journey was fraught with hardships and dangers. I assume that Guohuang [2]

1 Zeng Guoquan is also referred to as "ninth younger brother" because he was born the ninth child in the family.

2 Zeng Guohuang is also referred to as "fourth younger brother" because he was born the fourth child in the family.

计此时应有信，而折差久不见来，实深悬望。

予身体较九弟在京时一样，总以耳鸣为苦。问之吴竹如，云只有静养一法，非药物所能为力。而应酬日繁，予又素性浮躁，何能着实养静？拟搬进内城住，可省一半无谓之往还，现在尚未找得。予时时自悔，终未能洗涤自新。

九弟归去之后，予定刚日读经、柔日读史之法。读经常懒散不沉着。读《后汉书》，现已丹笔点过八本；虽全不记忆，而较之去年读前《汉书》，领会较深。九月十一日起同课人议每课一文一诗，即于本日申刻用白折写。予文、诗极为同课人所赞赏。然予于八股绝无实学，虽感诸君奖借之殷，实则自愧愈深也。待下次折差来，可付课文数篇回家。予居家懒做考差工夫，即借此课以摩厉考具，或亦不至临场窘迫耳。

and Guohua [1] have taken the provincial-level examination, and I expected to have received a letter from home by this time. The messenger has not appeared in ages, leaving me in a state of eager anticipation.

My health has not changed since Guoquan was in Beijing. I am always suffering from ringing in my ears. I have turned to Wu Zhuru for help and was told that rest is the only cure since no effective medicine exists. Considering an increase in work obligations combined with my restless temperament, how can I escape the chaos to cultivate a peaceful mind? I planned to move to the old town of Beijing to halve the time spent going to and from work, but I have yet to find suitable housing. I often regret that I have been unable to mend my ways and start life anew.

After Guoquan left for home, I decided to read the Confucian classics on odd-numbered days and history books on even-numbered days. My lack of concentration has made me lazy about reading the Confucian classics. So far, I have marked eight volumes of the *Book of the Latter Han* in red ink. Although I fail to remember everything, I have a deeper understanding of this book than I had of the *Book of Han* last year. Since September 11, some of us scholars who study together agreed to each write one essay and one poem for class. I must finish writing mine in the *baizhe* [2] style of script by five this evening. The other scholars have praised my prose and poetry, but I lack the scholarship needed to compose an eight-legged essay. Although their praise is appreciated, it only makes me feel more guilty. The next time the messenger comes, I will send some texts home. I do not want to prepare for business exams at home, so I would like to take this opportunity to practice my writing skills to avoid being embarrassed in future.

1 Zeng Guohua is also referred to as "sixth younger brother" because he was born the sixth child in the family.

2 *Baizhe* is a style of script usually used on the highest level of imperial examinations in the Qing Dynasty.

吴竹如近日往来极密，来则作竟日之谈，所言皆身心国家大道理。渠言有窦兰泉者（垿，云南人），见道极精当平实。窦亦深知予者，彼此现尚未拜往。竹如必要予搬进城住，盖城内镜海先生可以师事，倭艮峰先生、窦兰泉可以友事。师友夹持，虽懦夫亦有立志。子思、朱子言为学譬如熬肉，先须用猛火煮，然后用漫火温。予生平工夫全未用猛火煮过，虽略有见识，乃是从悟境得来。偶用功，亦不过优游玩索已耳。如未沸之汤，遽用漫火温之，将愈煮愈不熟矣。以是急思搬进城内，屏除一切，从事于克己之学。镜海、艮峰两先生亦劝我急搬。而城外朋友，予亦有思常见者数人，如邵蕙西、吴子序、何子贞、陈岱云是也。

蕙西尝言："'与周公瑾交，如饮醇醪'，我两人颇有此风味。"

Wu Zhuru [1] has been in close contact with me recently. When he visits, he spends the whole day discussing the principles of a sound mind and body and the state of national affairs. He told me about a man named Dou Lanquan [2] from Yunnan who is knowledgeable and honest. Dou knows me well, though we have yet to meet. Zhuru agrees that I should move to the old town so that I can look to Tang Jinghai [3] as my teacher and Wo Genfeng [4] and Dou Lanquan as my friends. With the support of good teachers and friends, even a coward will steel his resolve. Zisi and Zhu Xi once said that studying may be likened to boiling meat. We must first boil it over a fierce fire, and then simmer it over a gentle heat. I have never cooked with a fierce fire in my life, although I do have some small insight just from personal enlightenment. I may occasionally be studious simply because my interest has been aroused. My studying may be likened to unboiled soup that only tastes worse when boiled over a gentle heat. The gentler the heat, the less it cooks. Therefore, I have been eager to move to the old town, where I might eliminate all distracting thoughts and learn to practice self-restraint. Jinghai and Genfeng have urged me to move quickly as well. I also have several friends whom I would like to visit frequently but who do not live in the old town, such as Shao Huixi, Wu Zixu, He Zizhen, and Chen Daiyun.

Shao Huixi [5] once said, "Cheng Pu compared being friends with

---

1 Wu Tingdong (1793 – 1873), pseudonym Zhuru, a native of Huoshan County, Anhui Province, was a fifth-grade official at the Ministry of Punishment.

2 Dou Xu (1804 – 1865), pseudonym Lanquan, was a native of Luoping Prefecture (present-day Qujing City), Yunnan Province. He served as a director of the Ministry of Personnel, the imperial censor for Jiangxi Province, and other official positions.

3 Tang Jian (1778-1861), courtesy name Jinghai, a native of Shanhua County, Hunan Province, was a famous neo-Confucianist of the late Qing Dynasty.

4 Wo Ren (1804-1871), courtesy name Genfeng, was a famous neo-Confucianist of the late Qing Dynasty who had a Mongolian background. Like Zeng Guofan, Wo was also a student of Tangjian.

5 Shao Yichen (1810-1861), courtesy name Huixi, was a famous Confucianist of the late Qing Dynasty.

故每见辄长谈不舍。子序之为人，予至今不能定其品。然识见最大且精，尝教我云："用功譬若掘井，与其多掘数井而皆不及泉，何若老守一井，力求及泉而用之不竭乎？"此语正与予病相合。盖予所谓掘井多而皆不及泉者也。

何子贞与予讲字极相合，谓我"真知大源，断不可暴弃"。予尝谓天下万事万理皆出于乾坤二卦。即以作字论之：纯以神行，大气鼓荡，脉络周通，潜心内转，此乾道也；结构精巧，向背有法，修短合度，此坤道也。凡乾以神气言，凡坤以形质言。礼乐不可斯须去身，即此道也。乐本于乾，礼本于坤。作字而优游自得真力弥满者，即乐之意也；丝丝入扣转折合法，即礼之意也。

Zhou Yu to drinking rich wine.[1] I have been thinking that we have a similar friendship." Every time we meet, we enjoy a long talk and are reluctant to part. As for Wu Zixu,[2] I have yet to identify his character, but he boasts the greatest and most excellent insight. He once told me, "Working hard is like digging a well; rather than digging several wells that do not lead to water, one should do one's best to dig only one well that provides an inexhaustible supply of water." He pinpointed my problem with these few words, for I am just the kind of person who digs many wells that never lead to water.

He Zizhen[3] and I share very similar views on calligraphy. He believes that I have a firm grasp on the fundamental principles and must not abandon my studies. I often say that everything in the universe is based on the *qian* (heaven) and *kun* (earth) hexagrams from the *Zhou Book of Change*. Take calligraphy, for example. The principle of *qian* (heaven) lies in doing calligraphy with poetic charm, great momentum, flowing thought, and sharp concentration; the principle of *kun* (earth) lies in creating an exquisite structure, balancing light and dark lines, and combining long and short strokes. The principle of *qian* (heaven) focuses on expression; the principle of *kun* (earth) focuses on form and structure. Similarly, rites and music cannot be separated, not even for a moment. Music is based on *qian* (heaven), and rites are based on *kun* (earth). The meaning of music is embodied in the ease and power of the brush strokes; the meaning of rites is embodied in the meticulous attention and flawless artistry that ensure the brush strokes conform to the rules of calligraphy. I sometimes talk with

1 Cheng Pu and Zhou Yu were famous generals of the late Eastern Han Dynasty.

2 Wu Jiabin (1803-1864), courtesy name Zixu, a native of Nanfeng County, Jiangxi Province, was a famous scholar and poet of the late Qing Dynasty.

3 He Shaoji (1799-1873), courtesy name Zizhen, a native of Dao County (present-day Tongdao County), Hunan Province, was a poet, painter, and calligrapher of the late Qing Dynasty.

偶与子贞言及此，子贞深以为然，谓渠生平得力，尽于此矣。陈岱云与吾处处痛痒相关，此九弟所知者也。

写至此，接得家书。知四弟、六弟未得入学，怅怅然。科名有无迟早，总由前定，丝毫不能勉强。吾辈读书，只有两事：一者进德之事，讲求乎诚正修齐之道，以图无忝所生；一者修业之事，操习乎记诵词章之术，以图自卫其身。进德之事难以尽言，至于修业以卫身，吾请言之：

卫身莫大于谋食。农工商劳力以求食者也，士劳心以求食者也。故或食禄于朝，教授于乡，或为传食之客，或为入幕之宾，皆须计其所业，足以得食而无愧。科名者，食禄之阶也，亦须计吾所业，将来不至尸位素餐，而后得科名而无愧。食之得不得，穷通由天作主，予夺由人作主；业之精不精，则由我作主。然吾

Zizhen about this, and he is in total agreement. He also mentioned that any competence he has developed over his lifetime originated with this concept. As for Chen Daiyun, he and I share a common lot, as Guoquan knows.

Having written thus far, I have received a letter from home. I now know that neither Guohuang nor Guohua passed the provincial-level examination. How disappointing. Nevertheless, destiny determines whether and when we can establish our names through the imperial examination system. It cannot be forced. We study for only two reasons. The first is to improve our morality and seek sincerity, integrity, enlightenment, and family regulation with the goal of living a virtuous life; the second is to improve our capabilities and practice memorization and the art of writing with the goal of making a living. It is difficult to speak about improving morality. As for improving our capabilities for the sake of self-sustainment, allow me to tell you about it.

The key to self-sustainment is to make a living. Farmers, workers, and merchants rely on their labor for food; scholars rely on their minds for food. Therefore, if one wants to earn a salary as an official with the imperial government, make a living as a teacher in the countryside, sponge off the rich as a dependent, or serve as an aide to a high-ranking official, one must determine whether one's capabilities suit the position and whether one can make a living in that position with a clear conscience. The imperial examinations can serve as a ladder for becoming an official and drawing an official salary, but we must also consider the state of our own education to ensure that we are not holding down a job without doing any work or feeling ashamed of the reputation and position that we have achieved. It is for the heavens to decide whether we can make a living and whether we will succeed; it is for others to decide whether we will be awarded or punished; however, it is for ourselves to decide whether we will be proficient learners. I have

未见业果精，而终不得食者也。农果力耕，虽有饥馑必有丰年；商果积货，虽有壅滞必有通时；士果能精其业，安见其终不得科名哉？即终不得科名，又岂无他途可以求食者哉？然则特患业之不精耳。

求业之精，别无他法，曰专而已矣。谚曰“艺多不养身”，谓不专也。吾掘井多而无泉可饮，不专之咎也。诸弟总须力图专业。如九弟志在习字，亦不必尽废他业。但每日习字工夫，断不可不提起精神，随时随事，皆可触悟。四弟、六弟，吾不知其心有专嗜否？若志在穷经，则须专守一经；志在作制义，则须专看一家文稿；志在作古文，则须专看一家文集。作各体诗亦然，作试帖亦然，万不可以兼营并骛，兼营则必一无所能矣。切嘱切嘱，千万千万。此后写信来，诸弟各有专守之业，务须写明。且须详

yet to meet anyone who is proficient at his studies but unable to make a proper living. If farmers are diligent about cultivating the land, they will experience bumper harvests despite occasional crop failures. If merchants are diligent about keeping goods in stock, they will find that goods sell well despite being overstocked at times. Therefore, how is it possible that a scholar who is proficient at his studies would not gain a reputation and official position through the imperial examinations? And, even if he does fail to achieve these things, does he not have other ways to make a living? That is the reason why I believe one only needs to be concerned about being proficient in one's studies.

There is only one way to become proficient in one's studies: concentration. The proverb "he who has too many skills cannot sustain himself" criticizes a lack of concentration. My own experience of digging many wells but finding no water to drink is a good case in point. My younger brothers, you should strive to concentrate on a specialty. Guoquan, if you would like to focus on calligraphy, you need not abandon all other studies. However, you should never practice calligraphy without first mustering your spirits. You may be inspired by anything at any time. Guohuang and Guohua, do you have your own special interests? If you aspire to study Confucian classics, then be sure to specialize in one area; if you are interested in eight-legged essays, then you should focus on the writings of one particular expert; if you want to study classical Chinese prose, then you must focus on the collected writings of one writer. The same is true for composing different styles of poetry and eight-legged essays. Under no circumstances should you devote yourselves to various fields of study. That will leave you with no special skills. Please bear this in mind! In the future, you must each write to tell me what specialized area of study you have chosen. Please ask me detailed questions and write lengthy letters

问极言，长篇累牍，使我读其手书，即可知其志向识见。凡专一业之人，必有心得，亦必有疑义。诸弟有心得，可以告我共赏之；有疑义，可以问我共析之。且书信既详，则四千里外之兄弟不啻晤言一室，乐何如乎？

予生平于伦常中，惟兄弟一伦抱愧尤深。盖父亲以其所知者尽以教我，而我不能以吾所知者尽教诸弟，是不孝之大者也。九弟在京年余，进益无多，每一念及，无地自容。嗣后我写诸弟信，总用此格纸，弟宜存留，每年装订成册。其中好处，万不可忽略看过。诸弟写信寄我，亦须用一色格纸，以便装订。

谢果堂先生出京后，来信并诗二首。先生年已六十余，名望甚重，与予见面，辄彼此倾心，别后又拳拳不忘，想见老辈爱才之笃。兹将诗并予送诗附阅，传播里中，使共知此老为大君子也。

予有大铜尺一方，屡寻不得，九弟已带归否？频年寄黄芽白

so that I might understand your aspirations and experience. Those who concentrate on one area of study will certainly have their own insights and questions. Brothers, share your insights with me so that I might appreciate them with you, and share your questions with me so that I might analyze them with you. Furthermore, your detailed letters will close the distance of 4,000 li between us, allowing us to feel as though we were together in the same room. How wonderful would that be?

My whole life, I have felt deep guilt about failing to fulfill one role, that of an elder brother. Our father has taught me everything he knows, but I cannot teach my younger brothers everything I know. This is the most unfilial behavior. Guoquan stayed with me in Beijing for more than a year, but he made little progress. The thought of it overwhelms me with deep shame. Brothers, I will always write to you on this type of ruled paper in the future. Please hold on to my letters and bind them together into a book every year. The advantages of doing this should not be ignored. Brothers, please write to me on the same type of ruled paper so that I might also bind your letters together into a book.

After leaving the capital, Xie Guotang[1] sent me a letter and two poems. He is over sixty years old and enjoys a wonderful reputation. After the meeting, we developed a high regard for one another. And even now, after leaving the capital, he still remembers me. You can imagine how earnestly he took his role as an elder. Please read his poems and the poems that I wrote in response, which I have attached to this letter, and disseminate them in the countryside so that others might know this great gentleman.

I have a big copper ruler that I have looked for many times but have yet to find. Did Guoquan take it home? Have you had any luck planting the cabbage seeds that I send home every year? Did

1 Xie Guotang (? – ?), a native of Xiangxiang County, Hunan Province, was a scholar official at Hanlin Academy.

菜子，家中种之好否？在省时已买漆否？漆匠果用何人？信来并祈详示。

兄国藩手具

you buy paint when you were in the provincial capital? Who did you hire to do the painting? Please provide the details when you write back.

Your elder brother, Guofan

谕纪鸿 (1856)

此信写于咸丰六年（1856）九月二十九日。这是曾氏家书中极负盛名的一封。在这封家书中，他提出一个重要的观念：愿子孙做读书明理之君子。这一句话可视为曾氏家教中的精核。

家长对子女的教育，最终的目的是期待他们做一个与自己心中设想相符的人。大多的父母都期待子女今后出人头地、光彩耀人。曾氏不这样想，他期待子女做君子。在中国传统文化中，君子指的是品性好、人格健全的人，与财富、权力、名声等无关，而成为君子的途径，是读书明理。

字谕纪鸿儿：

家中人来营者，多称尔举止大方，余为少慰。凡人多望子孙为大官，余不愿为大官，但愿为读书明理之君子。勤俭自持，习劳习苦，可以处乐，可以处约。此君子也。余服官二十年，不敢稍染官宦气习，饮食起居，尚守寒素家风，极俭也可，略丰也可，

To Jihong (1856)

This letter was written on the 29th day of the ninth month in the sixth year of Emperor Xianfang's reign (1856). This is one of the most famous of Zeng Guofan's family letters. In it, he expresses an important concept to his children: his wish that they become superior people – learned and sensible. This may be regarded as the essence of education in the Zeng family.

Parents educate their children with the ultimate goal of helping them become the people their parents envisage them to be. Most parents hope that their children grow up to be wealthy, powerful, famous, extraordinary, and respected. Zeng thought differently. He hoped that his children would grow up to be superior people. In traditional Chinese culture, a superior person refers to a person of noble character and integrity, which has no connection to concepts such as money, power, and reputation. One becomes a superior person by studying and knowing the rules of propriety.

My son Jihong,

Most of the people who come to the military camp from our hometown commend you for having a dignified bearing. I am fairly pleased by this. Most people hope that their children become high-ranking officials. I do not share these hopes. I only want my children to grow up to be "superior people" who are learned and sensible. He who is industrious, frugal, and reserved, who can adjust to hard labor and suffering, and who can live a life of comfort and privation is a superior person. I have served as an official for two decades but still guard against becoming corrupted by the bad habits of officialdom. In my daily life, I still maintain humble

太丰则吾不敢也。凡仕宦之家，由俭入奢易，由奢返俭难。尔年尚幼，切不可贪爱奢华，不可惯习懒惰。无论大家小家、士农工商，勤苦俭约，未有不兴，骄奢倦怠，未有不败。尔读书写字不可间断，早晨要早起，莫坠高曾祖考以来相传之家风。吾父吾叔，皆黎明即起，尔之所知也。

凡富贵功名，皆有命定，半由人力，半由天事。惟学作圣贤，全由自己作主，不与天命相干涉。吾有志学为圣贤，少时欠居敬工夫，至今犹不免偶有戏言戏动。尔宜举止端庄，言不妄发，则入德之基也。手谕。（时在江西抚州门外）

and simple family traditions. I can be extremely frugal or a little lavish; however, I would never dare to be too lavish. It is easy for a family of officials to go from frugality to extravagance, but the reverse is difficult. As a young man, under no circumstances should you covet extravagance or make a habit of laziness. Regardless of wealth and connections, all families can flourish through hard work and thrift, be they scholars, farmers, artisans, or merchants. All families will decline through pride, extravagance, and laziness. Do not take a break from studying and practicing calligraphy. Rise early in the morning and maintain the family traditions that have been handed down by our forefathers. As you well know, both my father and my uncles rose at dawn.

All wealth, honor, and fame are predetermined equally by fate or human effort. Only studying to become a sage is determined entirely by oneself, with no connection to fate. Although I have the desire to become a sage, I failed to put enough effort into conducting myself properly and being respectful when I was young. Even now, I still cannot repress my jocular manner. However, you should carry yourself in a dignified manner and refrain from speaking carelessly. This is the foundation of moral integrity.(Written outside the gates of Fuzhou City, Jiangxi Province)

谕纪泽（1858）

此信写于咸丰八年（1858）七月二十一日。

曾氏在这封信里向儿子讲了些读书方法与为人的道理。在读书方法上，曾氏教给儿子四个字：看、读、写、作。看，即我们通常说的阅览，立足在“博”字上：博览群书，扩大知识面，加大信息量。读，用在经典名著上，或细读慢嚼，体悟其中的深刻之处；或高声吟咏，欣赏它的情趣声韵。写，写字，不是做书法家，而是做到又快又好，利于实用。作，勤作诗文。

为人之道，曾氏认为最重要的是两个字：敬与恕。敬，指待人待事的严肃恭谨的态度；恕，对别人应该存宽厚包容之心。

字谕纪泽儿：

余此次出门，略载日记，即将日记封每次家信中。闻林文忠

To Jize (1858)

This letter was written on the 21st day of the seventh month in the eighth year of Emperor Xianfeng's reign (1858).

In this letter, Zeng Guofan talks to his son about how to study and how he should conduct himself. Zeng sums up his advice on how to study in four words: skim, read, handwrite, and compose. Skimming refers to reading quickly for a broad understanding of the subject matter. It allows one to read extensively, expand one's knowledge base, and take in more information. Reading refers to carefully and slowly reading the classics to understand their deeper meaning. One may also want to chant the classics aloud to appreciate the cadence of the writing. Handwriting should be practiced not for the purpose of becoming a calligrapher but to develop a faster and more competent hand, which is quite practical. As for composing, Zeng believes that one should be diligent about writing poems and prose.

Zeng Guofan believes that the key to conducting oneself properly can be summarized in two words: respect and forgiveness. Respect refers to maintaining a solemn and respectful attitude toward people and things; forgiveness refers to being magnanimous and tolerant of others.

My son Jize,

While away from home this time, I have kept a diary, the pages of which I am enclosing in my letters home. I took up this practice after hearing about Lin Wenzhong's [1] family letters. When you were in the provincial capital, you refrained from going out except to visit the Ding and Zuo families. This has comforted me despite

1 Lin Zexu (1785 – 1850), posthumous honorary title Wenzhong, a native of Houguan County (present-day Fuzhou City), Fujian Province, was a famous statesman and literary writer of the late Qing Dynasty.

家书，即系如此办法。尔在省，仅至丁、左两家，余不轻出，足慰远怀。

读书之法，看、读、写、作，四者每日不可缺一。看者，如尔去年看《史记》《汉书》“韩文”《近思录》，今年看《周易折中》之类是也。读者，如《四书》《诗》《书》《易经》《左传》诸经，《昭明文选》、李杜韩苏之诗、韩欧曾王之文，非高声朗诵则不能得其雄伟之概，非密咏恬吟则不能探其深远之韵。譬之富家居积，看书则在外贸易，获利三倍者也，读书则在家慎守，不轻花费者也；譬之兵家战争，看书则攻城略地，开拓土宇者也，读书则深沟坚垒，得地能守者也。看书如子夏之“日知所亡”相近，读书与“无忘所能”相近，二者不可偏废。

至于写字，真行篆隶，尔颇好之，切不可间断一日。既要求好，又要求快。余生平因作字迟钝，吃亏不少。尔须力求敏捷，每日能作楷书一万则几矣。至于作诸文，亦宜在二三十岁立定规

the distance between us.

Studying requires four aspects of daily practice: skimming, reading, handwriting, and composing. Some works are for skimming. For example, last year, you skimmed the *Records of the Grand Historian*, the *Book of Han*, Han Yu's essays, and *Reflections on Things at Hand* (*Jin Si Lu*); this year, you skimmed books similar to *Eclectic Notes to the Zhou Book of Change*. Some works are for reading, including the *Four Books*, the *Book of Poetry*, the *Book of Documents, the Zhou Book of Change*, *Zuo's Commentaries on the Spring and Autumn Annals and Selections of Refined Literature*; poems by Li Bai, Du Fu, Han Yu, and Su Shi; and essays by Han Yu, Ouyang Xiu, Zeng Gong, and Wang Anshi. A failure to read them aloud and with expression makes it impossible to appreciate their grandeur; a failure to recite them quietly makes it impossible to explore their profound charm. Consider how rich families accumulate wealth. Skimming is like conducting foreign trade to earn triple the interest; reading is like managing your home conservatively, without reckless expenditures. Or consider how commanders fight wars. Skimming is like attacking cities to expand territory; reading is like digging trenches and building fortifications in order to maintain captured territory. Skimming may be likened to this saying by Zixia, [1] "Learn something new every day," and reading may be likened to another of his sayings, "Don't forget what you already know." Both should be given equal weight.

As for handwriting, you love practicing regular (*zhen*), running (*xing*), seal (*zhuan*), and ancient official (*li*) scripts; never let a day go by without practicing. Strive to write both beautifully and quickly. My slow handwriting has caused me much grief over the years. You must be faster. Writing ten thousand characters in regular script every day should do it. As for composing essays, one

1 Bu Shang (507 BC – ?), courtesy name Zixia, a native of the State of Jin, was a disciple of Confucius.

模；过三十后，则长进极难。作四书文，作试帖诗，作律赋，作古今体诗，作古文，作骈体文，数者不可不一一讲求，一一试为之。少年不可怕丑，须有狂者进取之趣，此时不试为之，则后此弥不肯为矣。

至于作人之道，圣贤千言万语，大抵不外敬恕二字。“仲弓问仁”一章，言敬恕最为亲切。自此以外，如立则见参于前也，在舆则见其倚于衡也；君子无众寡，无小大，无敢慢，斯为泰而不骄；正其衣冠，俨然人望而畏，斯为威而不猛。是皆言敬之最好下手者。孔言欲立立人，欲达达人；孟言行有不得，反求诸已。以仁存心，以礼存心，有终身之忧，无一朝之患。是皆言恕之最好下手者。尔心境明白，于恕字或易著功，敬字则宜勉强行之。此立德之基，不可不谨。

科场在即，亦宜保养身体。余在外平安，不多及。

should develop one's own style in one's twenties. After the age of thirty, any progress in that area is hard won. Try your hand at all kinds of writing, including essays and poems in the literary style of imperial examinations,[1] ancient and modern poetry styles, classical Chinese prose, and parallel prose. Young people should not fear becoming a laughingstock; they must be enterprising. If they fail to do so while they are young, they will never do it.

As for the way of conducting oneself, the thousands upon thousands of words that sages have written on the subject may be summarized with just two: respect and forgiveness. The section in *The Analects* in which Zhonggong[2] asks about humaneness argues that respect and forgiveness are the warmest qualities. Once developed, they are as obvious as though they were displayed before you as you stood or were leaning upon the beam of your carriage as you passed by. The superior man is composed but not arrogant, regardless of the number of people around him or the importance of the matter at hand. The superior man maintains a neat appearance; he has an air of dignity to inspire respect and awe while still being kind at heart. This is how best to be respectful. Confucius said that he who wants to be upright should help others be upright; he who seeks success should help others be successful. Mencius advised turning inward to seek the solution within ourselves when we encounter difficulties in life. By cherishing benevolence and propriety, we may have a lifelong concern but not one day will be a disaster. This is how best to be forgiving. In your heart, you understand that forgiveness may be easier to practice than respect, but you should do your best to practice the latter. This is the basis of morality. It should be implemented with caution.

The imperial examination will be held soon. Be sure to take

1 The essays and poems in the literary style of imperial examinations include essays on the Four Books, Confucian classics and rhymed poems.

2 Ran Yong (531 BC-?), courtesy name Zhonggong, a native of the State of Lu, was a disciple of Confucius.

涤生手谕（舟次樵舍下，去江西省城八十里）

再，此次日记，已封入澄侯叔函中寄至家矣。余自十二至湖口，十九夜五更开船晋江西省，二十一申刻即至章门。余不多及。又示。

care of your health. I am safe and sound away from home. That is all for today.

Your father, Disheng[1]

(The boat is scheduled to stop at Qiaoshe Town, 80 *li* from the capital of Jiangxi)

Also, this diary entry was sealed and sent home with my letter to your uncle Chenghou.[2] I arrived in Hukou on the 12th, then set sail in the small hours of the 19th for Jiangxi Province and arrived in Zhangmen Town[3] around mid-afternoon on the 21st. Once more, that is all for today.

1 Disheng was Zeng Guofan's pseudonym.

2 Chenghou was Zeng Guohuang's courtesy name.

3 Present-day Ganzhou City, Jiangxi Province.

致澄弟 (1860)

这封信写于咸丰十年（1860）闰三月二十九日。曾氏与他的四弟谈整治家庭的八个字：书、蔬、鱼、猪、早、扫、考、宝。这就是有名的治家八字诀。这八个字代表八个方面。书，家人要读书。蔬，要把蔬菜种好。鱼，要有鱼塘，把鱼养好。猪，喂好猪。早，家人要早起。扫，打扫庭院。考，对祖先的祭祀要重视。宝，善待亲戚邻里。

如果将这八个字用今天的语境来表达，即读书、做好副业、勤奋、整洁环境、孝敬亲长、睦邻。曾国藩认为，这些方面是衡量一个家庭、家族兴旺与否的标志。

澄侯四弟左右：

二十七日刘得四来，接弟十三日信，欣悉各宅平安。沅弟是日申刻到，又得详问一切，敬知叔父临终毫无抑郁之情，至为慰念。

余与沅弟论治家之道，一切以星冈公为法，大约有八个字诀。其四字即上年所称书、蔬、鱼、猪也，又四字则曰早、扫、考、

To My Brother Guohuang (1860)

In this letter written on the 29th day of the third leap month in the tenth year of Emperor Xianfeng's reign (1860), Zeng Guofan explains his principles for managing a household through eight words: books, vegetables, fish, pigs, early, sweeping, ancestors, and cherishing. This is his famous "eight-character formula for household management." Each Chinese character, or word, represents an aspect of family life. Books should be available for studying. Vegetables should be grown in the fields. Fish should be stocked and raised in a pond. Pigs should be well fed. Early is the time when family members should rise. Sweeping of the courtyard should be performed daily. Ancestors should be worshipped and offered sacrifices. And, finally, cherished is the way relatives and neighbors should be treated.

In the modern world, these eight words may be better explained as attending school, sustaining multiple income streams, being diligent, maintaining a clean environment, showing respect to elderly relatives, and being a good neighbor. Zeng believes that the prosperity of a family can be measured through these benchmarks.

My brother Chenghou,

On the 27th day, Liu Desi arrived with your letter dated the 13th day. I was happy to learn that everyone in the family is safe and sound. Guoquan arrived later in the afternoon, so I was able to ask him for more details. It was comforting to hear that our uncle passed away without any hint of despondency.

Following in our grandfather's footsteps, Guoquan and I devised an eight-character formula for household management. Four of the eight characters are the same ones that I wrote to you about last year: books, vegetables, fish, and pigs; the other four characters are early, sweeping, ancestors, and cherishing. Specifically,

宝。早者，起早也；扫者，扫屋也；考者，祖先祭祀，敬奉显考、王考、曾祖考，言考而妣可该也；宝者，亲族邻里，时时周旋，贺喜吊丧，问疾济急，星冈公常曰人待人无价之宝也。星冈公生平于此数端最为认真。故余戏述为八字诀，曰：书、蔬、鱼、猪、早、扫、考、宝也。此言虽涉谐谑，而拟即写屏上，以祝贤弟夫妇寿辰，使后世子孙知吾兄弟家教，亦知吾兄弟风趣也。弟以为然否？顺问近好。

国藩手草

early is the time when the family should rise. Sweeping the home should be performed daily. Ancestors, including our father, grandfather, and great-grandfather, as well as our mother, grandmother, and great-grandmother, should be worshipped and offered sacrifices. Cherished is how relatives and neighbors should be treated. In other words, we should socialize together often, offer our congratulations or condolences as circumstances arise, ask after the sick, and offer our assistance. Our grandfather liked to say that treating one another well is priceless; it is a belief he revered all his life. Hence, I playfully devised the following eight-character formula for managing a household: books, vegetables, fish, pigs, early, sweeping, ancestors, and cherishing. Although somewhat whimsical, I am considering writing the formula on a plaque to celebrate the birthday of you and your wife. This way, future generations can get a glimpse of our upbringing and the sense of humor we brothers share. What do you think? Please accept my kind regards.

Guofan

致澄弟（1861）

这封信写于咸丰十一年（1861）二月二十四日。曾氏在信中提出“八本”之说。他说，治家八字诀是祖父的思想，他只是作归纳而已，而这“八本”则完全是他基于自己阅历的总结，他对此很有自信。他的家族很看重这个“八本”，他们世代居住的富厚堂又名“八本堂”。

本者，根本也。曾氏认为，他所经历的人生世事，有八个大的方面，而在这八个大的方面中，都有它的根本所在。抓住它们的根本，尽力做好，那这方面的事情也就大致做好了。“八本”之说，不仅为人们提供了一个技术操作的蓝本，更重要的是告诉人们一种思维方式：找出事物的根本来，从根本做起。正因为此，“八本”在近代中国很流行，并启发人们创造出许多“本”来。

澄侯四弟左右：

上次送家信者，三十五日即到。此次专人，四十日未到。盖因乐平、饶州一带有贼，恐中途绕道也。

自十二日克复休宁后，左军分出八营在于甲路地方小挫，退

To My Brother Guohuang (1861)

In this letter, written on the 24th day of the second month in the 11th year of Emperor Xianfeng's reign (1861), Zeng Guofan proposes his eight-basis formula. He explains that, while the eight-character formula for household management is merely his summary of his grandfather's ideas, this eight-basis formula is entirely his creation. It is based on his own experience and is a concept he felt very confident about. His family valued it so highly that they even changed the name of the hall in which their family had lived for generations from Fu Hou Hall (Abundance Hall) to Ba Ben Hall (Eight-basis Hall).

Here it refers to essence or foundation. Zeng believed that his life could be defined through eight major aspects, each rooted in its own basis. Identifying and solidifying the basis of each thus enabled him to excel in that aspect of his life. The eight-basis formula not only provides a blueprint for daily practice but also outlines a new way for family members to think, namely to discover the root of things and begin from there. Consequently, the eight-basis formula has found a receptive audience in modern China, inspiring the derivation of countless other bases.

My brother Guohuang,

It took 35 days for my last letter to reach home. Despite assigning the task to a special messenger, 40 days have now passed with no sign of my most recent letter. The rebels in Leping and Raozhou [1] probably forced the messenger to make a detour.

After recapturing Xiuning County [2] on the 12th day, Zuo Zongtang split his army into eight battalions, which suffered a small

1 Leping, present-day Leping City under Jingdezhen City in Jiangxi Province; Raozhou, also known as Poyang, is present-day Poyang County in Jiangxi Province.

2 A county under present-day Huangshan City, Anhui Province.

扎景镇。贼幸未跟踪追犯，左公得以整顿数日，锐气尚未大减。目下左军进剿乐平、鄱阳之贼。鲍公一军，因抚、建吃紧，本调渠赴江西省，先顾根本，次援抚、建。因近日鄱阳有警，景镇可危，又暂留鲍军不遽赴省。胡宫保恐狗逆由黄州下犯安庆沅弟之军，又调鲍军救援北岸。其祁门附近各岭，二十三日又被贼破两处。数月以来，实属应接不暇，危险迭见。而洋鬼又纵横出入于安庆、湖口、湖北、江西等处，并有欲来祁门之说。看此光景，今年殆万难支持。然余自咸丰三年冬以来，久已以身许国，愿死疆场，不愿死牖下，本其素志。近年在军办事，尽心竭力，毫无愧怍，死即瞑目，毫无悔憾。

家中兄弟子侄，惟当记祖父之八个字，曰："考、宝、早、

setback in Jialu Village [1] and then retreated to Jingdezhen. [2] Fortunately, the enemy failed to pursue them, and a few days of rest and reorganization left their morale mostly intact. Zuo's army is now tackling the enemy forces in Leping and Poyang. Bao Chao's [3] army was initially directed to Jiangxi Province to help control the general situation and have remained there to support the official army in Fuzhou and Jianchang. [4] In response to a recent warning that Poyang and Jingdezhen were targets, Bao's army has been ordered to stay put for the time being. Hu Gongbao [5] worried that the rebel army might leave Huangzhou to attack Guoquan's army in Anqing. Hence, Bao's army was then ordered to assist on the northern bank of the Yangtze River. On the 23rd, the enemy captured two more areas near Qimen County. [6] Over the past few months, we have been overwhelmed by one danger after another. Foreign soldiers have been sweeping in and out of Anqing, [7] Hukou, [8] Hubei, Jiangxi, and other areas, and reports indicate they are approaching Qimen. All of this goes to say that it will be all but impossible to hold out against these challenges this year. Since the winter of the third year of Emperor Xianfeng's reign (1853), however, I have aspired to meet my death on the battlefield rather than in my bed. In recent years, I have dedicated everything I have to the military. I have a clear conscience and can greet death with no regrets.

My brothers and nephews, remember the eight words that our grandfather emphasized: ancestors, cherishing, early, sweeping,

1 A village in present-day Wuyuan County, Jiangxi Province.

2 Present-day Jingdezhen City in Jiangxi Province.

3 Bao Chao (1828 – 1886), courtesy name Chunting, a native of Fengjie County, Chongqing Municipality was a famous military officer of the Xiang Army.

4 Fuzhou and Jianchang were both prefectures in Jiangxi Province. Present-day Jianchang, however, is a town in Nancheng County under Fuzhou City, Jiangxi Province.

5 Gongbao was the honorary name granted by Emperor Xianfeng to Hu Linyi. Hu (1812-1861), a native of Yiyang City, Hunan Province, was a famous military official of the late Qing Dynasty.

6 A county under present-day Huangshan City in Anhui Province.

7 Present-day Anqing City in Anhui Province.

8 A county under present-day Jiujiang City, Jiangxi Province.

扫、书、蔬、鱼、猪。”又谨记祖父之三不信，曰：“不信地仙，不信医药，不信僧巫。”余日记册中又有八本之说，曰：“读书以训诂为本，作诗文以声调为本，事亲以得欢心为本，养生以戒恼怒为本，立身以不妄语为本（即不扯谎也），居家以不晏起为本，作官以不要钱为本，行军以不扰民为本。”此八本者，皆余阅历而确有把握之论，弟亦当教诸子侄谨记之。无论世之治乱，家之贫富，但能守星冈公之八字与余之八本，总不失为上等人家。余每次写家信，必谆谆嘱咐。盖因军事危急，故预告一切也。

余身体平安。营中虽欠饷四月，而军心不甚涣散，或尚能支持，亦未可知。家中不必悬念。顺问近好。

兄国藩手草

books, vegetables, fish, and pigs. And remember the things that he distrusted: geomancers, medicine, and monks and shamans. In my diary, I have also compiled eight bases: exegesis is the basis for studying; intonation is the basis for composing poetry; love is the basis for serving one's parents; abstaining from anger is the basis of good health; refraining from wild talk (not telling lies) is the basis for conducting oneself; abstaining from rising late is the basis for running a household; ignoring monetary considerations is the basis for being an official; and not harassing the people is the basis for deploying the military. These eight bases are summarized from my own experience. My younger brothers should also teach my offspring to keep them in mind. Regardless of the state of the world or the economic condition of our family, we will always be considered a respectable family so long as we remember the eight words of our grandfather and the eight bases I summarized above. I must emphasize this in every letter I write home, for the war is at a crucial stage. I would like to explain everything to you while I still can.

I remain in good health. Although the army has received neither pay nor food for four months, morale has yet to slacken. Perhaps it will continue to hold out. There is no need for the family to worry about me. Please accept my kind regards.

Your elder brother, Guofan

谕纪泽、纪鸿 (1862)

此信写于同治元年（1862）四月二十四日。曾氏在此信中提出一个重要的观点：读书可变化气质。

曾氏一生手不释卷，临死前一天还在读《理学宗传》。他说君子有三乐，第一乐便是“读书声出金石，飘飘意远”。在高声朗诵前人的诗文中，他的精神得以自由驰骋，从而体会到无穷的乐趣。

他在给子弟的信中，多次谈到读书的重要性。这些重要之点大致包括以下五个部分：获取知识、明白事理、增进智慧、滋润心灵、提升境界。除第一个部分外，其他四个都属于变化气质的范畴，也就是说“腹有诗书气自华”。多读书，气质自然华美。

字谕纪泽、纪鸿儿：

今日专人送家信，甫经成行，又接王辉四等带来四月初十之信，尔与澄叔各一件，借悉一切。

尔近来写字，总失之薄弱，骨力不坚劲，墨气不丰腴，与尔身体向来轻字之弊正是一路毛病。尔当用油纸摹颜字之《郭家

To Jize and Jihong (1862)

In this letter, written on the 24th day of the fourth month in the first year of Emperor Tongzhi's reign (1862), Zeng Guofan argues that reading can change a person's temperament.

Zeng read throughout his life. The day before his death, he was still reading *A Genealogy of Neo-Confucianism* (*Li Xue Zong Zhuan*). He once explained that a gentleman experiences three kinds of joy, the first of which is "the sonorous sound of reading aloud and the broadmindedness it instills." Reciting ancient literary works in a loud voice frees one's mind. It is an inexhaustible source of joy.

In this letter to his descendants, he repeatedly discusses the importance of reading, which may be thought of as acquiring knowledge, following reason, enhancing wisdom, enriching the soul, and upgrading one's ideology. Aside from acquiring knowledge, the remaining four points may be categorized as ways of improving one's temperament. In other words, being well-read nurtures a natural elegance. The more one reads, the better one's temperament.

My sons Jize and Jihong,

Today, I assigned a special messenger to deliver my letter home. Soon after his departure, I received the letters brought by Wang Huisi and others that were dated the tenth day of the fourth month. This includes one each from you and your uncle Guohuang. Thus, I know how everything is going at home.

Recently, your handwriting has appeared weak. Your strokes lack vigor and richness. This is just like your body, which has always been plagued by frailty. You should use oiled paper to copy *Guojiamiao* in Yan Zhenqing's style or to copy *Langya Stele* and *Xuanmi Pagoda* in Liu Gongquan's style. Consider this to coun-

庙》、柳字之《琅琊碑》《玄秘塔》，以药其病。日日留心，专从厚重二字上用工。否则字质太薄，即体质亦因之更轻矣。人之气质，由于天生，本难改变，惟读书则可变化气质。古之精相法者，并言读书可以变换骨相。欲求变之之法，总须先立坚卓之志。即以余生平言之，三十岁前最好吃烟，片刻不离，至道光壬寅十一月二十一日立志戒烟，至今不再吃。四十六岁以前作事无恒，近五年深以为戒，现在大小事均尚有恒。即此二端，可见无事不可变也。尔于厚重二字，须立志变改。古称金丹换骨，余谓立志即丹也。满叔四信偶忘送，故特由驲补发。此嘱。

涤生示

ter the weakness in your handwriting. Let decorum be your focus every day. Otherwise, frailty shall define not only your handwriting but also your constitution. A person's temperament is inborn and, hence, difficult to change. Indeed, reading is the only way to amend it. Ancient physiognomists asserted that reading could transform the configuration of a person's bones. If we want to find a way to transform the configuration of our bones, we must first establish unwavering resolve. Take my life for example. Before the age of 30, I was a smoker, and I smoked nonstop. I resolved to quit on the 21st of the 11th month in the 22nd year of Emperor Daoguang's reign (1842) and have not smoked since. Before the age of 46, I lacked perseverance. After spending the past five years trying to correct this fault, I now have perseverance for matters big or small. These two examples prove that there is nothing we cannot change. You must steel your resolve to uphold decorum. The ancients claimed that an elixir could change one's bones. I believe determination is that elixir. I forgot to include four letters intended for your uncle Guobao. They will be sent home by regular post. Take care.

Your father, Disheng

致沅弟（1863）

此信写于同治二年（1863）七月二十一日。

曾氏在这封信里提出一个很重要的观点，即凡办大事，以识为主，以才为辅；凡成大事，人谋居半，天意居半。

什么是识？识，指个人的见识、眼光、思考能力等。它是才能范畴中最重要之点。识有大有小，小识可以让我们有好策划、金点子；大识可以让我们产生睿智的决策、富有远见的预判。决策与预判，在大事中更为要紧。所以，要办大事，必须在识上有过人之处。

所谓人谋，指人的主观谋划。所谓天意，指主观之外的一切因素的综合。曾氏认为，一件大事的成功，人谋与天意各占一半。

沅弟左右：

二十日接十六日信，二十一日接十一日交雷哨官信，具悉一切。

杏南未愈而萧、伍复病，至为系念。亲兵独到而丁道之匠头

To My Brother Guoquan (1863)

This letter was written on the 21st of the seventh month in the second year of Emperor Tongzhi's reign (1863).

In this letter, Zeng Guofan argues, "All great achievements are dependent primarily on knowledge rather than talent. Moreover, their success is determined equally by man-made plans and Heaven's will."

What is knowledge? Knowledge refers to an individual's experiences, insights, reflections, etc. It is the determining factor in regard to talent. Knowledge may be superficial or deep. The former may help with planning and spark creativity. The latter may help develop a keen intellect for making strategic decisions and far-sighted plans, both of which are vital to great achievements. Therefore, achieving great things is dependent upon acquiring exceptional knowledge in certain areas.

A man-made plan simply refers to a person's subjective plan, and Heaven's will refers to the synthesis of all elements outside of the human subjective element. Zeng believes that man-made plans and Heaven's will are each equally responsible for great achievements.

My brother Guoquan:

Having received your letter dated the 16th on the 20th and your letter dated the 11th via sentry officer Lei on the 21st, I am now caught up-to-date about everything.

Peng Xingnan's [1] illness has yet to improve, and I am concerned that Xiao and Wu have also taken ill. Ding Gongchen's [2] trusted soldiers are here, but the craftsmen he sent have yet to arrive.

1 Peng Xingnan was one of Zeng Guofan's cousins.

2 Ding Gongchen (1800 – 1875), a native of Jinjiang City, Fujian Province, was a mechanical engineer of the late Qing Dynasty.

未到。丁道以前二年在福建寄信来此，献硼炮之技。去年十一月到皖，已试验两次，毫无足观。居此半年，苟有长技，余方求之不得，岂肯弃而不用。渠在此无以自长，愿至金陵一为效用，余勉许之。至欲在雨花台铸炮，则尽可不必。待渠匠头来此，如需用他物，或可发给，若需锅铁及铸炮等物，则不发也。

凡办大事，以识为主，以才为辅；凡成大事，人谋居半，天意居半。往年攻安庆时，余告弟不必代天作主张。墙濠之坚，军心之固，严断接济，痛剿援贼，此可以人谋主张者也。克城之迟速，杀贼之多寡，我军士卒之病否，良将之有无损折，或添他军来助围师，或减围师分援他处，或功隳于垂成，或无心而奏捷，此皆由天意主张者也。譬之场屋考试，文有理法才气，诗不错平仄抬头，此人谋主张者也。主司之取舍，科名之迟早，此天意主张者也。若恐天意难凭，而必广许神愿，行贿请枪；若恐人谋未

While in Fujian Province two years ago, Ding Gongchen sent me a letter offering to share cannon-making technology. When I was in Anhui Province in the 11th month last year, we attempted the process twice, but the firepower of the cannons failed to live up to expectations. He lived here for half a year. He has special skills, which are most welcome, so how could I possibly give him up? Feeling unchallenged here, he wanted to go to Jinling [present-day Nanjing], where he felt he could be more effective. I reluctantly agreed. He plans to cast cannons in Yuhuatai, which is unnecessary. When his craftsmen arrive, you may supply them with necessary equipment but not iron pots and other items for casting cannons.

All great achievements are dependent primarily on knowledge rather than talent. Moreover, their success is determined equally by man-made plans and Heaven's will. When your army attacked Anqing, I told you that you cannot force Heaven's hand. As human beings, we can plan to build solid walls and trenches, maintain strong morale, cut off enemy provisions, and exterminate enemy reinforcements. However, it is the will of Heaven to decide when a town is captured, how many enemy soldiers are killed, whether our soldiers become sick, whether brilliant generals are killed, whether the enemy has reinforcements, whether some of our forces are redirected to reinforce other areas, whether a promising win results in a debacle, or whether victory unfolds unexpectedly. For example, when sitting in the examination hall, a candidate may depend on reason and literary talent to write an essay or compose a poem in good form with level and oblique tones. However, it is the will of Heaven to decide who will pass the examination and when scholars will be established through the imperial examination system. It would be folly to plead with the gods, worship Buddha, or bribe another to take one's place at an examination out

臧，而更多方设法，或作板绫衣以抄夹带，或蒸高丽参以磨墨。合是皆无识者之所为。弟现急求克城，颇有代天主张之意。若令丁道在营铸炮，则尤近于无识矣。愿弟常存畏天之念，而慎静以缓图之，则善耳。顺问近好。

兄国藩手草

of fear that the will of Heaven is unreliable. It would also be folly to try out all possible means, wear silk clothing to hide notes on slips of paper, or steam Korean ginseng to polish ink for good luck out of fear that your plans are lacking. That is the way of one who lacks knowledge. Now, you are eager to capture the enemy city and prepared to make decisions on Heaven's behalf. Ordering Ding Dao to cast cannons at camp is similar to the way of one who lacks knowledge. It would be better for you to remain in awe of Heaven and slowly and carefully make your plans. Please accept my kind regards.

Your brother, Guofan

致沅弟（1864）

此信写于同治三年（1864）正月二十六日。

在大哥的指导下，一向热衷事功、做人强势的曾老九，慢慢地对人生与事业有所思索、有所开悟，于是做大哥的进一步启迪九弟：功名富贵皆人世浮荣，唯胸次浩大是真正受用。这两句话是他的真切体验。

功名富贵这些东西，人们在未得到之前，总认为它千好万好，得到之后，才知道其实不过如此，况且还有不少随之而来的麻烦事。而胸次浩大，乃属于生命本身。它可以让人时时刻刻有着光风霁月、海阔天空般的愉悦，这才是人生的真正享受。

沅弟左右：

二十五日接十八日来信，二十六日接二十二夜来信。天保城以无意得之，大慰大慰。此与十一年安庆北门外两小垒相似，若再得宝塔梁子，则火候到矣。

To My Brother Guoquan (1864)

This letter was written on the 26th day of the first month in the third year of Emperor Tongzhi's reign (1864).

Zeng Guoquan, who had always yearned for success and power, began thinking deeper and becoming more enlightened about his personal and professional lives under his eldest brother's guidance. Consequently, Zeng Guofan attempted to offer him further inspiration. He posited that fame, fortune, rank, and honors are all human vanity. Only broad-mindedness provides genuine benefits. These two sentences encapsulate Zeng Guofan's own life experiences.

Prior to attaining them, people believe that fame, fortune, rank, honors and the like are wonderful beyond measure. Once attained, however, they realize that these are not only nothing special but also quite often accompanied by trouble. Broad-mindedness is woven into life itself. It makes it possible for people to experience genuine pleasure at any time in "the light breeze and the clear moon" [1] and the boundless sea and sky.

My brother Guoquan,

I received your letter dated the 18th on the 25th and your letter dated the evening of the 22nd on the 26th. Tianbao Town [2] was recaptured unexpectedly, which was a great comfort. This was similar to the situation with the two small barracks outside the north gate of Anqing in the 11th year of Emperor Xianfeng's reign (1861). The time may be right to make another attempt to recapture Baotaliangzi.

1 Here, "the light breeze and the clear moon" symbolize the state of being open and aboveboard.

2 Tianbao Town was a military fortress built on top of Zhongshan Mountain by the Taiping rebel army.

弟近来气象极好，胸襟必能自养其淡定之天，而后发于外者有一段和平虚明之味。如去岁初奉不必专折奏事之谕，毫无怫郁之怀，近两月信于请饷请药毫无激迫之辞，此次于莘田、芝圃外家渣滓悉化，皆由胸襟广大之效验，可喜可敬。如金陵果克，于广大中再加一段谦退工夫，则萧然无与，人神同钦矣。富贵功名皆人世浮荣，惟胸次浩大是真正受用。余近年专在此处下功夫，愿与我弟交勉之。

闻家中内外大小及姊妹亲族无一不和睦整齐，皆弟连年筹画之功。愿弟出以广大之胸，再进以俭约之诫，则尽善矣。喜极答函，顺问近好。

国藩手草

Brother, life has been going smoothly for you recently. Broad-mindedness can cultivate detachment and tranquility in the form of peacefulness and clear-mindedness. You felt neither anger nor despondency upon receiving an edict at the beginning of last year for failing to submit special memorials to the throne. Writing letters over the past two months, you refrained from using passionate or urgent language in pleas for military pay and ammunition. The grudges between Li Youshu's (courtesy name Shentian) and Li Zongwei's (courtesy name Zhipu) in-laws have also been resolved thanks to your broad-mindedness, which is gratifying and admirable. If Jinling [Nanjing] is conquered, and you augment your broad-mindedness with the virtues of humility and detachment from fame and fortune, you may hold yourself aloof from the world and win the admiration of both the people and the gods. Fame, fortune, rank, and honors are all human vanity. Only broad-mindedness provides genuine benefits. This is an area that I have worked hard to improve in recent years. I hope we can encourage each other.

I have heard that harmony and order prevail among all members of our family, including close and extended relatives, the young and the elderly, and elder and younger sisters. This can be attributed to your careful planning over the past few years. I hope that your broad-mindedness, coupled with thrift and temperance, will become evermore refined. I am overjoyed to answer your letter. Please accept my kind regards.

Your brother, Guofan

致澄弟(1864)

此信写于同治三年(1864)六月初四日。

曾氏常常对家人说“有福不可享尽,有势不可使尽”的话,借此提醒子弟们在享福时,不可忘记先人的勤苦节俭;在有权势的时候,要知万一哪天失势后可能遇到的困境。

有福不可享尽,有势不可使尽,这实际上就是居安思危的意识。它的用意在于对人性中的贪婪无厌和得意忘形等弱点加以抑制,使人不至于过于放纵,过于膨胀,从而减少犯错的可能性,也可以减少社会的忌妒与愤恨。富贵之家宜常存此忧患感。

澄弟左右:

六月四日接五月二十三日信,初一日接十一日信,具悉一切。震四果尔早世,四妹适朱家,万缘皆空。吾骨肉中今年何多变也!老弟终日奔驰劳苦,身体吃得住否?深为系念。

此间近状平安。大女儿病六七日,今已全愈。沅弟病亦愈矣,

To My Brother Guohuang (1864)

This letter was written on the fourth day of the sixth month in the third year of Emperor Tongzhi's reign (1864).

Zeng Guofan often told his family, "Neither exhaust all your good fortune nor utilize all your power and influence." This served as a warning to younger generations to remember the hard work and frugality of their ancestors as they themselves enjoyed a life of ease and comfort, and to devise contingency plans while the family still maintained power and influence in the event they one day fall on hard times.

In practice, this is the same mentality as being vigilant in times of peace. The purpose is to control human weaknesses, such as avarice, insatiability, and complacency, to prevent people from becoming overindulgent or overinflated, thus reducing the risk of their mistakes, jealousy, and resentment from others. This mentality should be engrained in wealthy and honorable families.

My brother Guohuang,

Having received your letter dated the 23rd day of the fifth month on the fourth day of the sixth month, and your letter dated the 11th day was received on the 1st. I am now caught up-to-date about everything. I cannot believe that Guozhi [1] passed away so young. She married into the Zhu family, and now all is vanity. How can so many misfortunes befall our family this year! Can your health withstand all the long hours you work? This concerns me greatly.

Everything here is fine. My eldest daughter had been ill for six

1 Zeng Guozhi was one of Zeng Guofan's younger sisters.

闻二十五六日每日又骑行百余里。余命泽儿往看沅病，初二归来云“尽可放心”，但六月尚盖棉被三床，体亦弱矣。弟能从此少管公事，甚慰甚慰。余蒙先人余荫忝居高位，与诸弟及子侄谆谆慎守者但有二语，曰“有福不可享尽，有势不可使尽”而已。福不多享，故总以俭字为主，少用仆婢，少花银钱，自然惜福矣；势不多使，则少管闲事，少断是非，无感者亦无怕者，自然悠久矣。余详日记中，顺问近好。

外李北冈一信，阅毕专人送去。

or seven days but has now recovered. Guoquan has also gotten better. I heard that on the 25th and 26th, he rode more than 100 *li* each day. I asked Jize to check on him. He returned on the second day of the sixth month, saying, "You can rest easy." I know, however, that Guoquan is still weak as it is the sixth month, and he still uses three quilts to keep warm in bed. I am delighted to learn that you can relinquish some of your official duties in the future. Our ancestors' legacy has enabled me to occupy a high position of which I am unworthy. My advice to my brothers and the younger generations can be summarized in two sentences, "Neither exhaust all your good fortune nor utilize all your power and influence." Good fortune should be enjoyed in moderation. By prioritizing frugality, employing fewer servants, and spending less money, we naturally cherish our blessings. By wielding less power, we interfere less in the business of others and make fewer judgments about right and wrong. With neither anyone to feel indebted toward us nor anyone for us to fear, our family will naturally prosper for years to come. You may consult the enclosed journal entry for more details on the subject. Please accept my kind regards.

I have also written a letter to Li Beigang.[1] Please read it and assign someone to deliver it to him.

1 Li Xukuan, courtesy name Beigang, a native of Xiangxiang County, was a military officer of the late Qing Dynasty.

谕纪泽、纪鸿（1871）

同治十年（1871）十一月，在自知来日无多的病痛折磨中，曾氏写下了一份遗嘱。

作为一位有担当、有强烈责任感的家长，他对子孙的长远关怀，不是形而下的财富的遗留，而是形而上的思想的传授。他将多年的人生思考凝聚为“慎独、主敬、求仁、习劳”八个字，作为最后的家训传给二子，希望他们牢记于心，传之于后，长保曾氏家族的兴旺不衰。

曾氏家族现已传至八代。前五代中代代都有杰出人物，后三代中也个个清清白白。它是近现代著名的人才辈出的家族。这是曾氏家教家风培育的结果。

一曰慎独则心安。自修之道，莫难于养心。心既知有善知有恶，而不能实用其力，以为善去恶，则谓之自欺。方寸之自欺与否，盖他人所不及知，而己独知之。故《大学》之“诚意”章，两言慎独。果能好善如好好色，恶恶如恶恶臭，力去人欲，以存

To Jize and Jihong (1871)

In the 11th month of the tenth year of Emperor Tongzhi's reign (1871), aware that his time was short and tormented by pain, Zeng Guofan wrote the following last testament for his descendants.

As a parent with a strong sense of duty to his family, Zeng expressed his loving concern for his descendants by leaving them a legacy of ideas rather than riches. He distilled the years he spent reflecting on life into the following four points: "exercise caution in one's private life, hold reverence, pursue benevolence, and practice labor." As his last instructions for his two sons, Zeng hoped that they would keep these four points in mind and eventually pass them on to future generations to ensure long-term prosperity.

The Zeng family has evolved for eight generations. The first five each boasted outstanding individuals, and the last three have each been without blemish. In modern times, the Zeng family has been celebrated for its wealth of talented people, which may be attributed to education and family traditions.

First, exercising caution in one's private life bestows peace of mind. The most challenging aspect of educating oneself is cultivating mental calm. Recognizing both good and evil, yet unable to effectively use its power to eliminate evil, the mind deceives itself. Whether or not an individual deceives himself is beyond the knowledge of others, but the individual himself knows. Therefore, exercising caution in one's private life is discussed twice in the section "Making Thoughts Sincere" in the *Great Learning*. If an individual loves good as much as he loves beauty, detests evil as much as he detests a stench, and strives to eliminate human desires and preserve heavenly principles, then he is able to practice

天理，则《大学》之所谓自慊，《中庸》之所谓戒慎恐惧，皆能切实行之。即曾子之所谓自反而缩，孟子之所谓仰不愧、俯不怍，所谓养心莫善于寡欲，皆不外乎是。故能慎独，则内省不疚，可以对天地质鬼神，断无行有不慊于心则馁之时。人无一内愧之事，则天君泰然，此心常快足宽平，是人生第一自强之道，第一寻乐之方，守身之先务也。

二曰主敬则身强。敬之一字，孔门持以教人，春秋士大夫亦常言之，至程朱则千言万语不离此旨。内而专静纯一，外而整齐严肃，敬之工夫也；出门如见大宾，使民如承大祭，敬之气象也；修己以安百姓，笃恭而天下平，敬之效验也。程子谓上下一于恭敬，则天地自位，万物自育，气无不和，四灵毕至。聪明睿智，皆由此出。以此事天飨帝，盖谓敬则无美不备也。吾谓敬字切近

the self-restraint of the *Great Learning* and the caution and fear of the *Doctrine of the Mean*. Zengzi proposed finding oneself to be right after self-examination. Mencius declared that one is worthy before Heaven and feels no shame before man; he also declared that nothing cultivates mental calm more than a lack of desire. Therefore, if an individual can exercise caution in private, then he will find no faults when engaged in introspection. He will be able to withstand the questions of the universe and supernatural beings, for if he cannot feel at ease with what he has done, his noble spirit will be exhausted. If an individual has done nothing with a sense of shame, then he will feel very much at ease and remain happy, satisfied, relieved, and calm. This is the best way to improve oneself, seek happiness, and preserve one's integrity.

Second, holding reverence strengthens the body. The Confucian school used the word "reverence" to educate people; the literati of the Spring and Autumn period often discussed it; the Cheng brothers and Zhu Xi even anchored their thousands of words to it. The work of reverence is to treat people and things by being peaceful and single-minded internally and neat and solemn externally; the spirit of reverence is to behave as though one were visiting a noble guest when going out and to rule the people as though one were offering sacrifices to one's ancestors; the effect of reverence is improving oneself to appease the people and upholding purity and respect to pacify the world. The Cheng brothers said that when superiors and subordinates are united in reverence, heaven and earth will be properly positioned, all living things will be self-nurturing, harmony will prevail, and the four supernatural beings[1] will show themselves. This is the source of wisdom and intelligence. If we use reverence to serve heaven and the emperor, then nothing beautiful will be lacking. I believe that the immediate

1 The four auspicious animals in ancient China were the unicorn, the phoenix, the turtle, and the dragon.

之效，尤在能固人肌肤之会、筋骸之束。庄敬曰强，安肆曰偷，皆自然之征应，虽有衰年病躯，一遇坛庙祭献之时，战阵危急之际，亦不觉神为之悚，气为之振，斯足知敬能使人身强矣。若人无众寡，事无大小，一一恭敬，不敢懈慢，则身体之强健，又何疑乎？

三曰求仁则人悦。凡人之生，皆得天地之理以成性，得天地之气以成形，我与民物，其大本乃同出一源。若但知私己，而不知仁民爱物，是于大本一源之道已悖而失之矣。至于尊官厚禄，高居人上，则有拯民溺、救民饥之责。读书学古，粗知大义，即有觉后知、觉后觉之责。若但知自了，而不知教养庶民，是于天之所以厚我者辜负甚大矣。

孔门教人，莫大于求仁，而其最切者，莫要于欲立立人、欲达达人数语。立者自立不惧，如富人百物有余，不假外求；达者四达不悖，如贵人登高一呼，群山四应。人孰不欲己立己达，若

effect of reverence lies in strengthening an individual's tendons and bones. Reverence gradually improves one's strength, whereas indulgence gradually makes one weak – this is a natural progression. Despite being old and sick, when the time comes to offer sacrifices at the altar or the temple or to deploy military troops in a crisis, I cannot help but be frightened and excited. This is sufficient evidence that reverence can strengthen the body. Regardless of the number of people or the importance of things, holding each with reverence will surely help one become strong and healthy. Can there be any doubt?

Third, pursuing benevolence brings joy. For an ordinary individual, one's nature is determined by the principles of the universe, and one's form is shaped by the energy of the universe. My life originated in the same way as any ordinary person. If I am selfish and fail to understand how to love all people and things, then I violate or even abandon the way of the origin of life. As for well-paid officials who set themselves far above the people, they should shoulder the responsibility of saving them from drowning and starvation. Scholars who read the classics to learn from the ancients should bear the burden of enlightening those who have yet to learn from the ancients. If an individual only learns for himself and does not understand how to educate others, he will be unworthy of Heaven's blessings.

In a Confucian education, nothing is more important than pursuing benevolence. The most fundamental point is for those who want to be established to help establish others and for those who want to be distinguished to help others gain distinction. Those who stand on their own have no fear, just as the rich who possess an abundance of everything have no need for outside assistance. Those who are distinguished have access to directions, just as those of high rank hear a response from the surrounding

能推以立人达人，则与物同春矣。后世论求仁者，莫精于张子之《西铭》。彼其视民胞物与，宏济群伦，皆事天者性分当然之事。必如此，乃可谓之人；不如此，则曰悖德，曰贼。诚如其说，则虽尽立天下之人，尽达天下之人，而曾无善劳之足言，人有不悦而归之者乎？

四曰习劳则神钦。凡人之情，莫不好逸而恶劳，无论贵贱智愚老少，皆贪于逸而惮于劳，古今之所同也。人一日所着之衣所进之食，与一日所行之事所用之力相称，则旁人韪之，鬼神许之，以为彼自食其力也。若农夫织妇终岁勤动，以成数石之粟数尺之布，而富贵之家终岁逸乐，不营一业，而食必珍羞，衣必锦绣，酣豢高眠，一呼百诺，此天下最不平之事，鬼神所不许也，其能久乎？

mountains when they climb up to make a public appeal. How can an individual be unwilling to be established and distinguished? If he can continue to help others become established and distinguished, then he can empathize with the rest of the world. Later generations have yet to produce any work that discusses pursuing benevolence as well as Zhang Zai's "West Inscription" (Xi Ming Jiang Yi). Zhang Zai regarded all living things as fellow beings because they all serve Heaven and possess their own respective nature. It is in this way that a person can be called human. Otherwise, he will be considered in violation of morality and hence a thief. As they say, if a person helps everyone become established and distinguished and bears responsibilities without exaggerating his own work, how can the people not be happy and follow him?

Fourth, practicing labor wins the admiration of the gods. Ordinary people tend to love leisure and hate labor. Regardless of status, intelligence, age, or time period, all people prefer to indulge in ease and comfort and avoid practicing labor. If the clothes an individual wears and the food he eats are equivalent to the labor he has performed that day, he will be recognized by others and praised by supernatural beings because he relies on his own ability to make a living. Farmers and weavers only earn a few *dan* of grain and a few *chi*[1] of cloth annually for their hard work, whereas people with fortune and rank enjoy comfort and pleasure all year round. They perform no labor but eat delicacies and wear brocade and satin clothes. After becoming inebriated, they sleep like a log. When awake, they have hundreds of attendants at their beck and call. This is the greatest unfairness in the world. Even supernatural beings will not allow such behavior. Is it possible for those with fortune and high rank to enjoy such leisure and pleasure for an extended time?

1 One *chi* equals 0.33 meters, or about one foot.

古之圣君贤相，若汤之昧旦丕显，文王日昃不遑，周公夜以继日坐以待旦，盖无时不以勤劳自励。《无逸》一篇，推之于勤则寿考，逸则夭亡，历历不爽。为一身计，则必操习技艺，磨炼筋骨，困知勉行，操心危虑，而后可以增智慧而长才识。为天下计，则必己饥己溺，一夫不获，引为余辜。大禹之周乘四载，过门不入，墨子之摩顶放踵，以利天下，皆极俭以奉身，而极勤以救民。故荀子好称大禹、墨翟之行，以其勤劳也。军兴以来，每见人有一材一技、能耐艰苦者，无不见用于人，见称于时。其绝无材技、不惯作劳者，皆唾弃于时，饥冻就毙。故勤则寿，逸则夭，勤则

In ancient times, wise emperors and capable ministers motivated themselves with hard work. For example, Emperor Tang of the Shang Dynasty rose before dawn to ponder how to fully develop his moral career; Emperor Wen of the Zhou Dynasty worked all day so that he had yet to eat when the sun set in the west; the Duke of Zhou, who is commended for his role in founding the Zhou Dynasty, worked late into the night and early hours of the morning. According to the essay "Against Leisure" (*Wu Yi*) from the *Book of Documents*, the diligent man will enjoy longevity, while the man who enjoys comfort will meet an early death. From the perspective of our personal lives, we should strive to learn and practice skills, exercise our bodies, and redouble our efforts to gain knowledge upon realizing that our knowledge is limited. This is the only way to develop our talents and increase our knowledge. From the perspective of the outside world, we must be responsible for the welfare of the people because we are at fault if even one person is not freed from suffering. Emperor Yu of the Xia Dynasty travelled by four kinds of transport to tame the Yellow River and passed his home without entering it. Mozi served the interests of others at great self-sacrifice. They both maintained their integrity through extreme frugality and devoted themselves to saving the people. Xunzi was fond of discussing the conduct of Emperor Yu and Mozi, mainly due to their diligence. Since fighting began against the Taiping rebel army, anyone with talent and skill who is capable of working hard has been employed and created a good reputation. Those who are unaccustomed to labor and without talent or skill have been cast aside to die from hunger and cold. Thus, diligence leads to longevity, and leisure leads to an early death. Talented people who work hard are employed, and comfort-seeking people without any talent are abandoned by society. A diligent person can create wealth and benefit society, thus winning the es-

有材而见用，逸则无能而见弃，勤则博济斯民，而神祇钦仰，逸则无补于人，而神鬼不歆。是以君子欲为人神所凭依，莫大于习劳也。

余衰年多病，目疾日深，万难挽回，汝及诸侄辈身体强壮者少，古之君子修己治家，必能心安身强而后有振兴之象，必使人悦神钦而后有骈集之祥。今书此四条，老年用自儆惕，以补昔岁之愆，并令二子各自勖勉，每夜以此四条相课，每月终以此四条相稽，仍寄诸侄共守，以期有成焉。

teem and admiration of supernatural beings. A person who longs for comfort and pleasure neither creates wealth nor benefits society and thus will never be esteemed or admired by supernatural beings. Therefore, practicing labor is the greatest reason for a gentleman to be respected and supported by the gods and the people.

I am now old and plagued by illness. The disease attacking my eyes grows worse by the day. Among you and your cousins, only a few are strong and sturdy. However, self-cultivation and household management required gentlemen in ancient times to be peaceful-minded and physically strong, which are signs of rejuvenation. They were required to bring the people joy and earn the esteem of the gods, which are signs of different talents converging. I have written the four points above for myself as a way of compensating for the mistakes of my early years. I have also written them for my two sons as a way of encouraging each other. Study these four points every evening and measure yourselves against them at the end of every month. I will mail a copy of this letter to my nephews so that they, too, may observe the four points and achieve success.

图书在版编目(CIP)数据

曾国藩诗文选/尹飞舟,乐国斌译;唐浩明编.—长沙:岳麓书社,2024.12

(汉英对照湖湘经典丛书)

ISBN 978-7-5538-1732-3

Ⅰ.①曾… Ⅱ.①尹…②乐…③唐… Ⅲ.①古典诗歌—诗集—中国—清后期—汉、英②古典散文—散文集—中国—清后期—汉、英 Ⅳ.①I215.22

中国版本图书馆 CIP 数据核字(2022)第 174737 号

ZENG GUOFAN SHIWEN XUAN

曾国藩诗文选

译　　者:尹飞舟　乐国斌

编　　者:唐浩明

责任编辑:张丽琴　刘　文

责任校对:舒　舍

封面设计:格局创界文化传播

岳麓书社出版发行

地址:湖南省长沙市爱民路 47 号

直销电话:0731-88804152　0731-88885616

邮编:410006

版次:2024 年 12 月第 1 版

印次:2024 年 12 月第 1 次印刷

开本:960mm×640mm　1/16

印张:25.5

字数:280 千字

ISBN 978-7-5538-1732-3

定价:78.00 元

承印:湖南省众鑫印务有限公司

如有印装质量问题,请与本社印务部联系

电话:0731-88884129